South Pasadena Historical Landmarks 2018

Lily Anderson

South Pasadena Historical Landmarks 2018
© Lily Anderson
www.realilystudio.com
First Edition © 2018
ISBN-13:978-1721267811
ISBN-10:1721267816
All rights reserved

10 9 8 7 6 5 4 3 2 1

FORWARD

South Pasadena is situated between Pasadena and Los Angeles and over the past 130 years has somehow managed to preserve its small town character. The land that became South Pasadena was originally part of the Spanish San Pasqual Rancho. In 1873, 27 stockholders of the California Colony of Indiana bought 1500 acres covering the area that now includes Altadena, Pasadena, and South Pasadena. Large tracts were settled by 40 families. They used the land to grow orange groves and fruit trees.

In 1886 the central area incorporated into the city of Pasadena. The areas of Altadena and South Pasadena declined to be included. In 1887 Pasadena passes an anti-saloon ordinance. All the saloons moved just south of the Pasadena border. In 1888 South Pasadena incorporated and the first order of business was to pass its own anti-saloon ordinance. Word for word it was identical to Pasadena's.

With readily available and inexpensive rail transportation from the east, South Pasadena enjoyed a land boom. The southern California climate made the area a nationwide resort and tourist destination. In 1903 the Pacific Electric Short Line made commuting to Los Angeles easy and inexpensive. South Pasadena became Los Angeles's first suburb.

South Pasadena is dedicated to preserving its rich history of architecturally significant buildings and streetscapes. Here are the 53 current landmarks or sites that tell the story of South Pasadena's History. Enjoy!

Lily Anderson

2018

Table of Contents

1 Adobe Flores and Cactus Garden - 1845

2 South Pasadena War Memorial Building – 1921

3 Oaklawn Bridge and Waiting Station – 1906

4 Garfield House – 1904

5 Meridian Iron Works - 1887

6 Wynyate - 1887

7 Watering Trough and Wayside Station – 1906

8 South Pasadena Bank Building – 1904

9 Oaklawn Portals – 1905

10 South Pasadena Public Library - 1907

11 Miltimore House – 1911

12 Ashbourne Drive and Chelton Way – 1891

13 Clokey Oak Tree

14 Ashbourne – Chelten Hybrid Oak Tree

15 Andrew O. Porter House – 1874

16 Raymond Hill Waiting Station - 1903

17 Howard Longley House - 1897

18 Cawston Ostrich Farm Site – 1896

19 Cathedral Oak Monument - 1952

20 Manuel Garfias Adobe Site – 1852

21 Leo Longley House - 1887

22 Grace Brethren Church – 1907

23 Tanner – Behr House – 1917

24 Lloyd Morrison House – 1925

25 Rialto Theatre – 1925

26 Mission Hotel – 1923

27 Baranger Studios – 1925

28 Grokowski House 1928

29 Vivekananda House – circa 1880

30 School Administration Building – 1925

31 Lewis-Markey Building – 1928

32 Eddie House and Memorial Park – 1910

33 St. James Episcopal Church – 1907

34 Century House – 1888

35 Adobe Eulalia Perez – 1924

36 Bissell House – 1887

37 Pettee Building – 1933

38 Garfias Spring

39 Mabel Packard House – 1914

40 Washburn House – 1910

41 Torrance-Childs House - 1903

42 Knox-Merwin - Porter House - circa 1875

43 East Wynyate - 1896

44 Chouinard House – 1907

45 Municipal Plunge Building – 1936

46 Smith & Williams Building – 1958

47 Burwood – 1910

48 Riggins House – 1885

49 Fair Hope Building – 1911

50 Huntzinger House – 1910

51 Fleet House -1947

52 Whit Smith House- 1947

53 Raab Family Homestead – Circa 1875

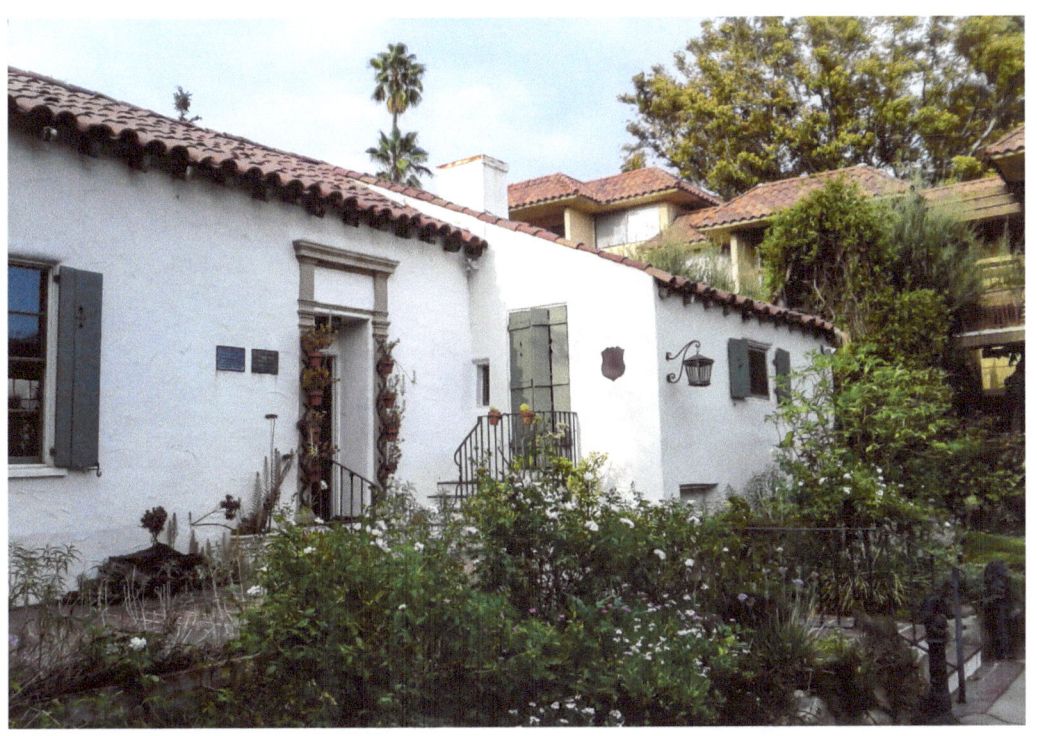
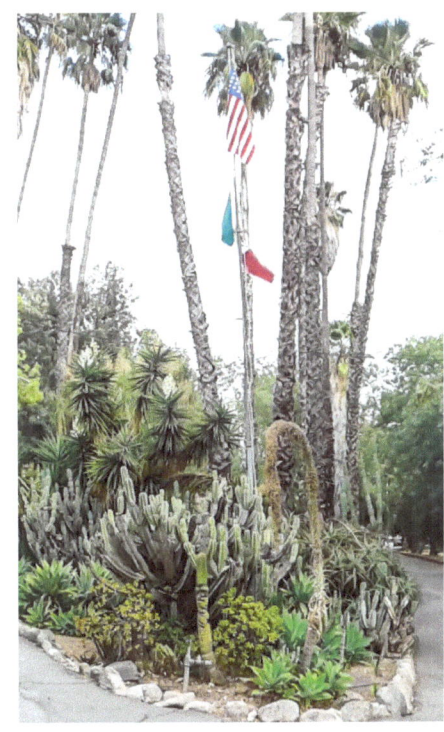
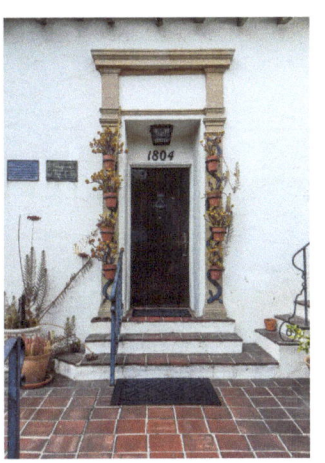
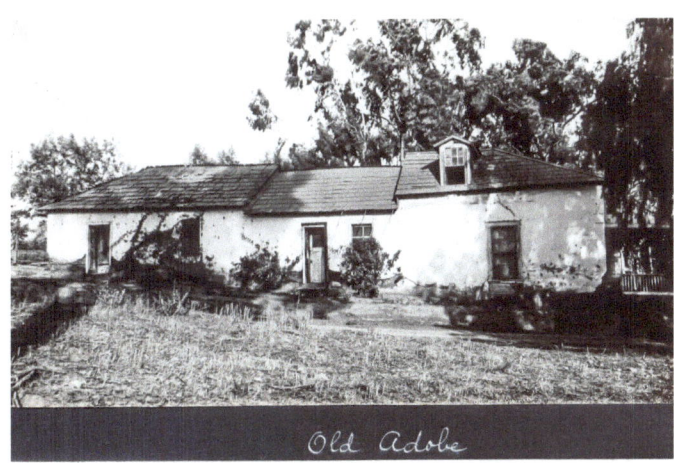
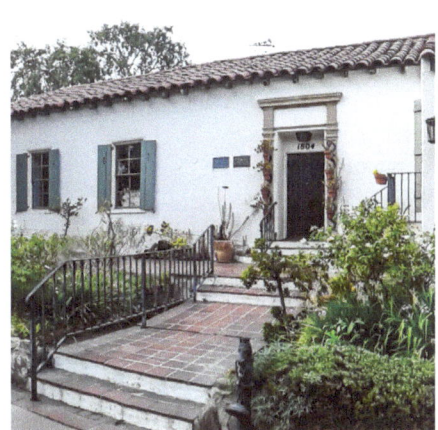
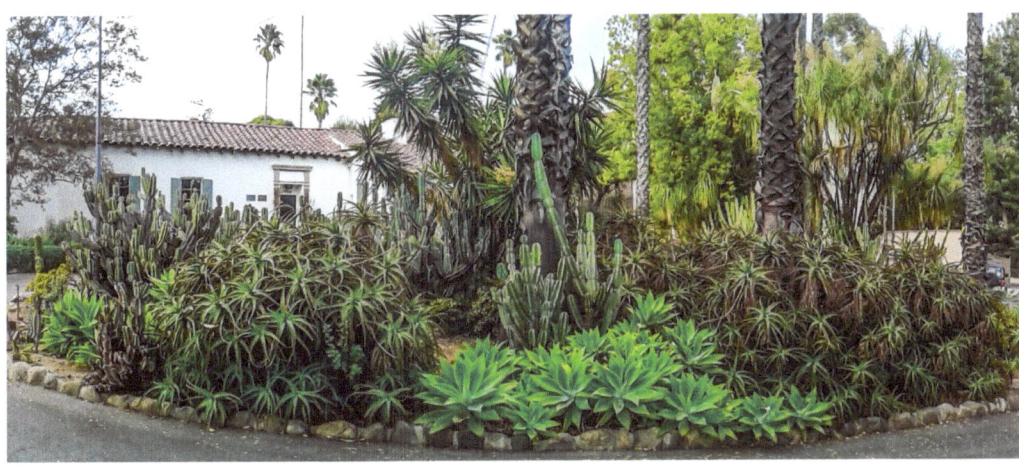
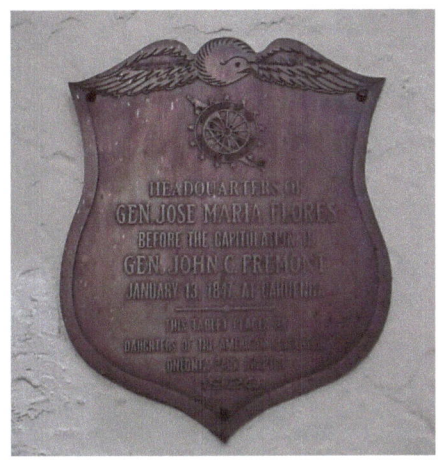

Adobe Flores and Cactus Garden - 1845

Spanish Adobe – First building in the area.

1

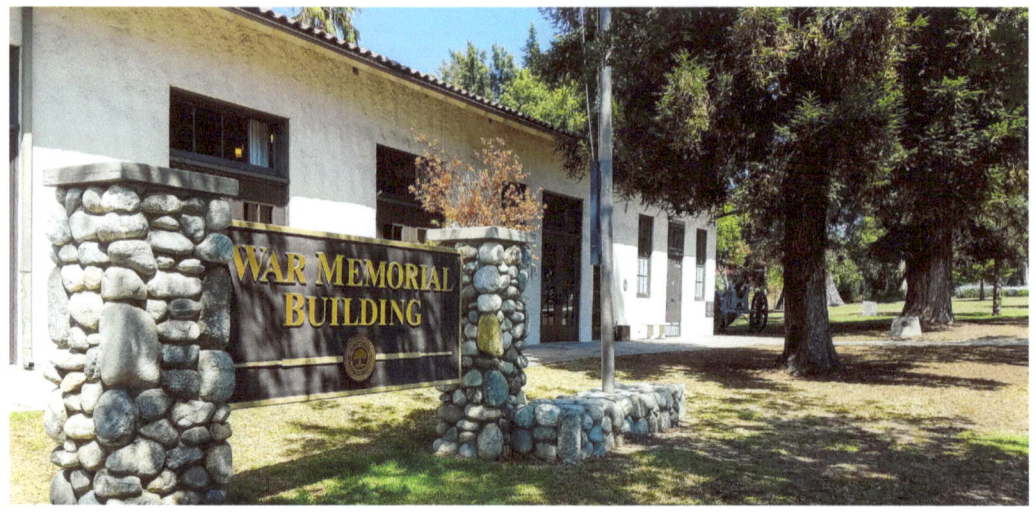
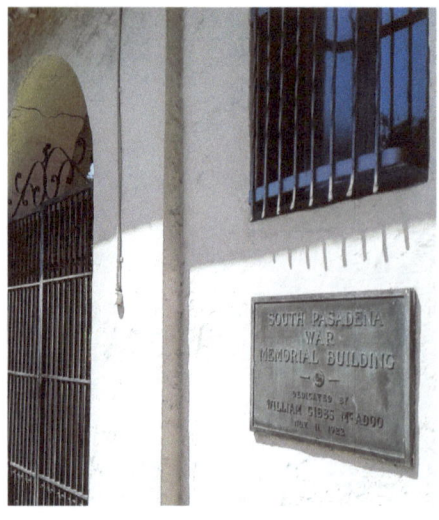
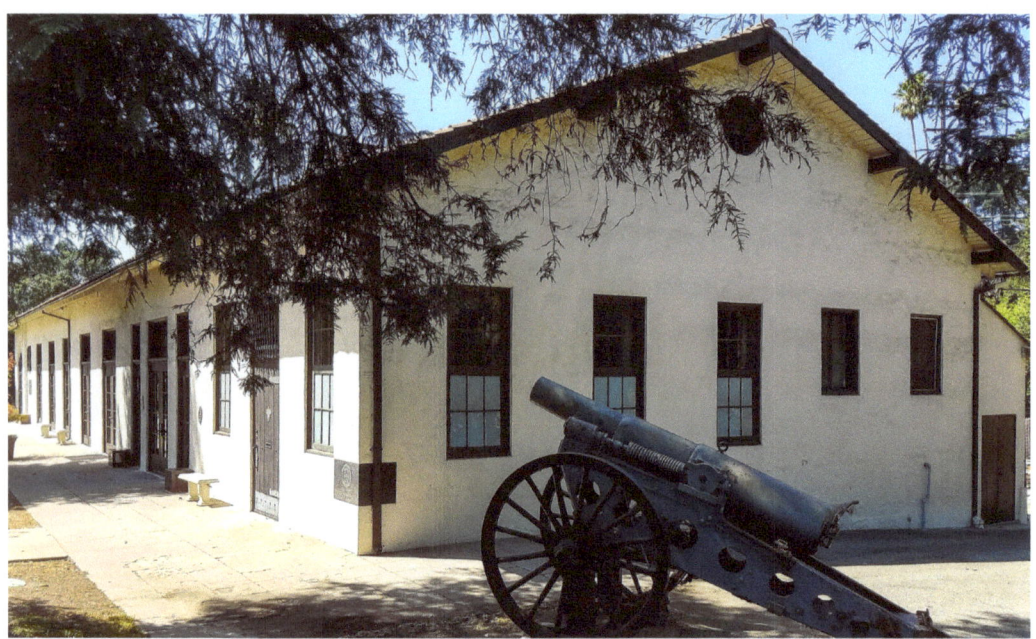
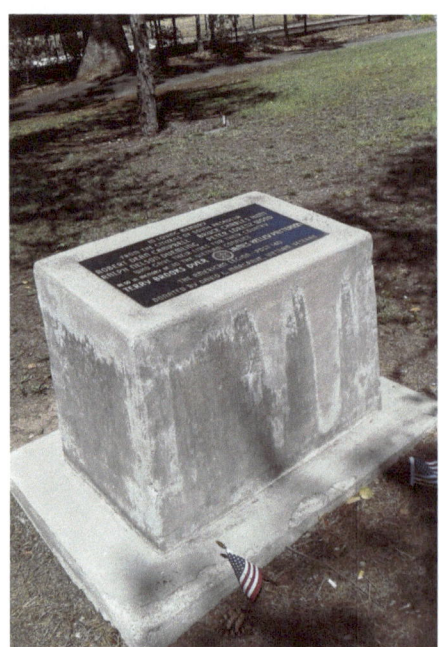
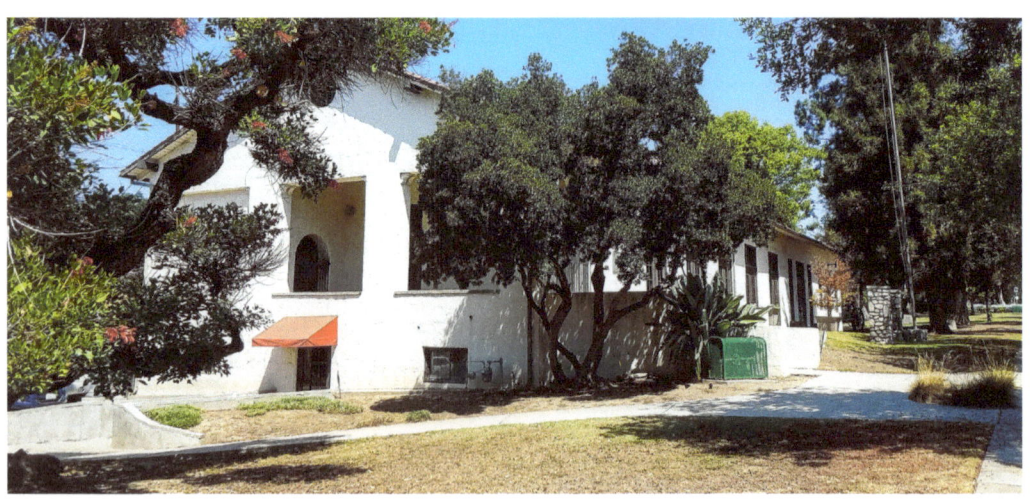
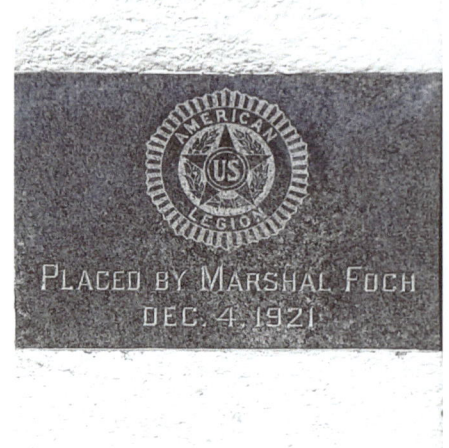

South Pasadena War Memorial Building – 1921

Spanish Revival – Norman Marsh, Architect

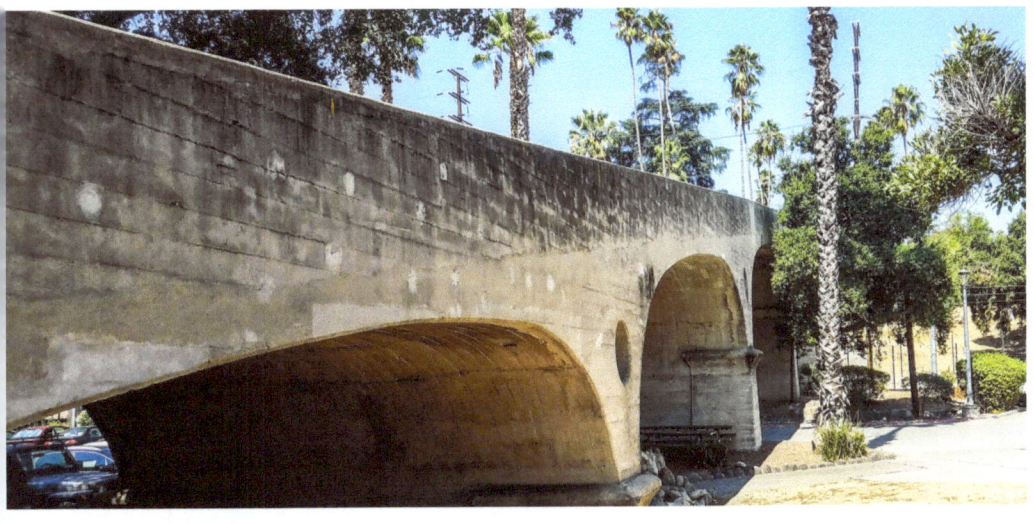
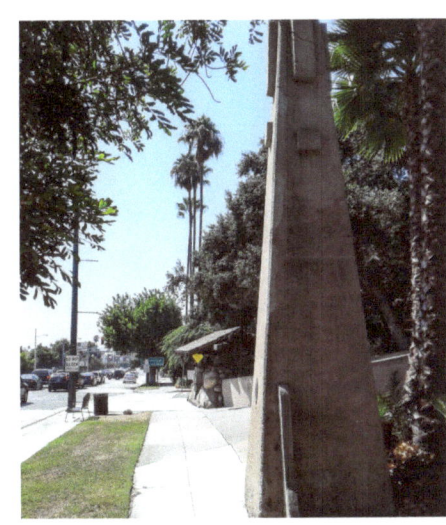
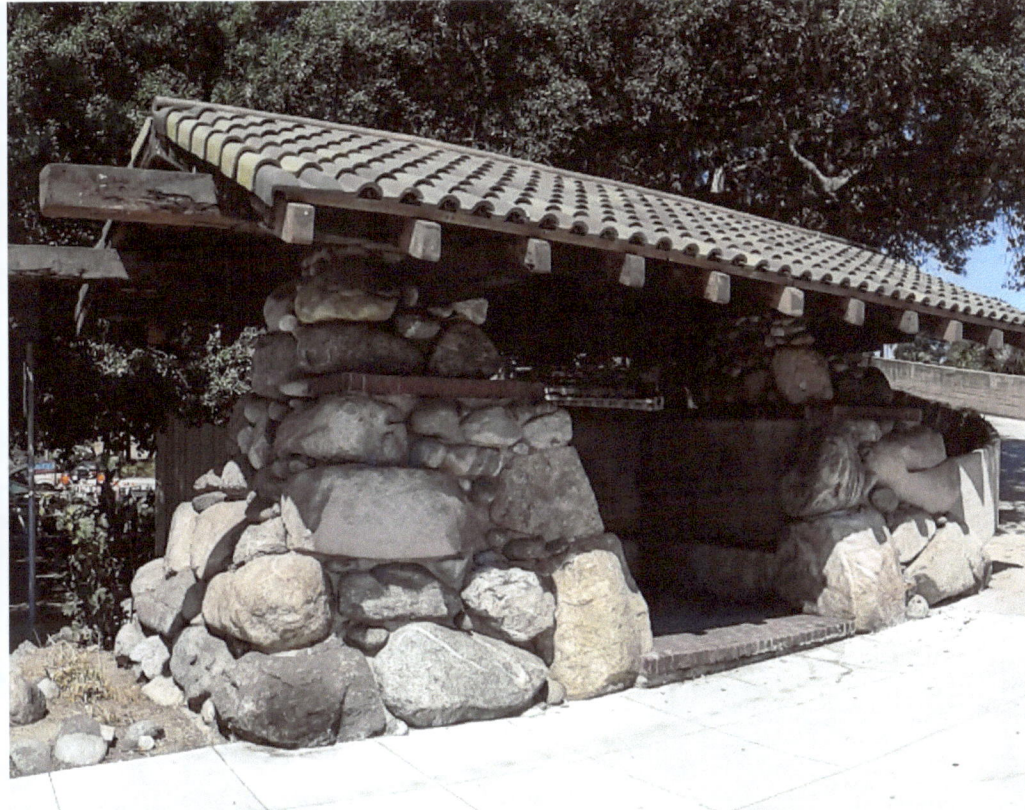
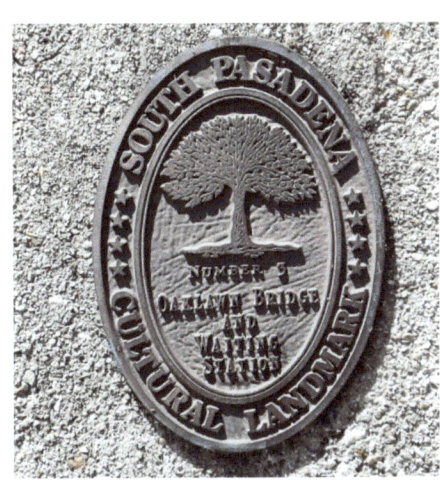
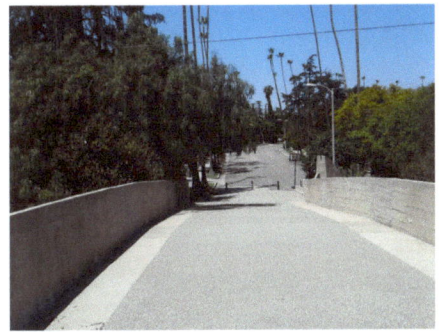
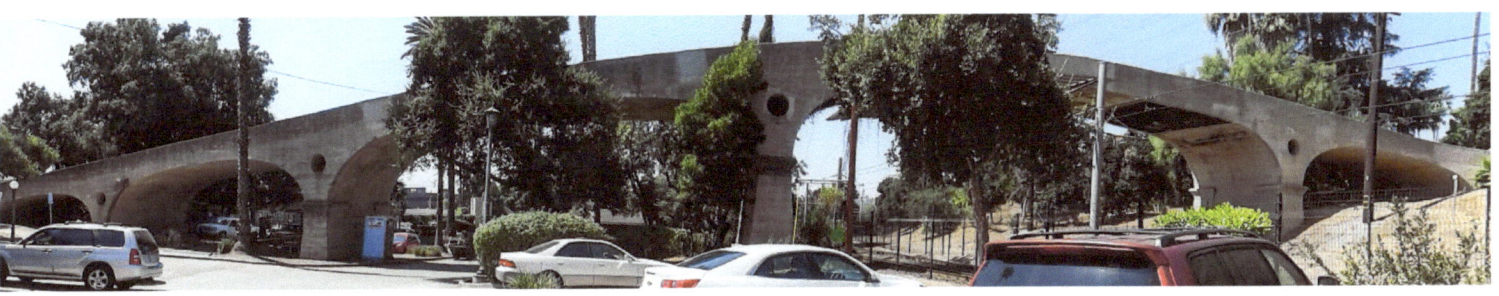

Oaklawn Bridge and Waiting Station – 1906

Craftsman Style – Designed by Charles and Henry Green

3

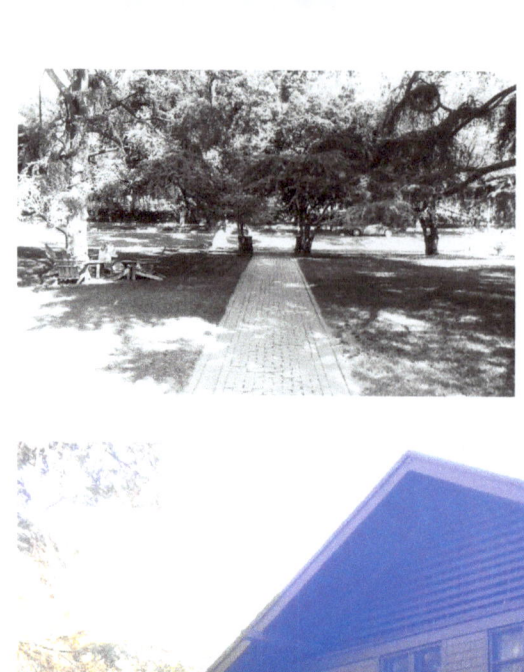
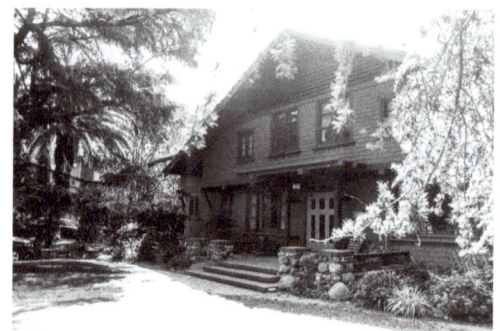
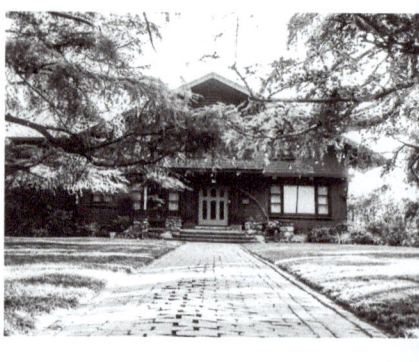
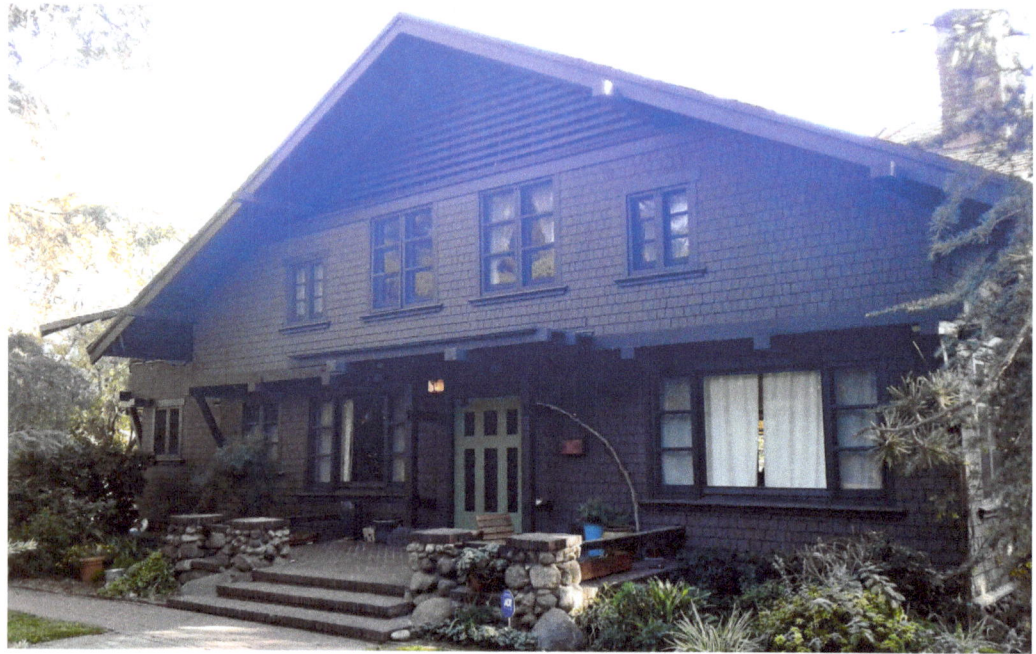
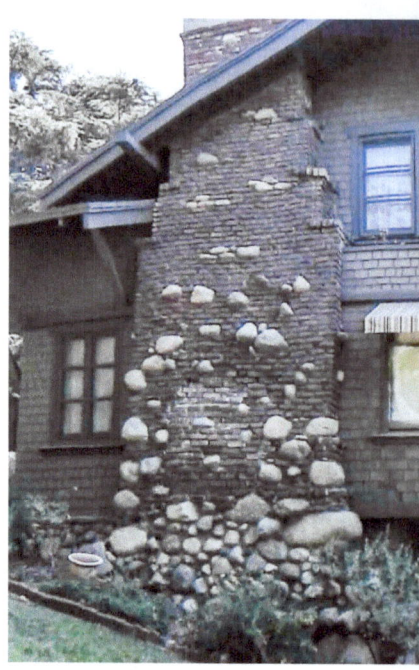
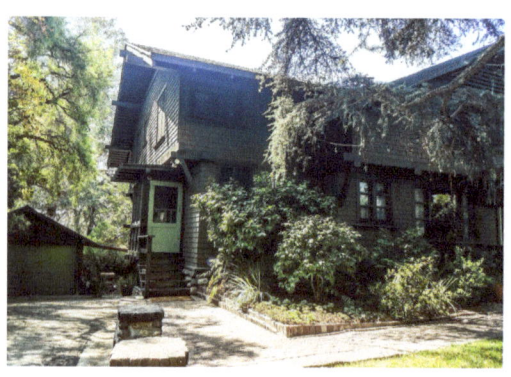
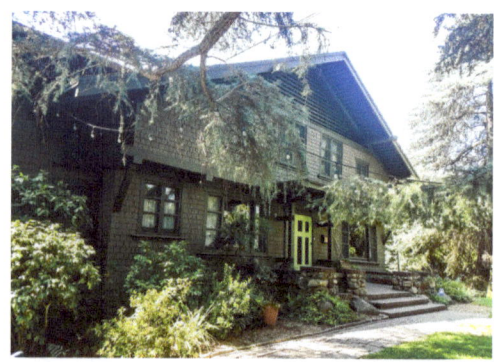
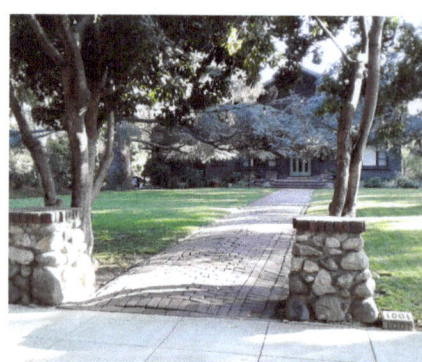
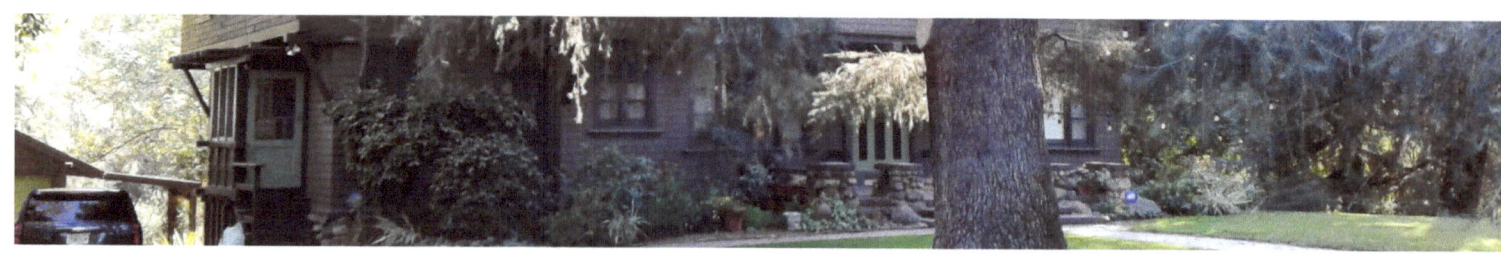

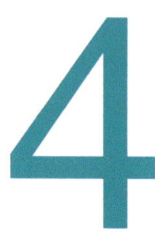

Garfield House – 1904

Craftsman Style – Charles and Henry Greene, Architects

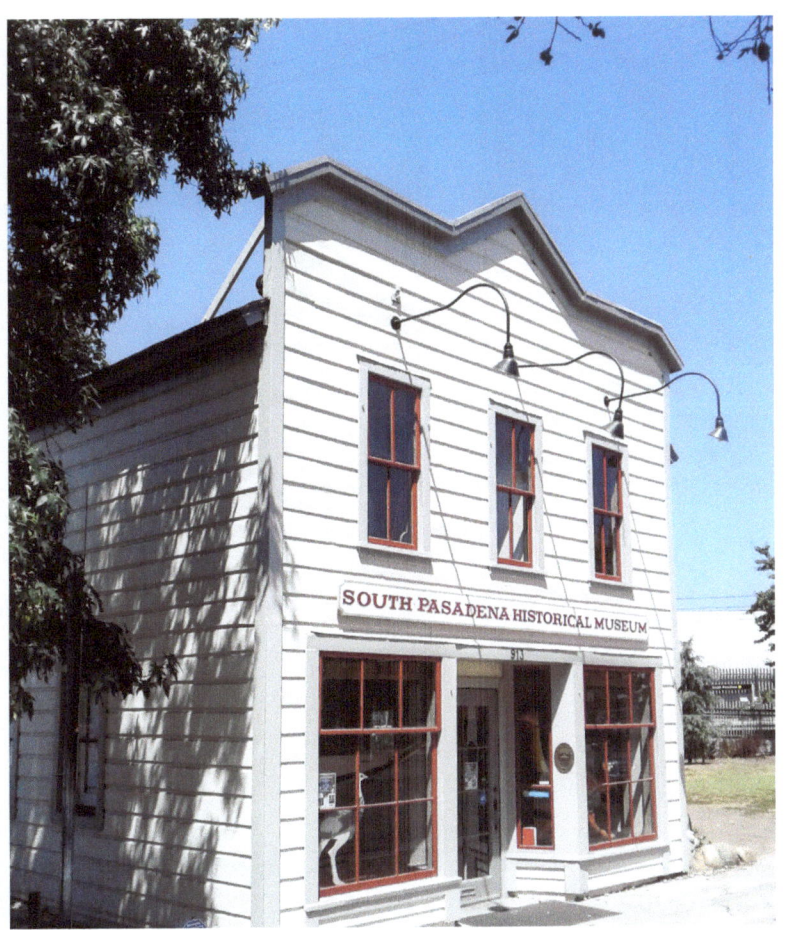
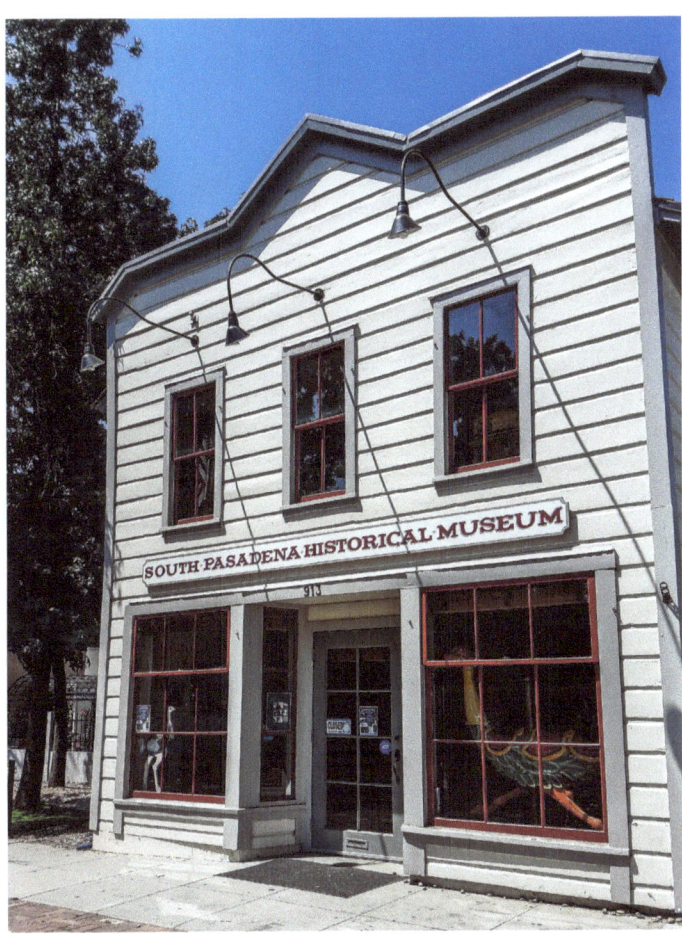
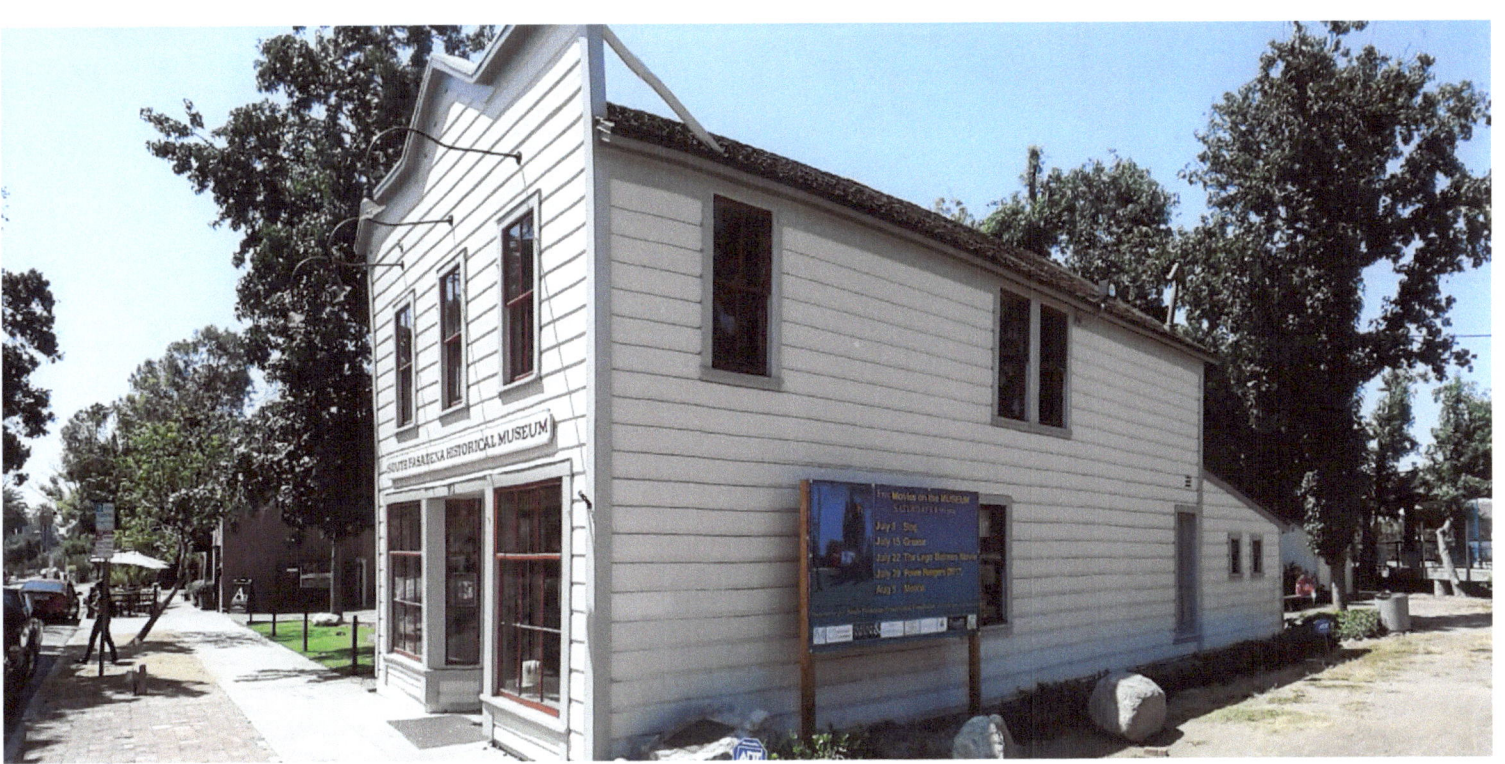

Meridian Iron Works - 1887

Victorian era store front – Architect unknown

5

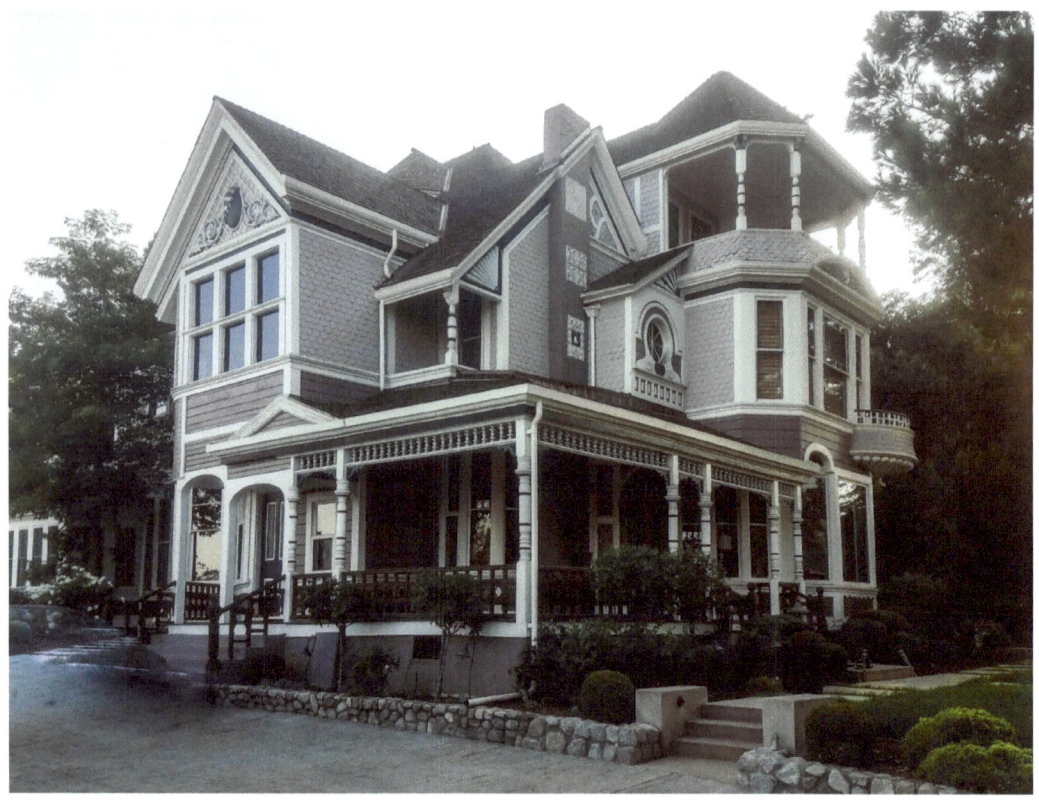
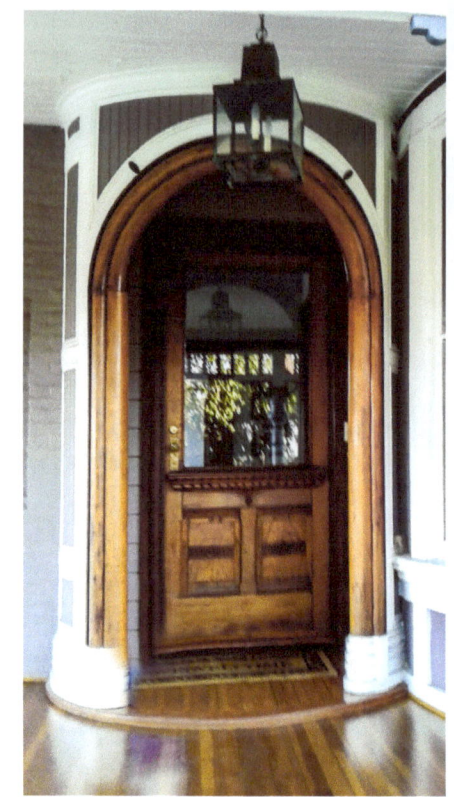
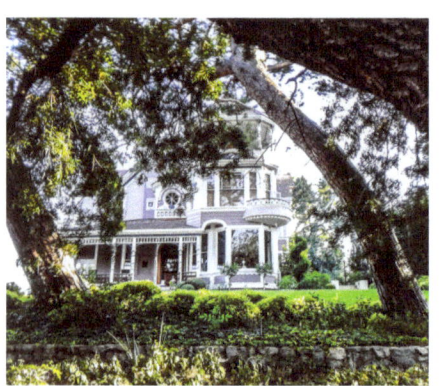
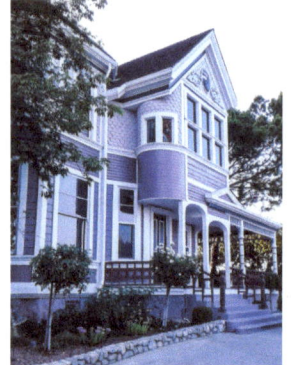
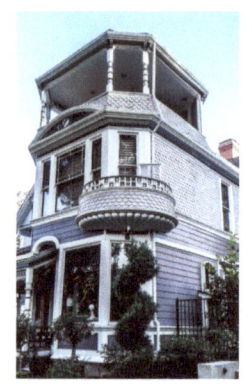
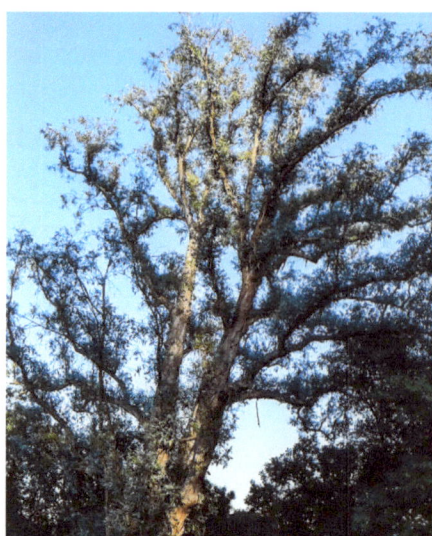
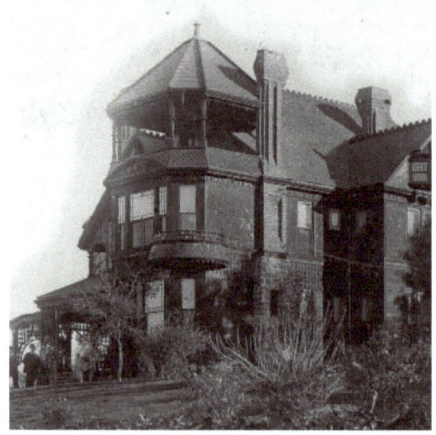
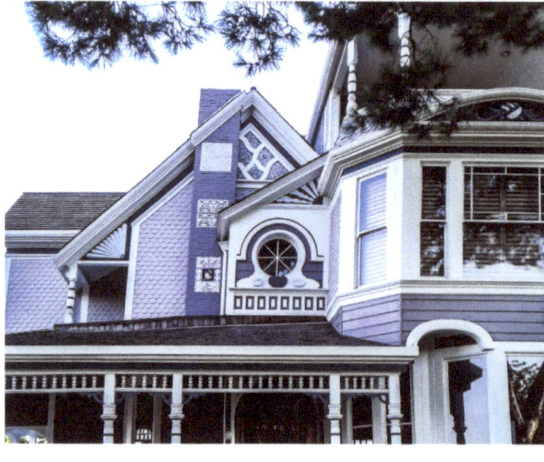
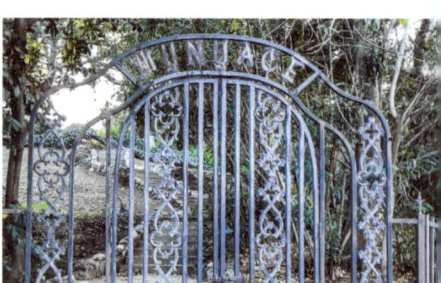

6

Wynyate - 1887

Queen Anne Victorian – W. R. Norton, Architect

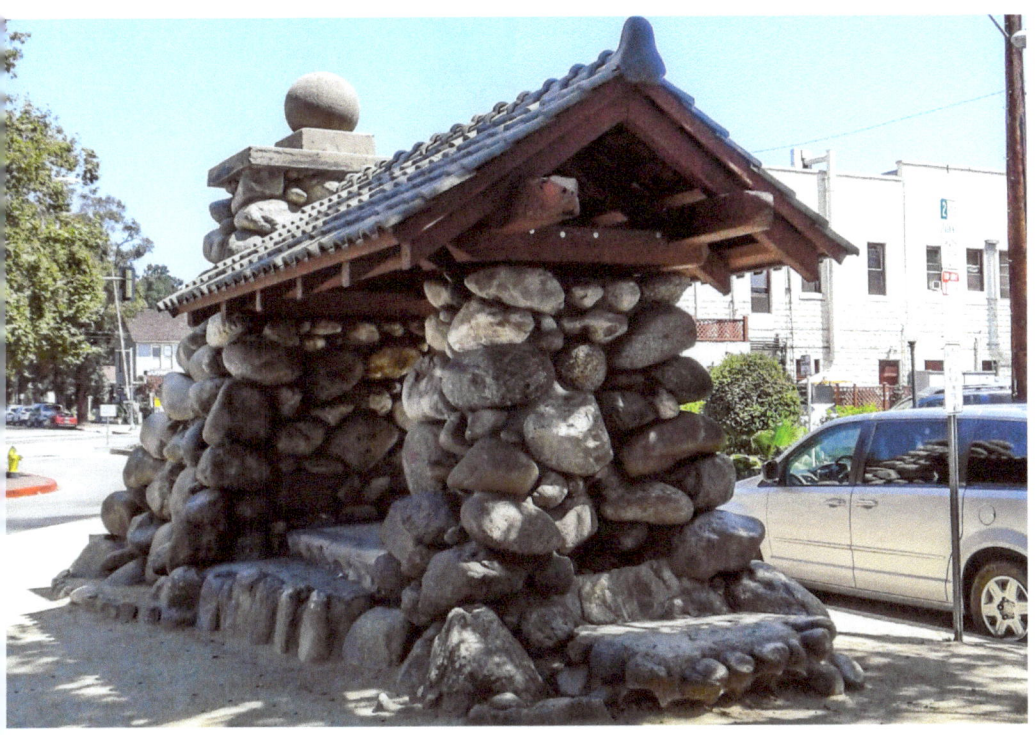
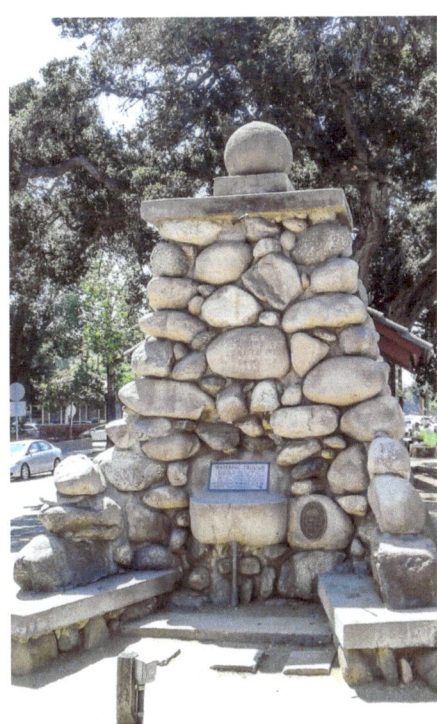
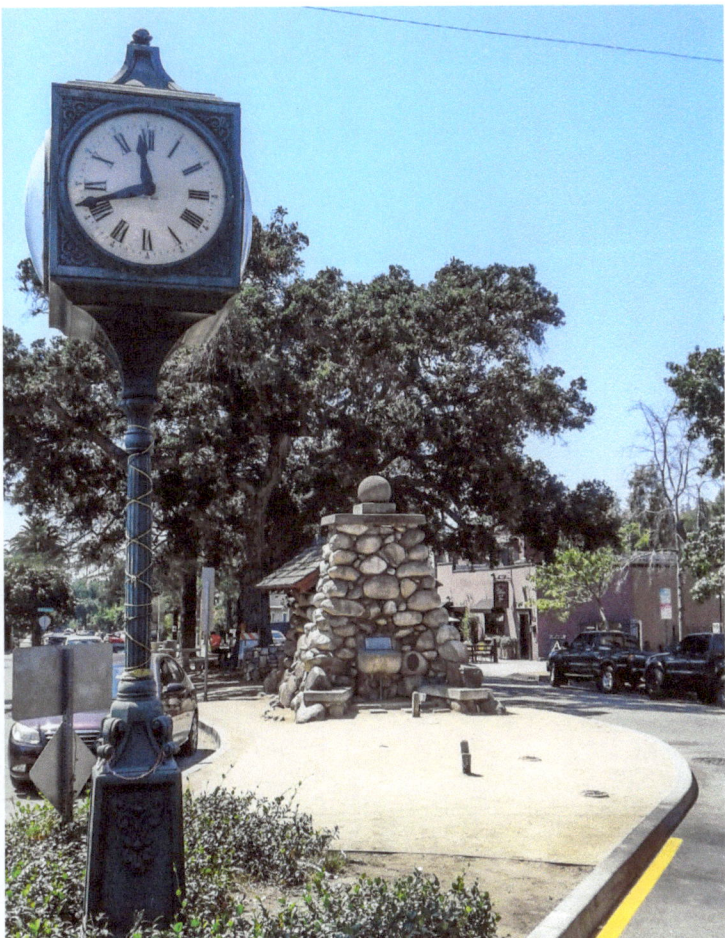
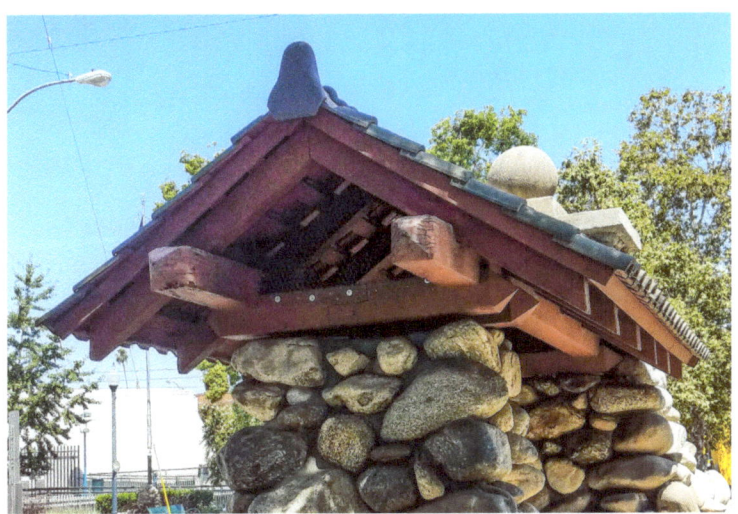
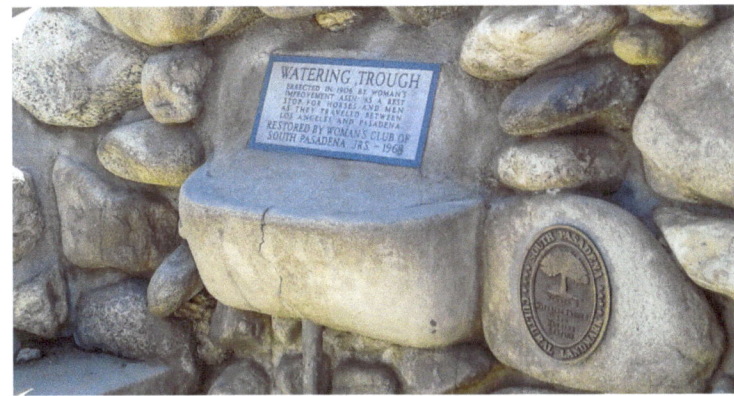

Watering Trough and Wayside Station – 1906

Craftsman Style - Designed by Norton Marsh

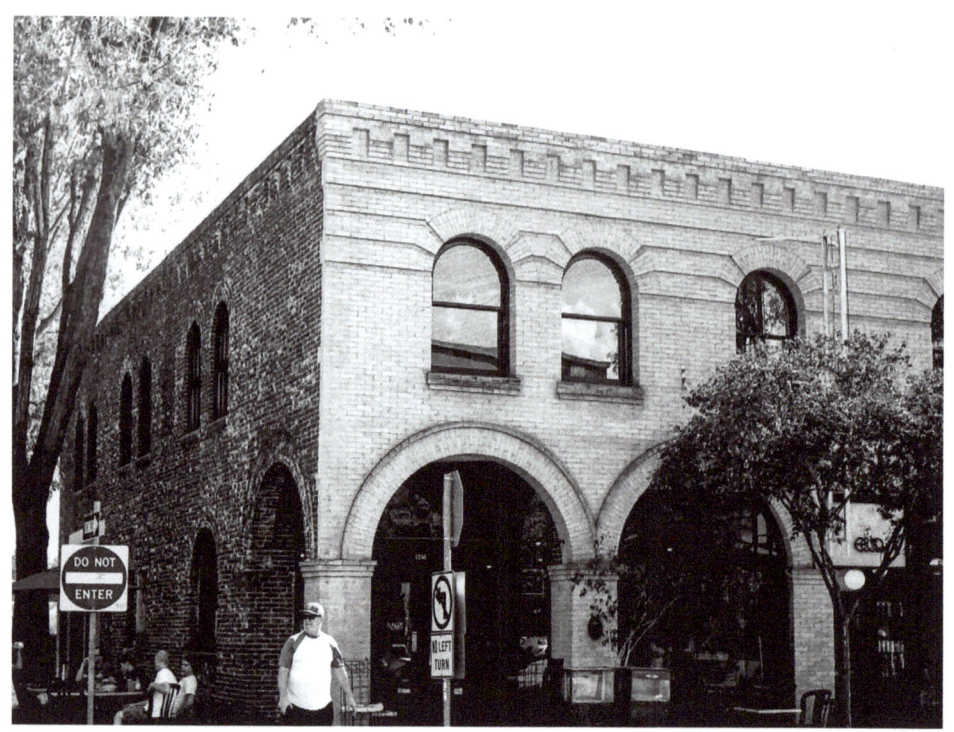
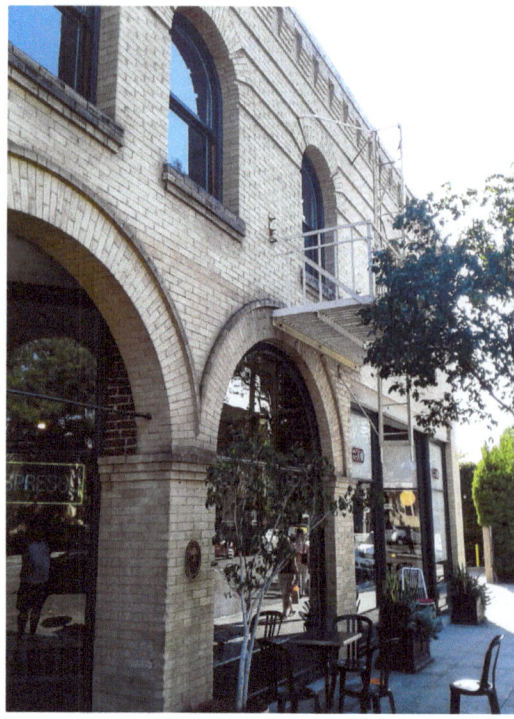
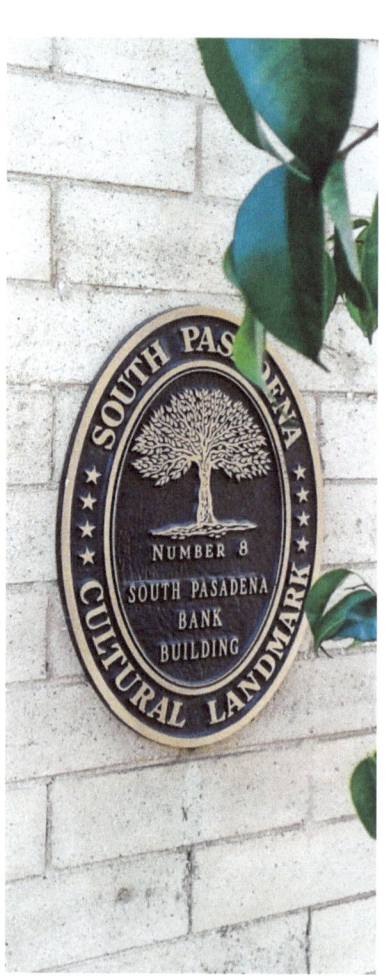
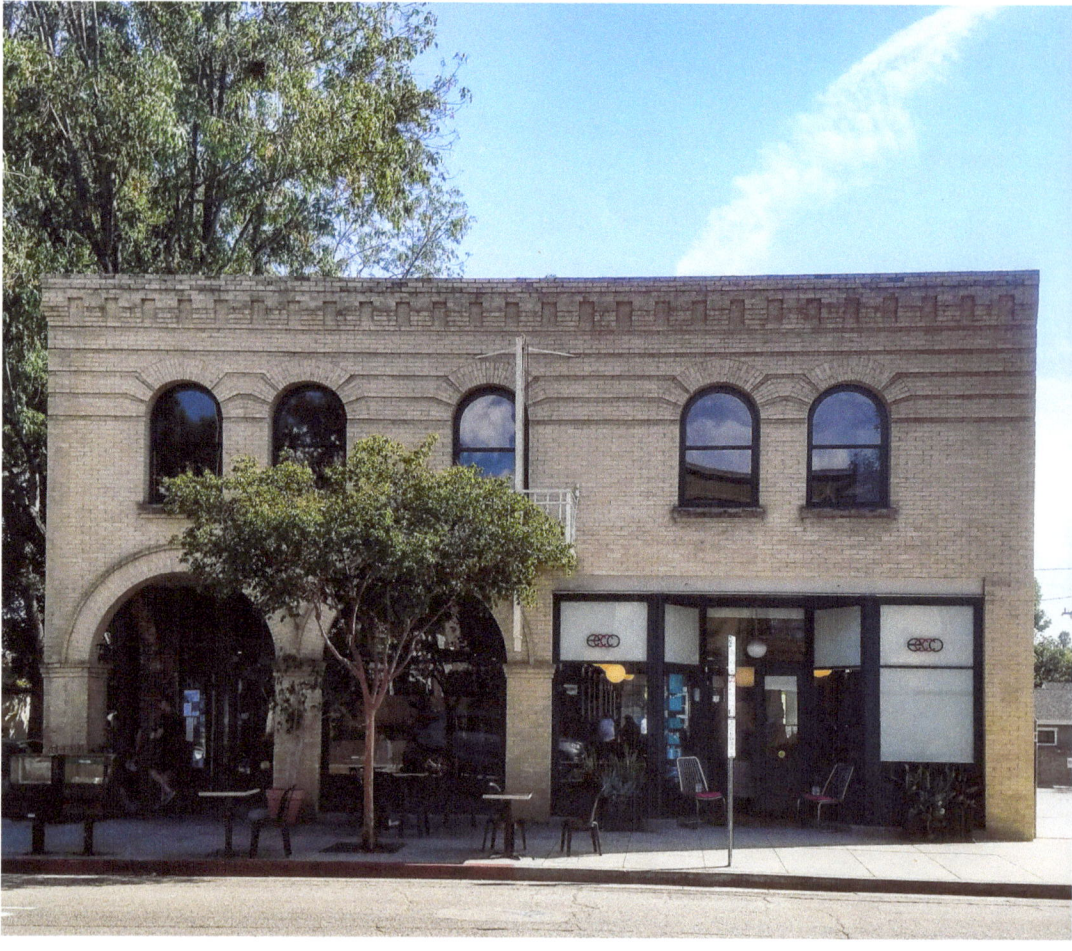

8

South Pasadena Bank Building – 1904

Brick Commercial Building - Architect unknown

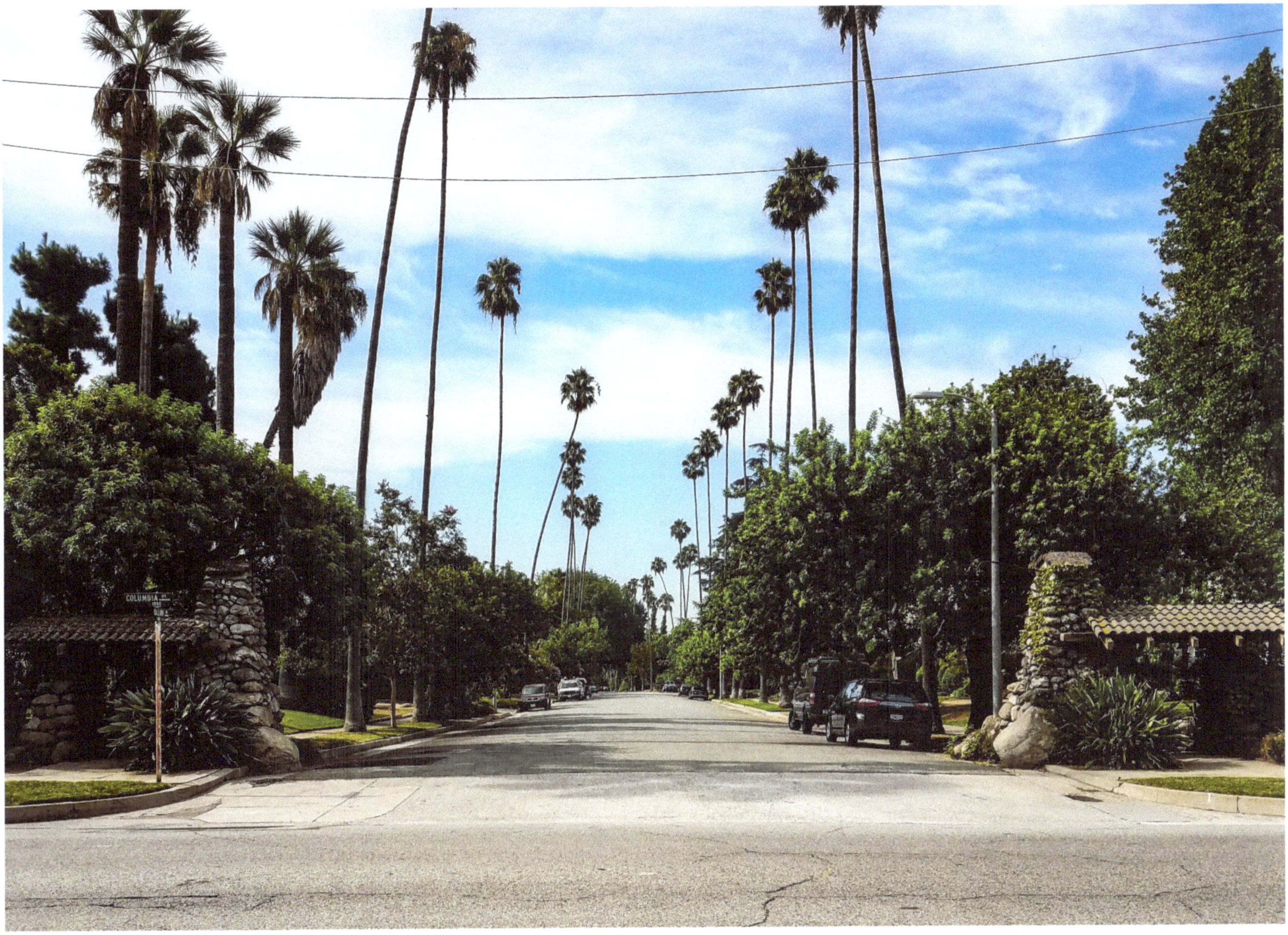

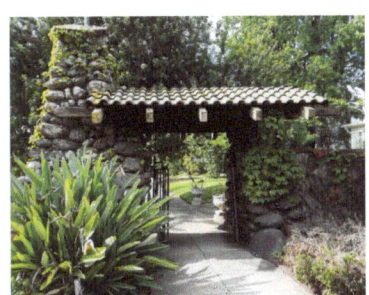
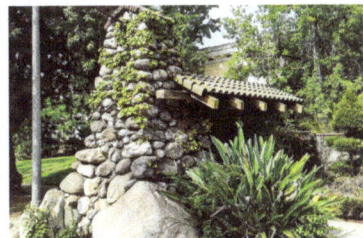
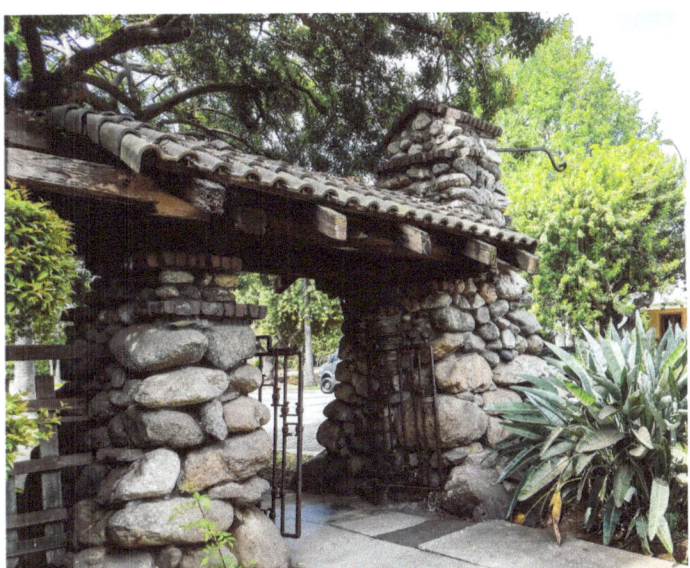
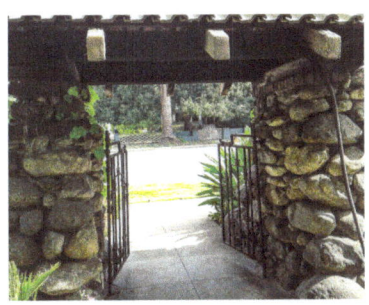
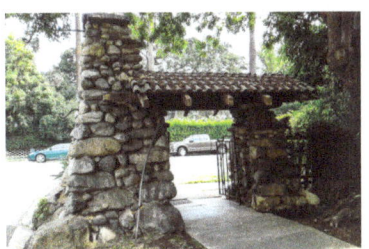

Oaklawn Portals – 1905

Craftsman Style – Designed by Charles and Henry Green

9

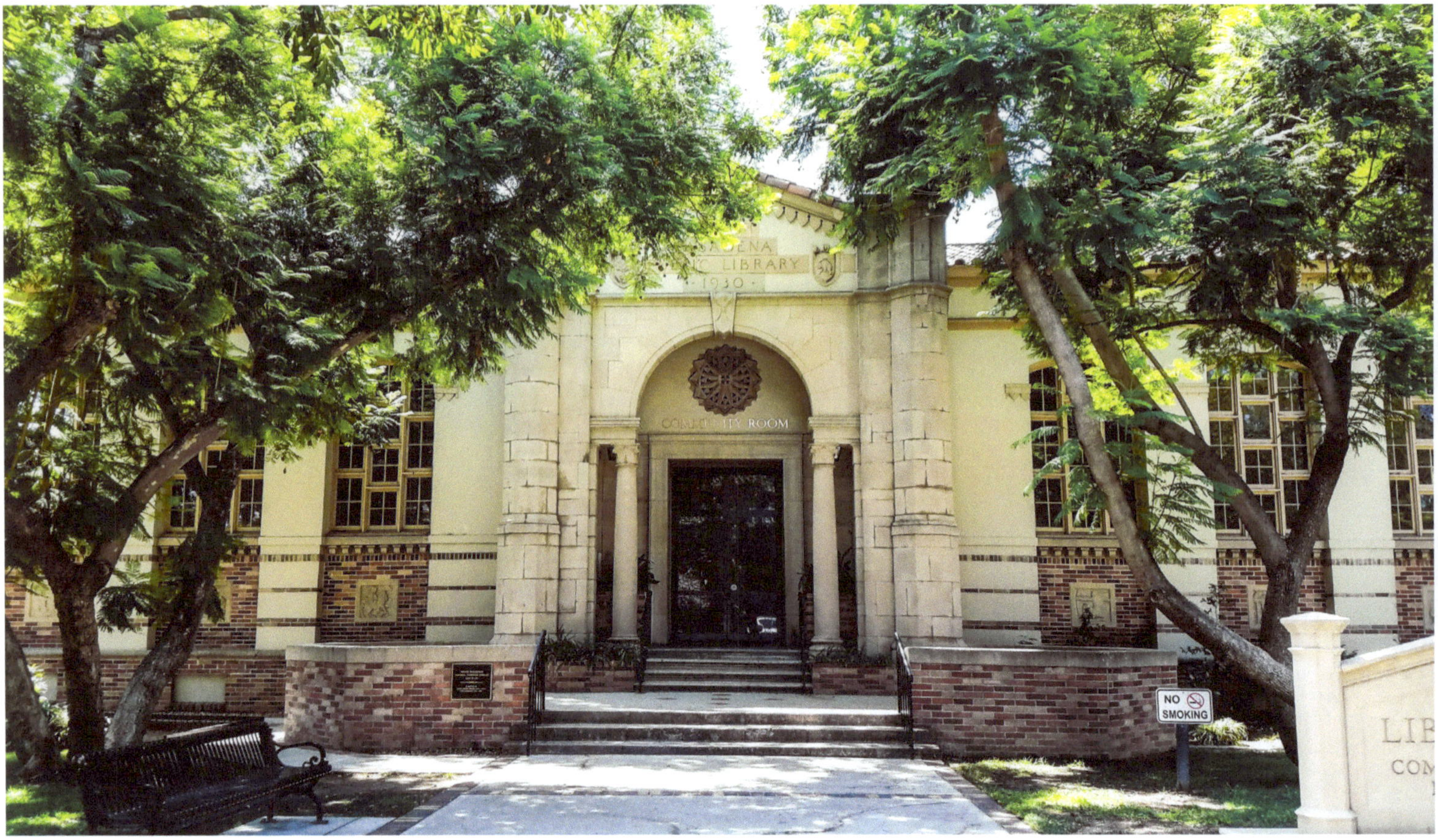

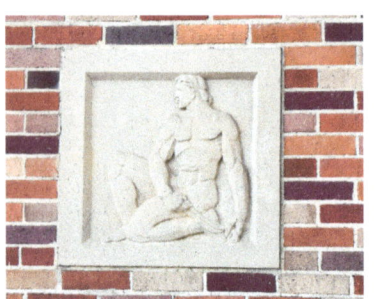
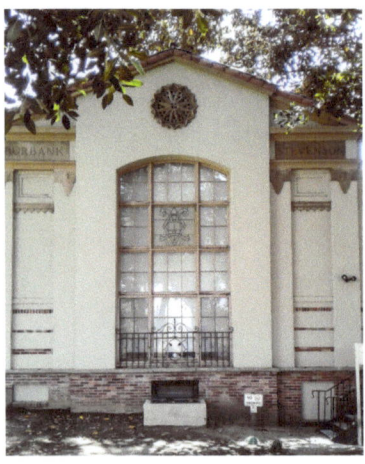
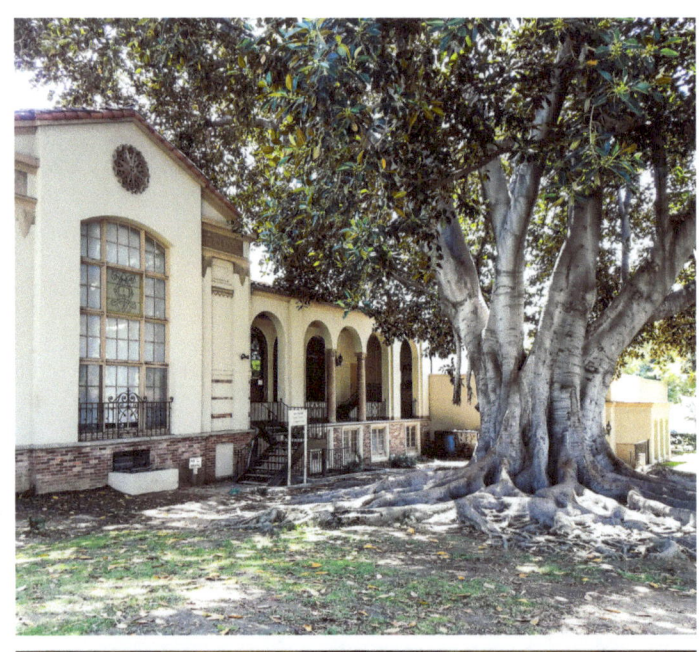
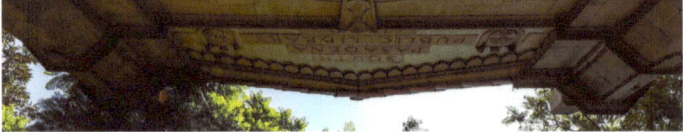
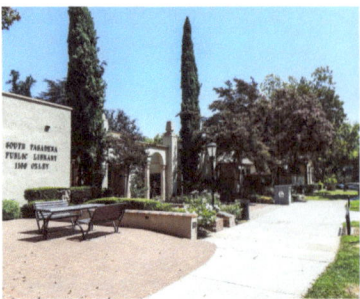
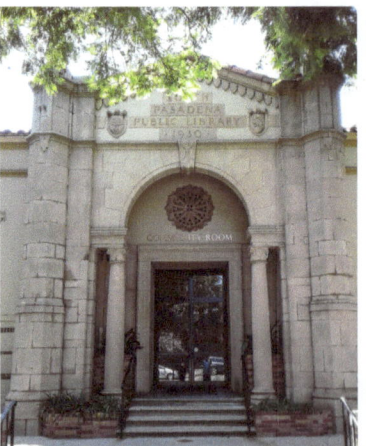
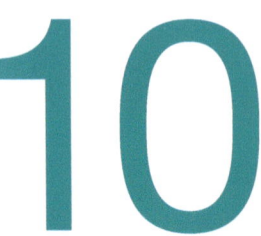

10 South Pasadena Public Library - 1907

Neo Classical Style - Norman Marsh, Architect

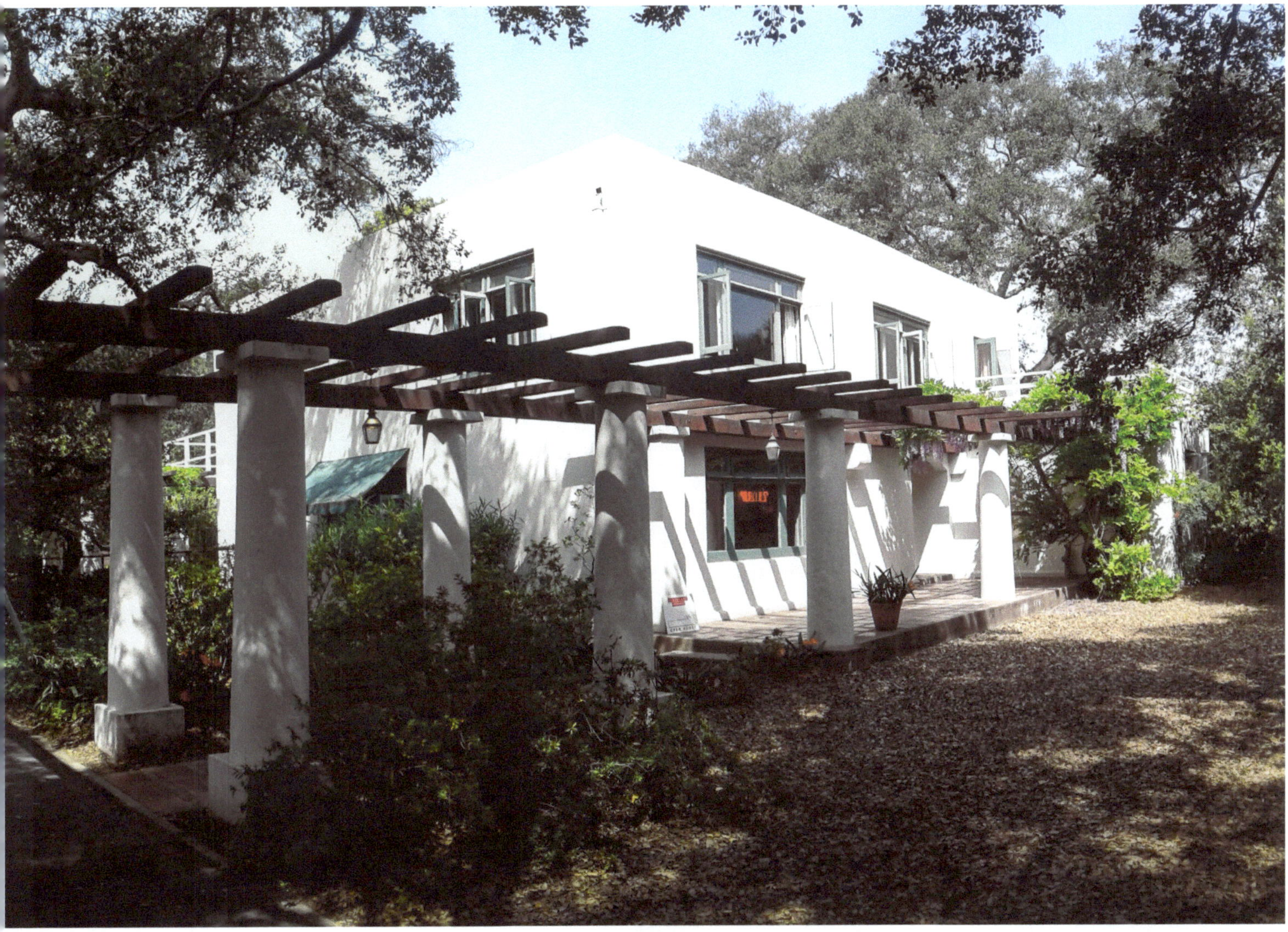

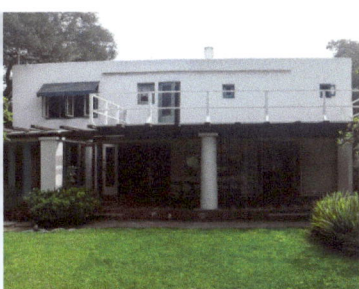
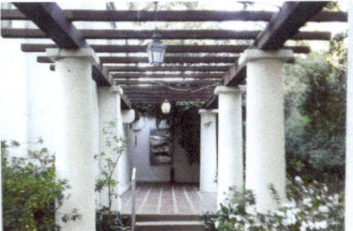
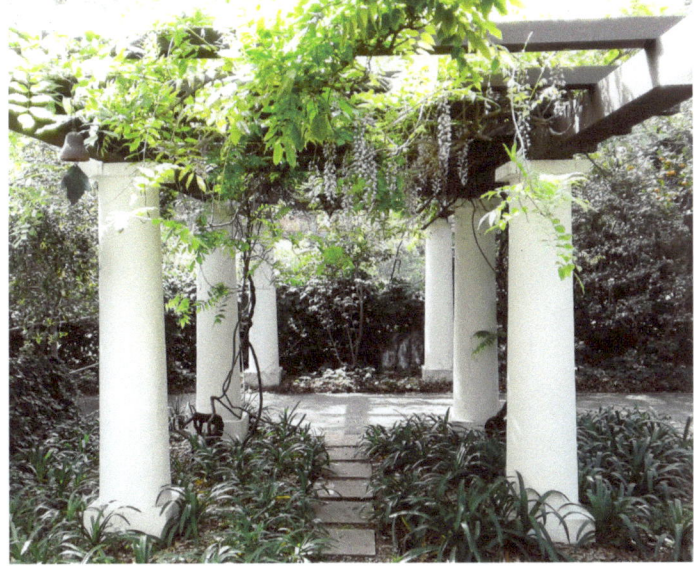
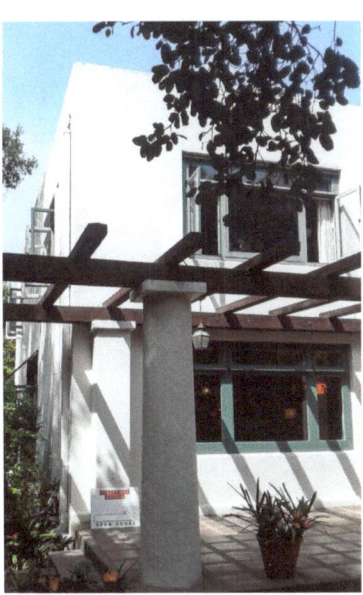

Miltimore House – 1911

Early International Style – Irving Gill, Architect

11

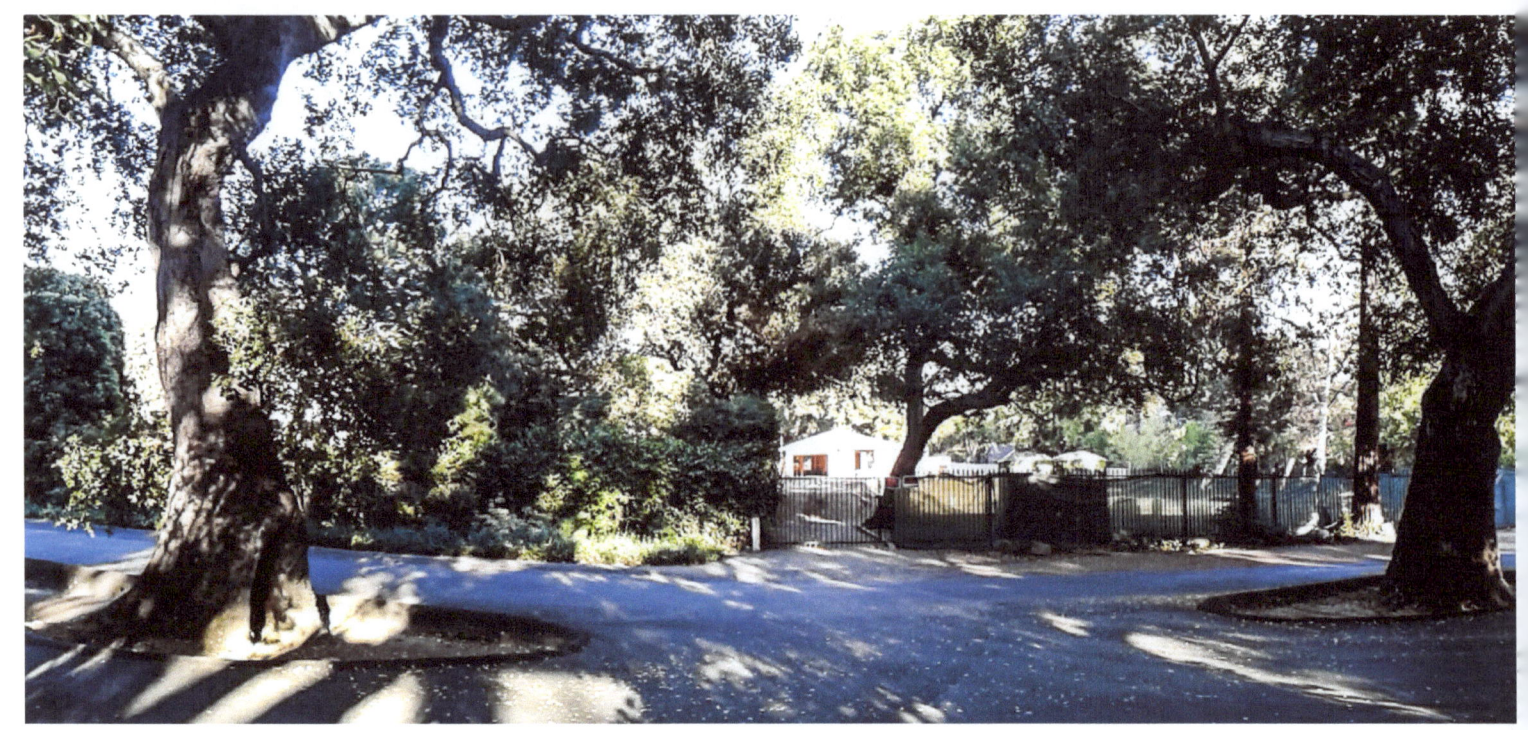
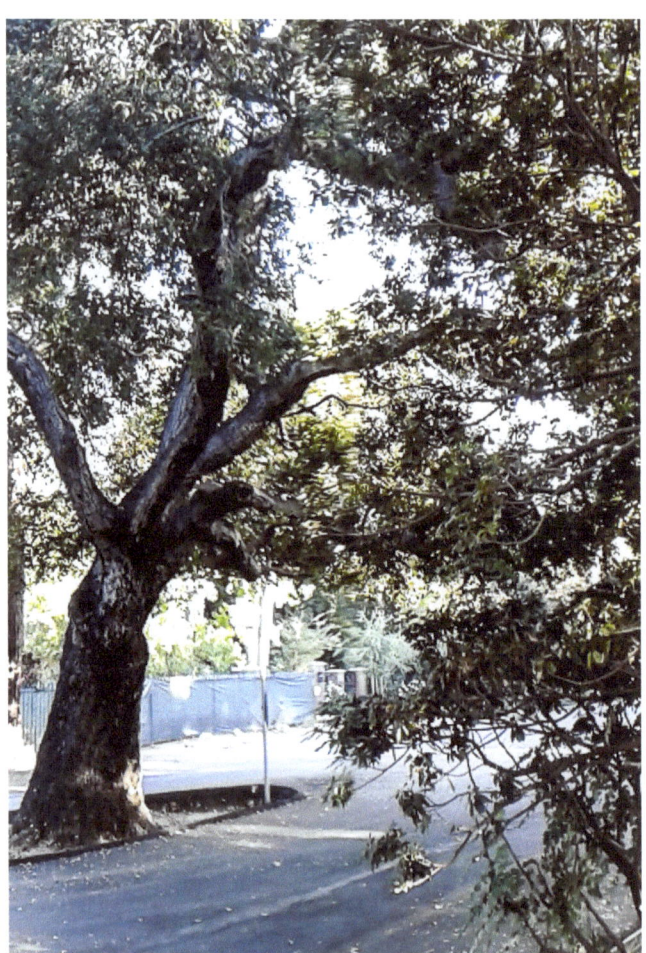
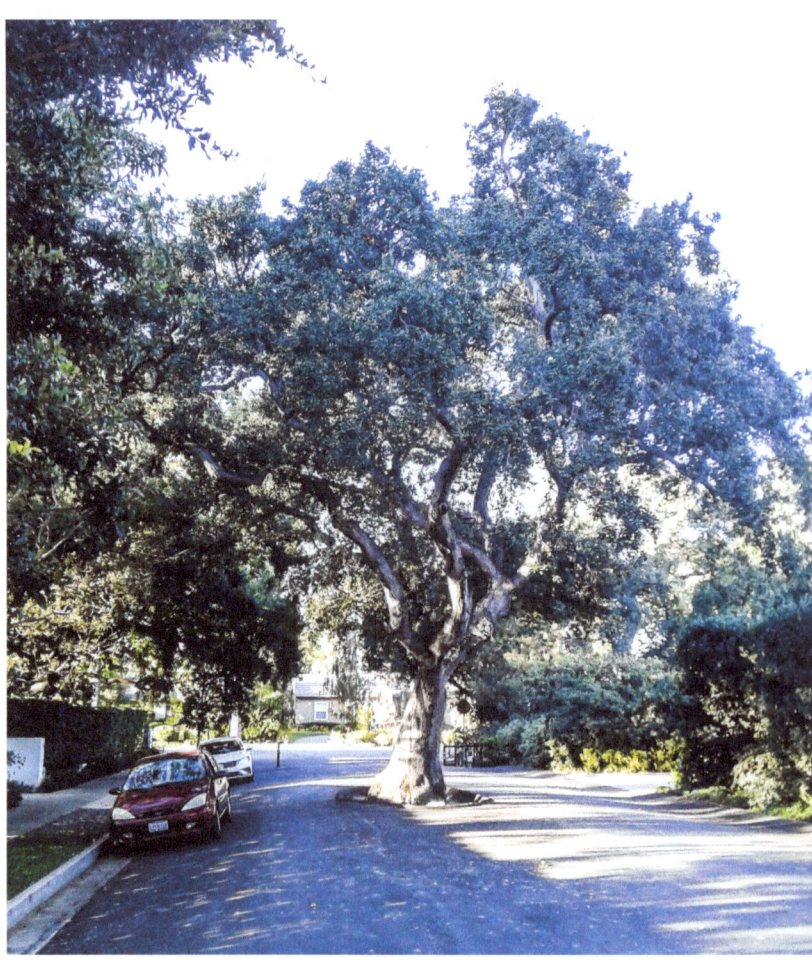

12 Ashbourne Drive and Chelton Way – 1891
Original oak trees remain in the middle of the street.

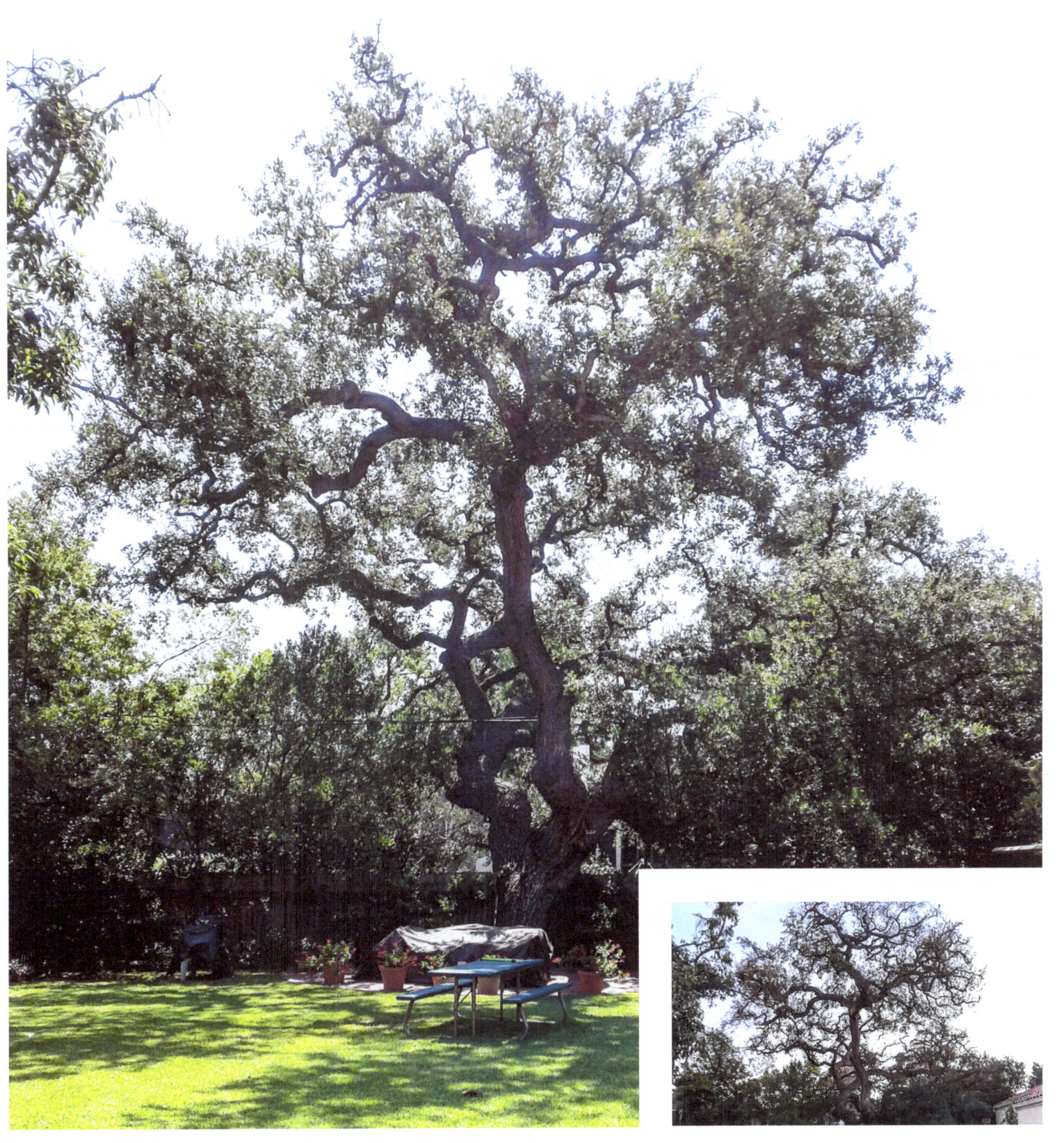

Clokey Oak Tree

200 year old deciduous hybrid oak tree

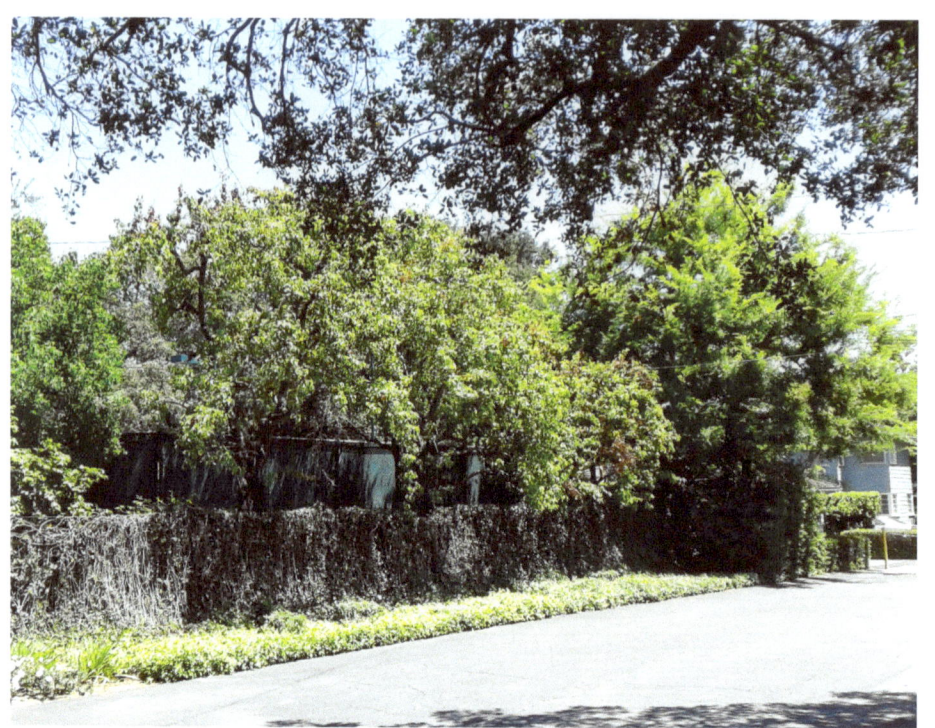
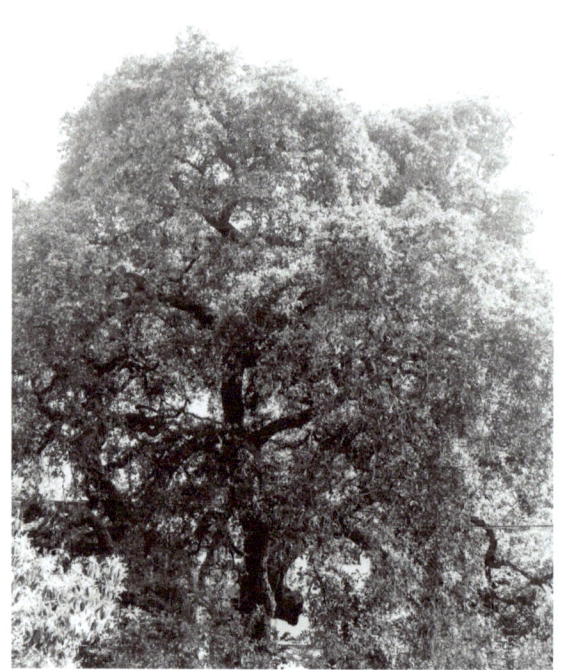

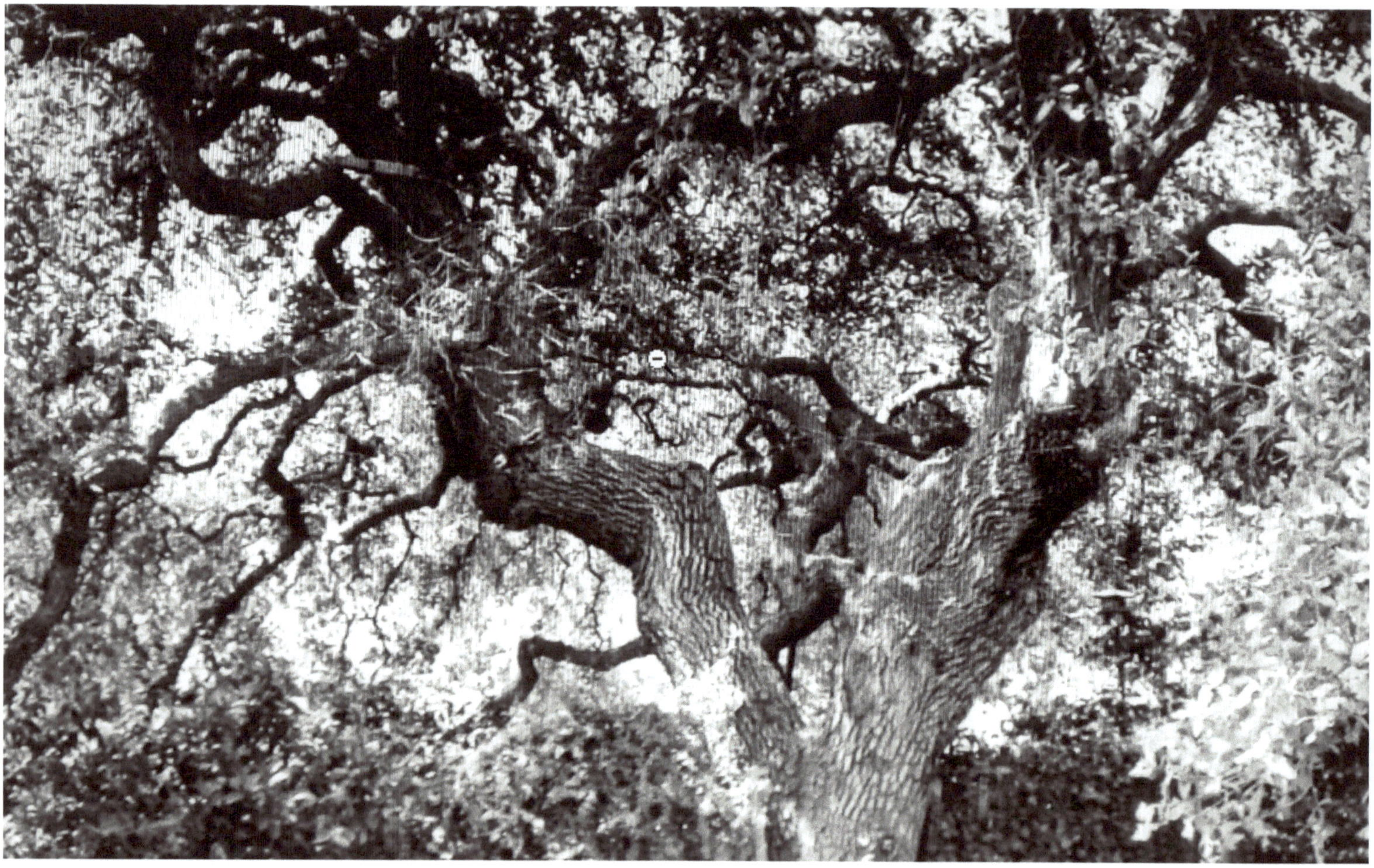

14

Ashbourne – Chelten Hybrid Oak Tree

Deciduous Hybrid Oak Tree – died in 1981

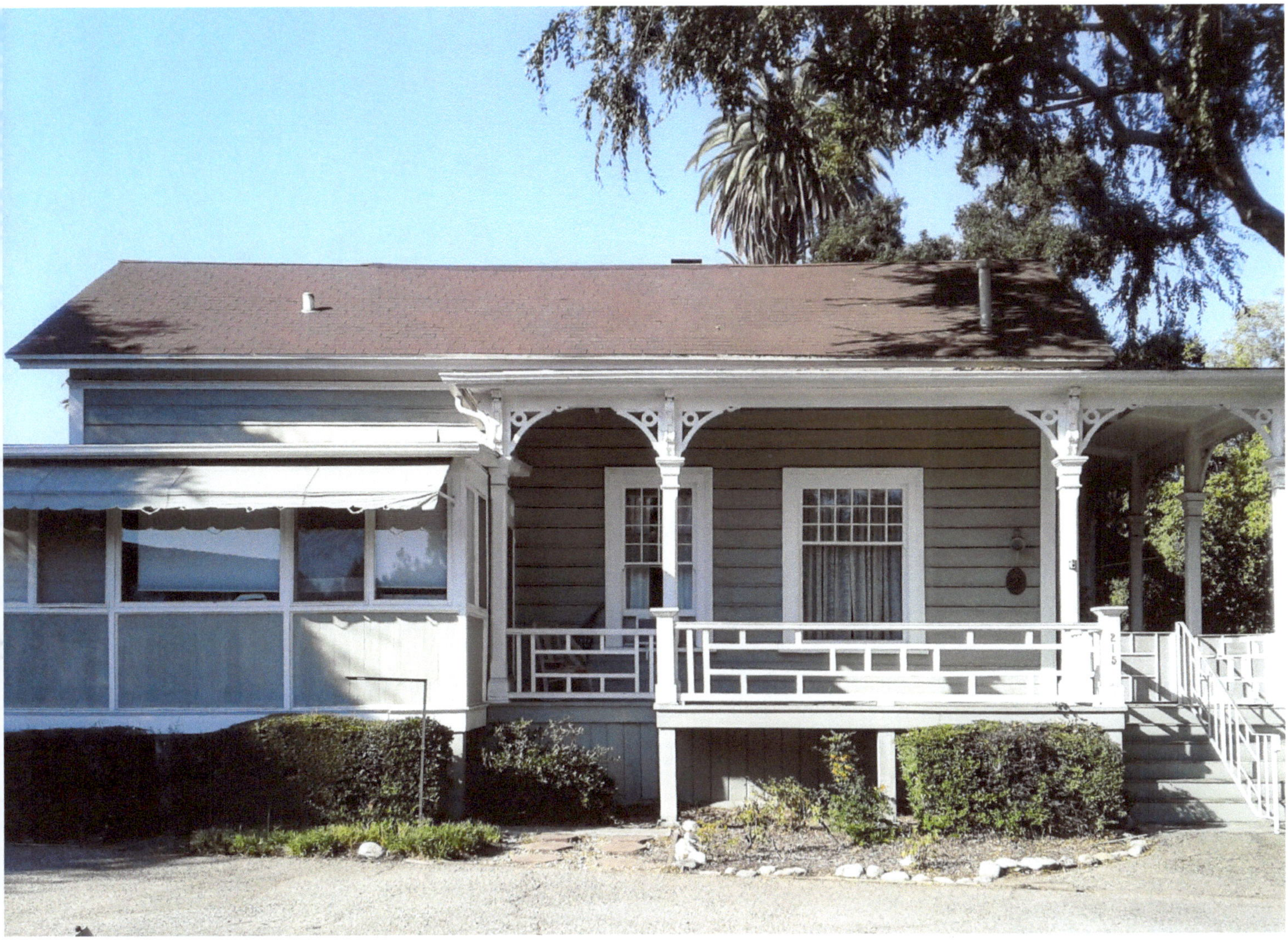

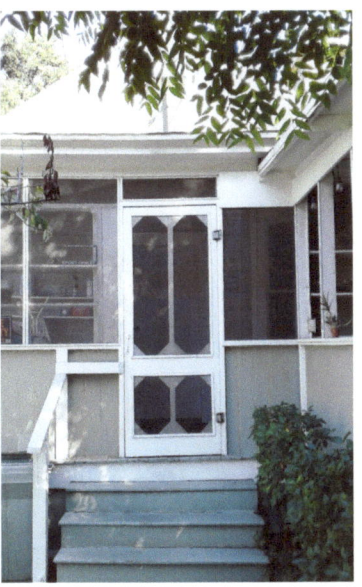
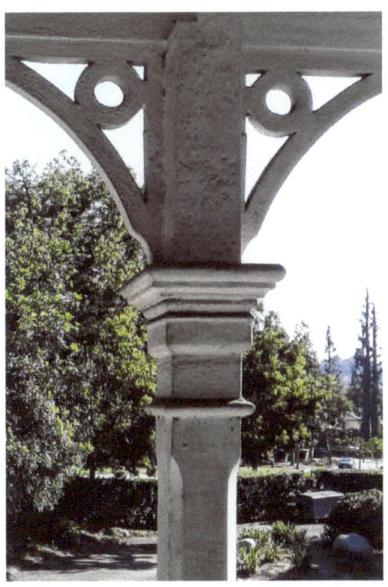
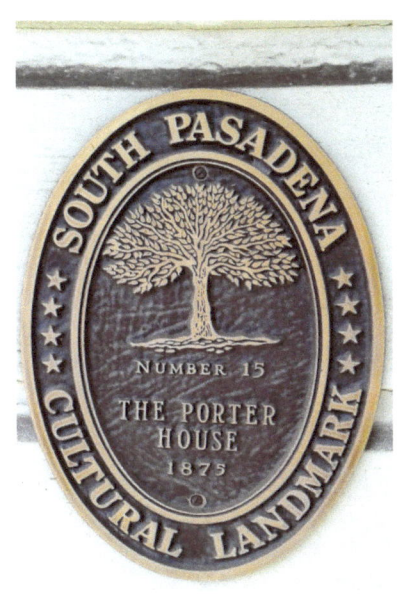
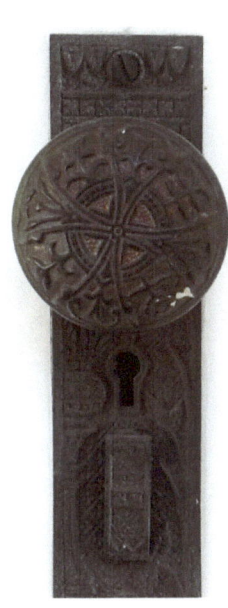

Andrew O. Porter House – 1874

Folk Victorian – Architect unknown

15

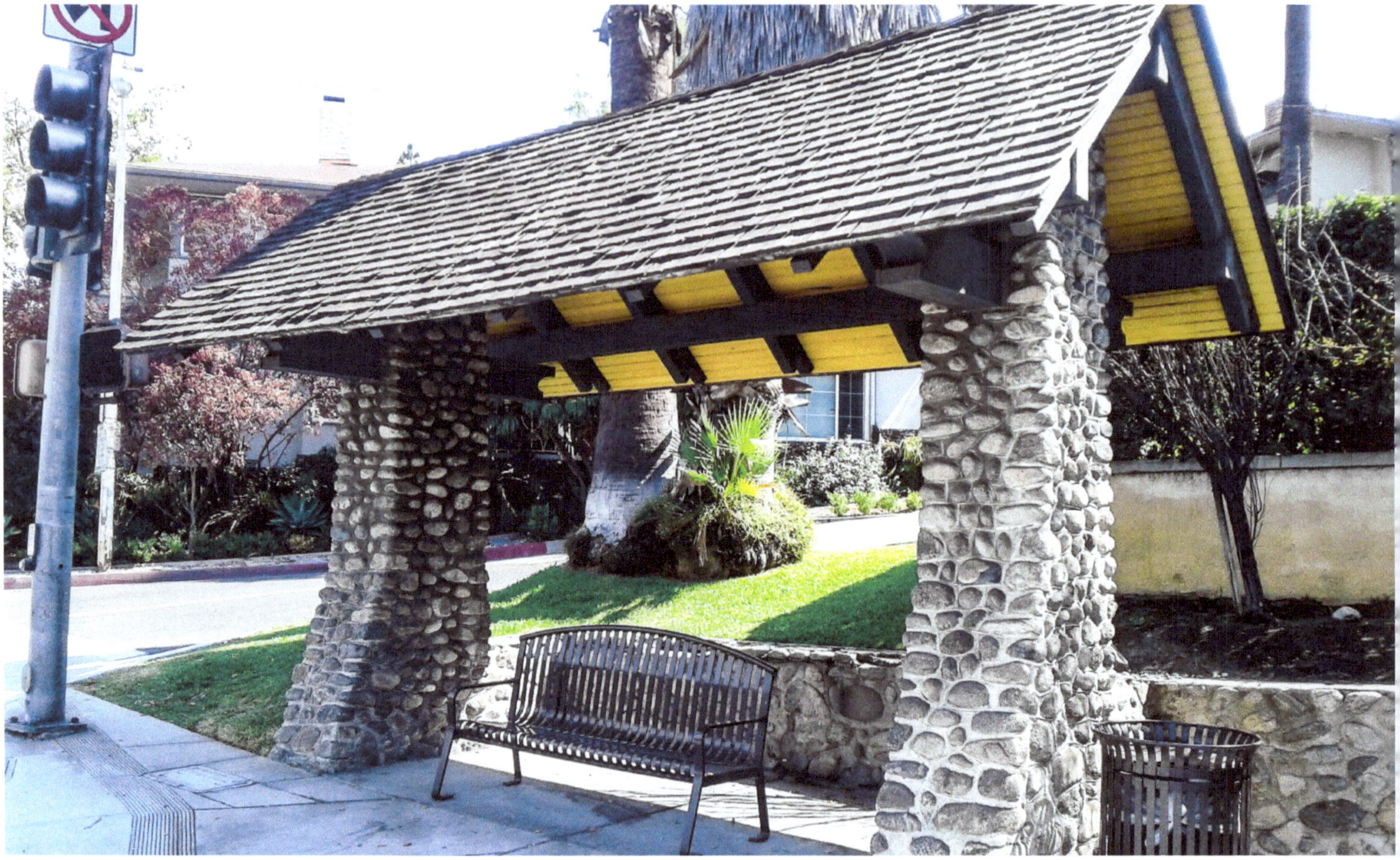

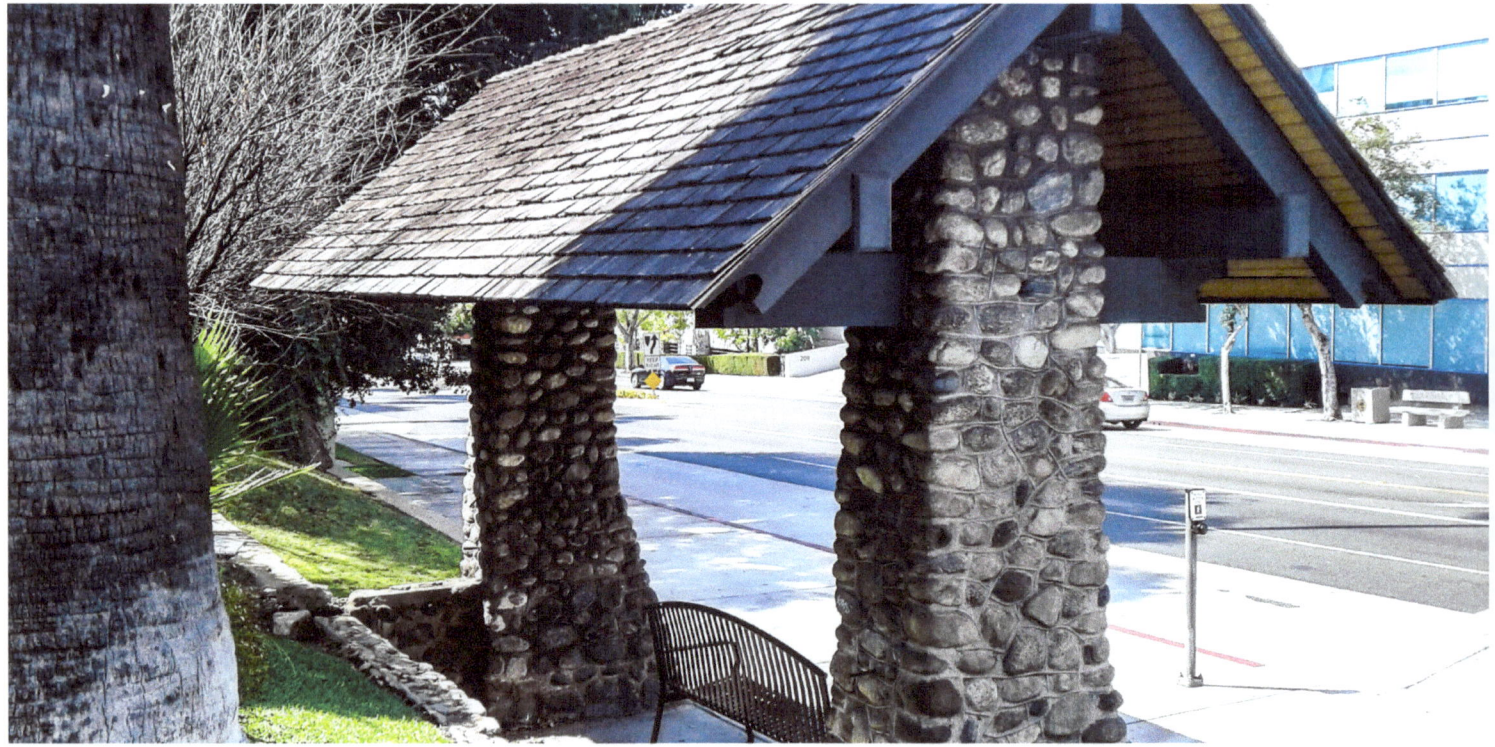

16 Raymond Hill Waiting Station - 1903

Craftsman shelter for trolley car riders

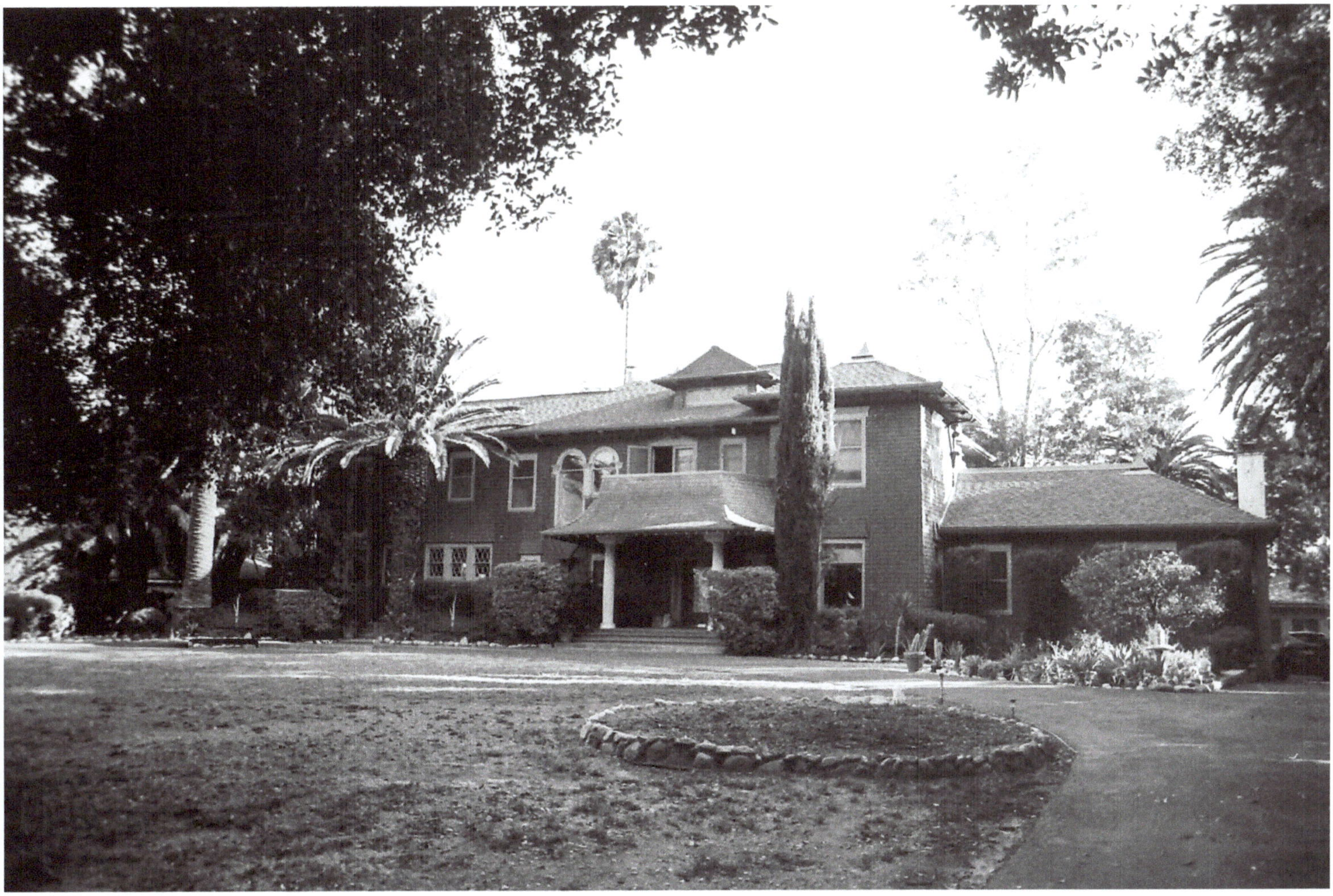

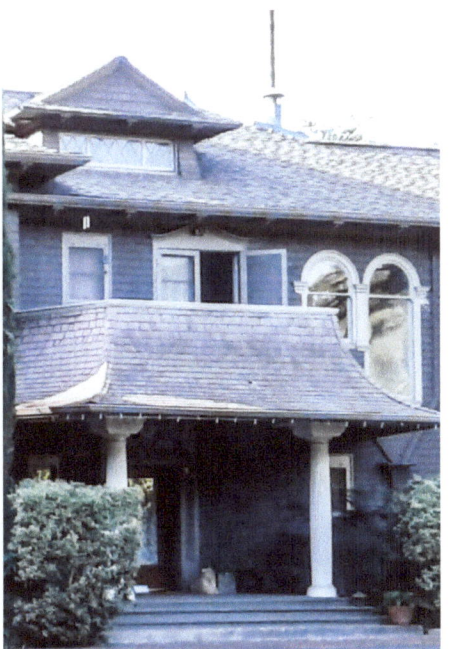
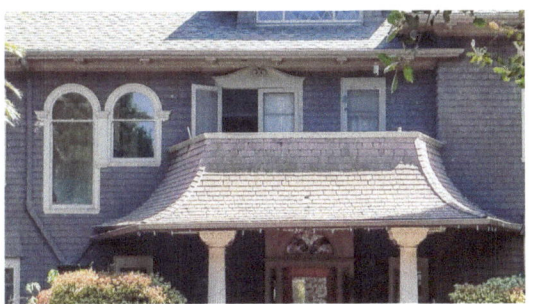
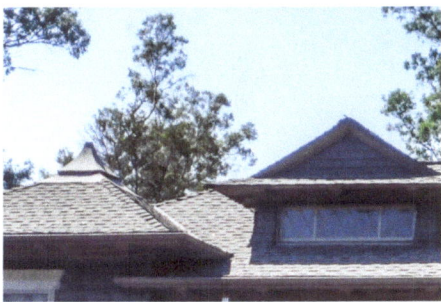
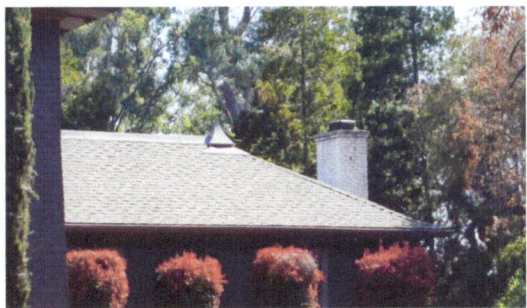
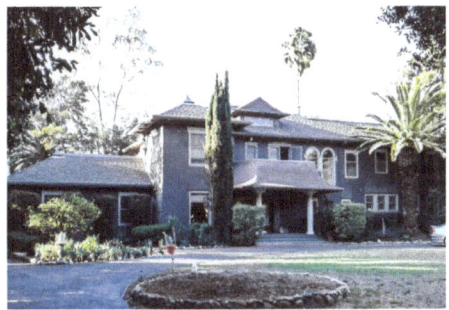

Howard Longley House - 1897

Eclectic Shingle Victorian style

Charles and Henry Greene, Architects

17

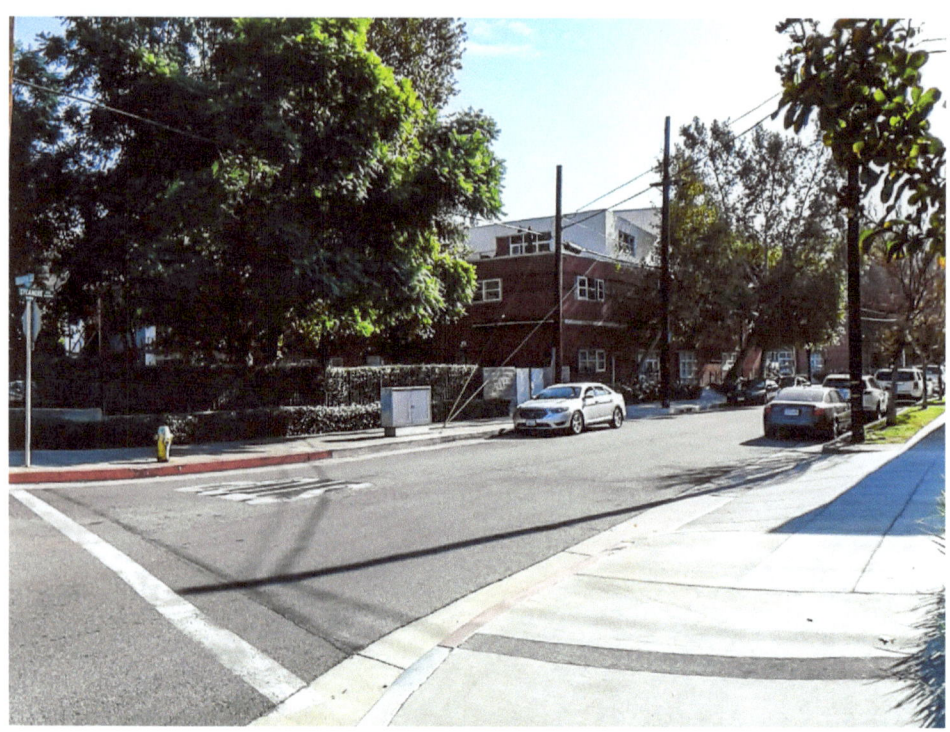
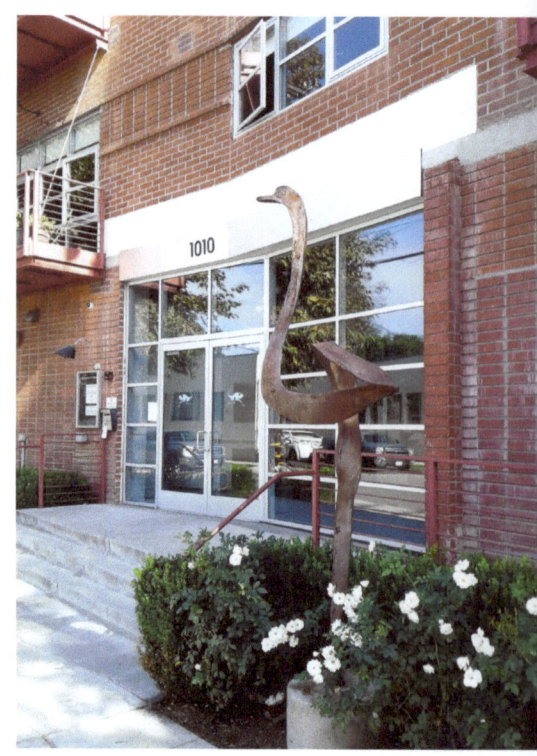
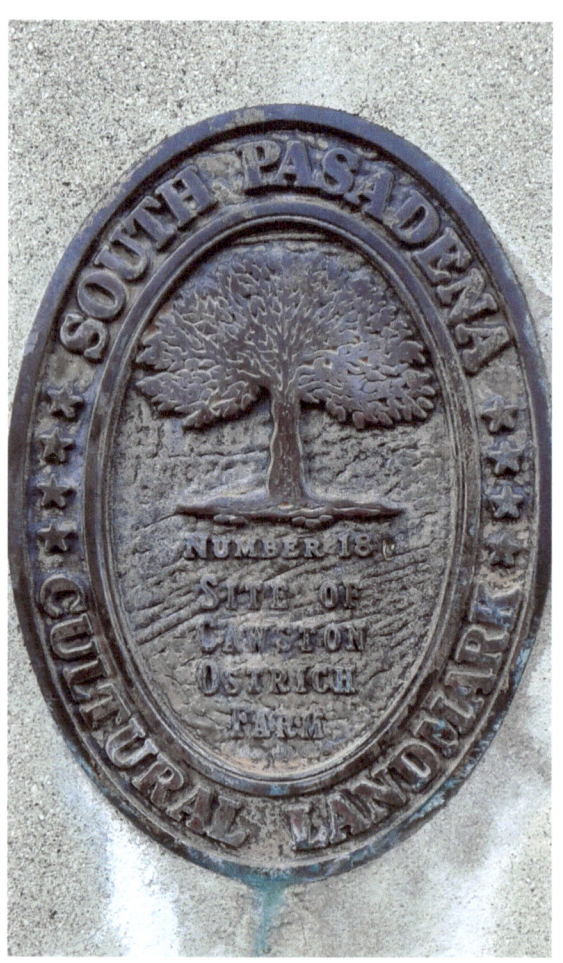
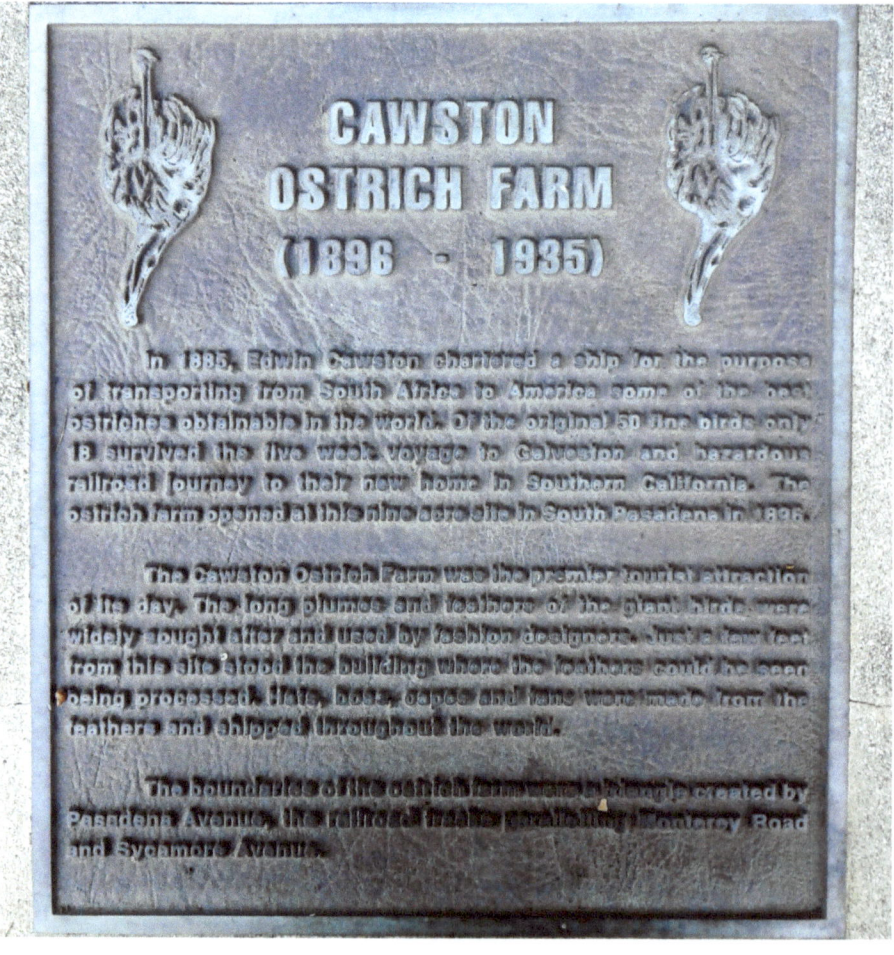

18

Cawston Ostrich Farm Site – 1896

Tourist attraction closed in 1935

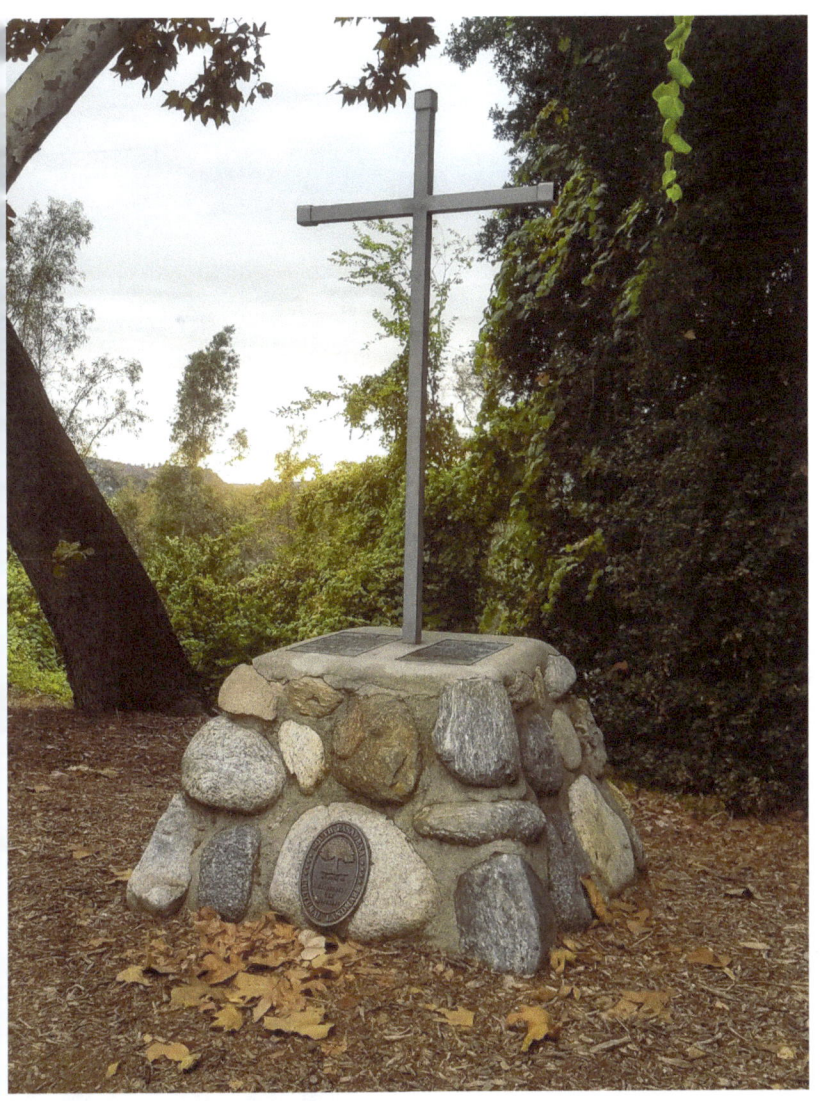
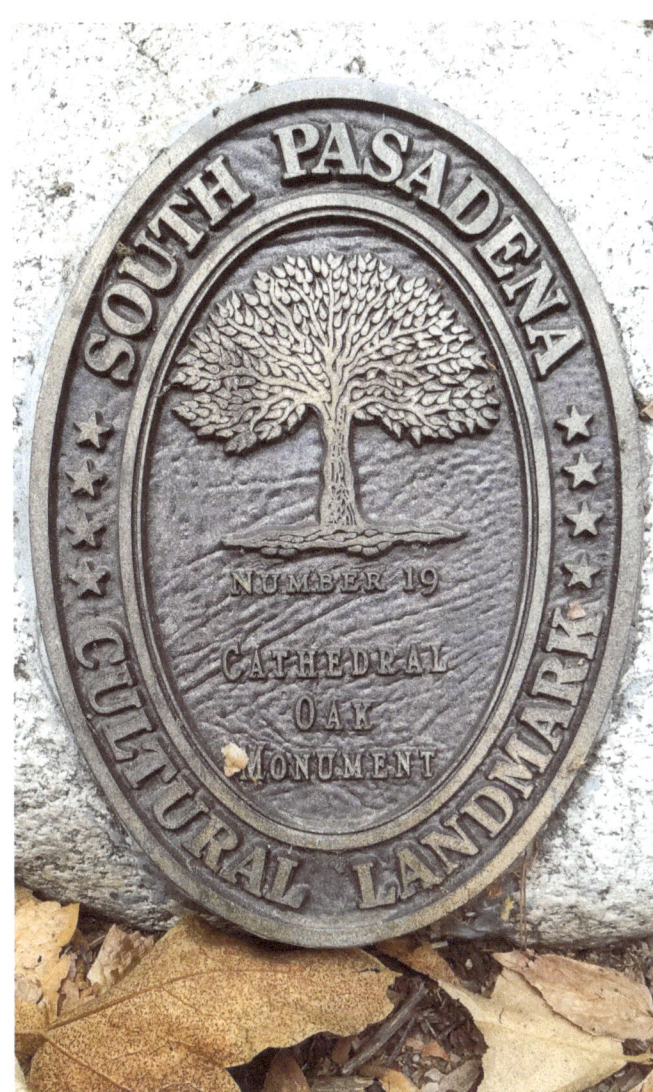
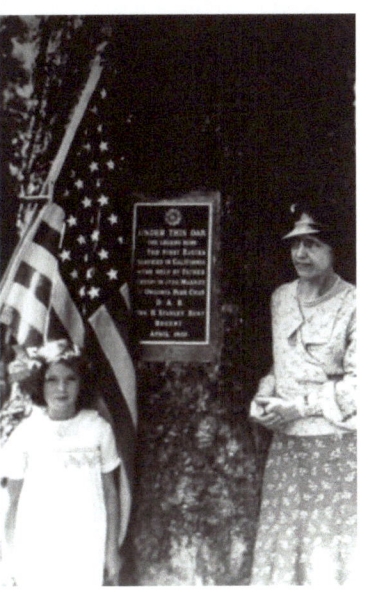
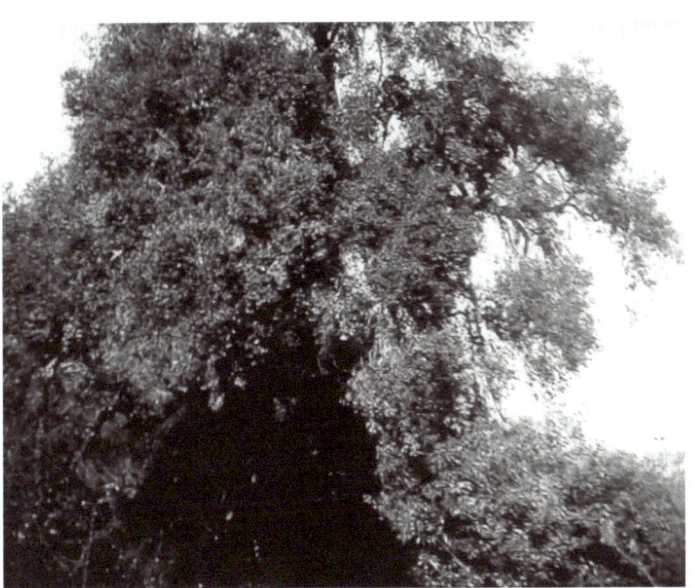
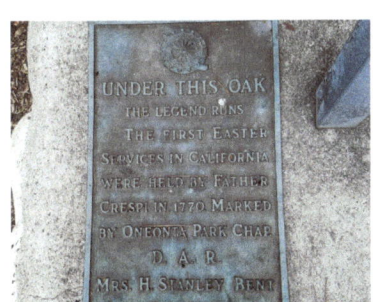
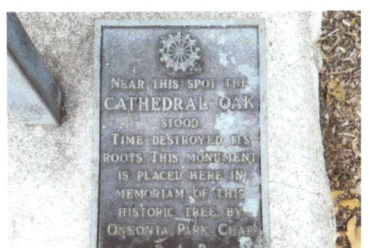

Cathedral Oak Monument - 1952

Mission Style Cross – Designed by Ruth Shellhorn

19

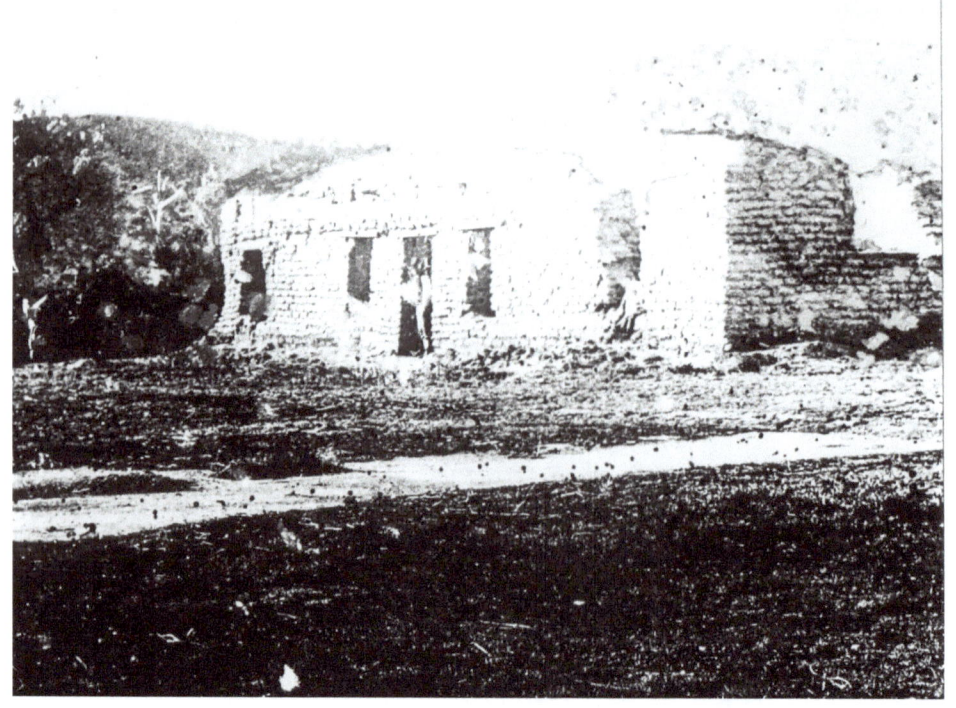
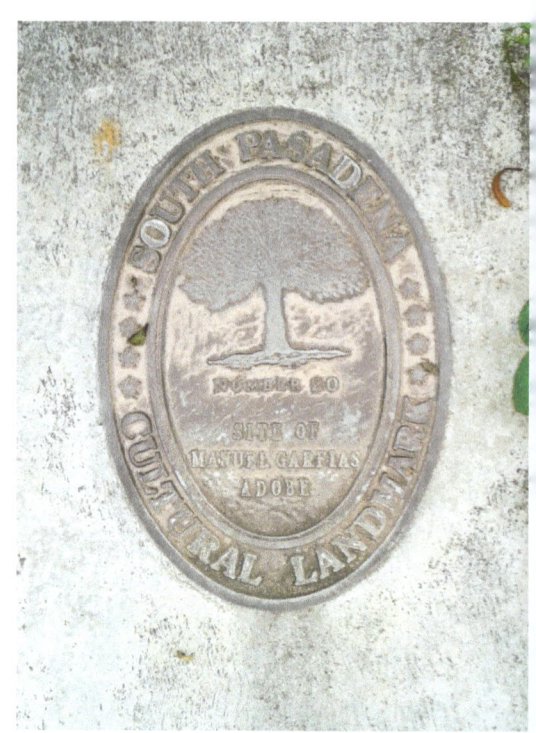

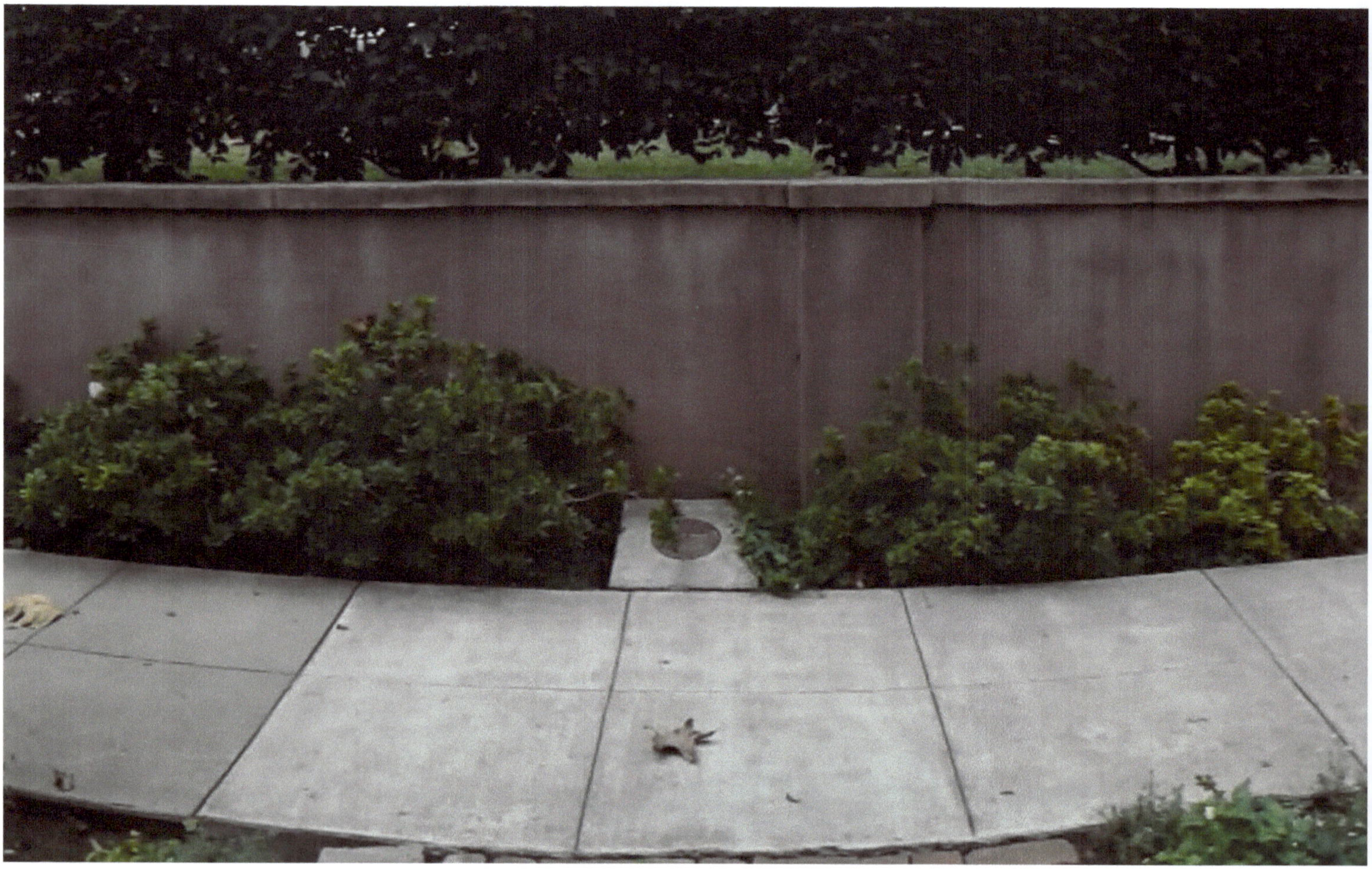

20 Manuel Garfias Adobe Site – 1852

First Adobe built in area – abandoned in 1880

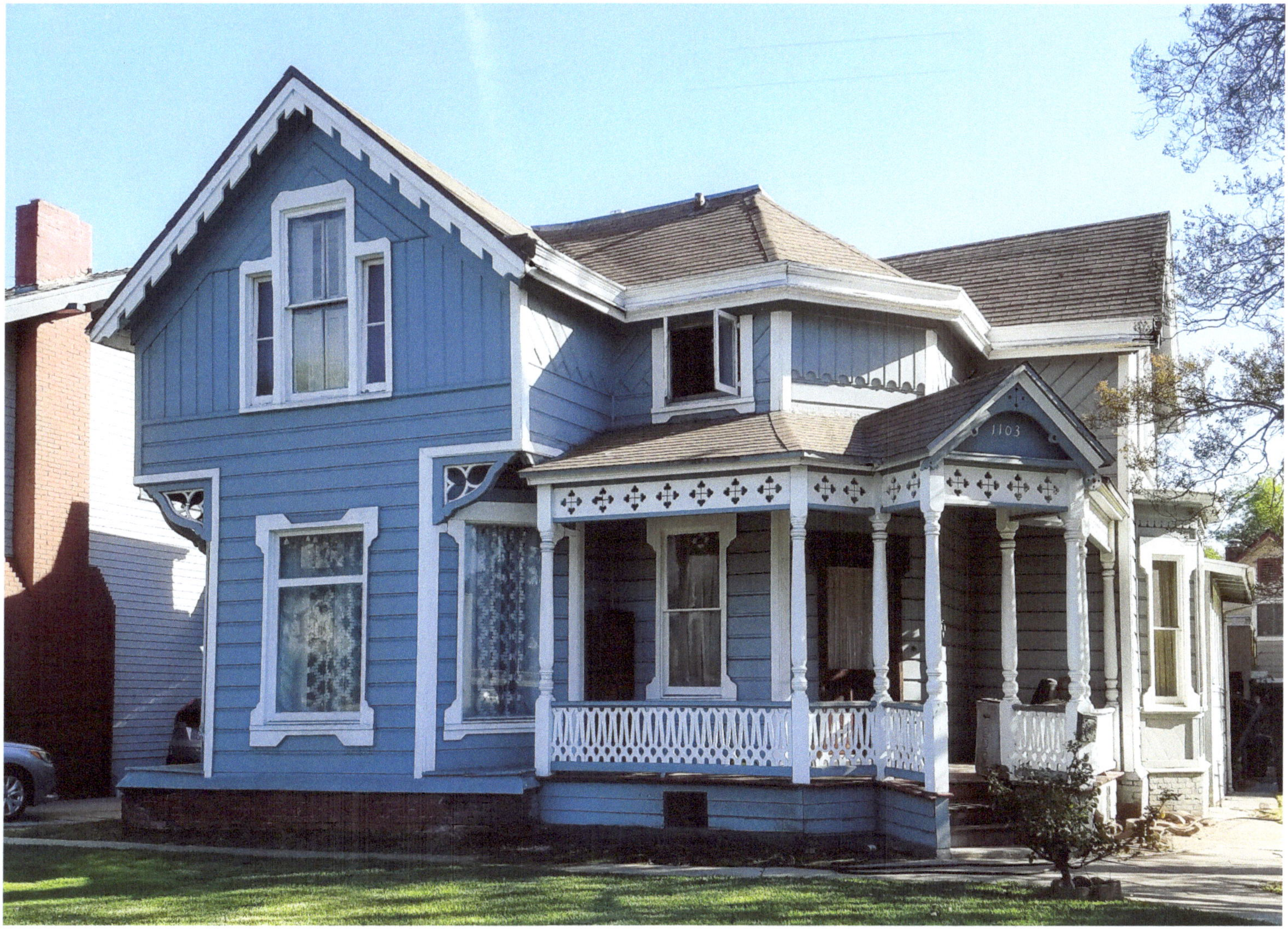

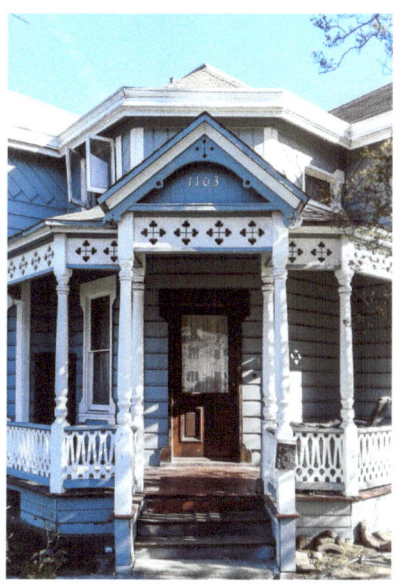
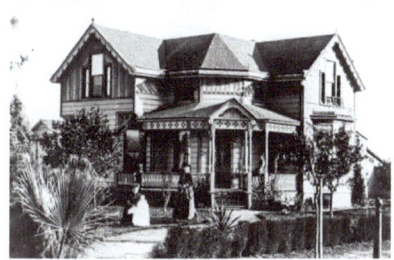
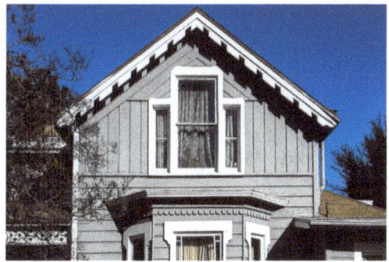
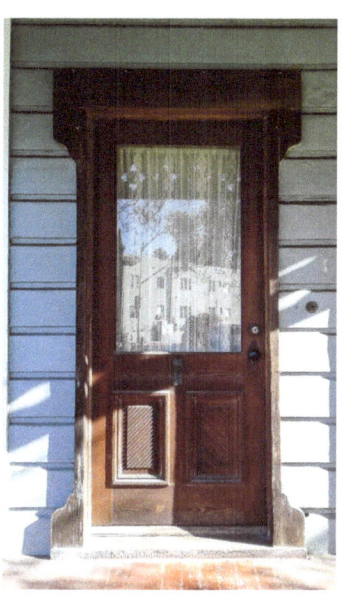
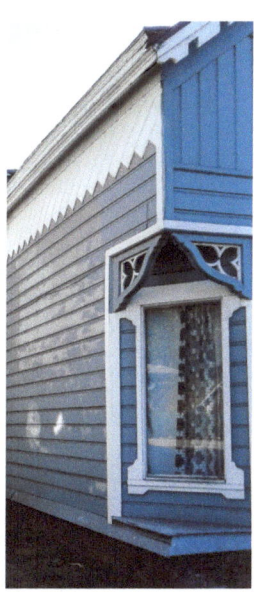

Leo Longley House - 1887

Folk Victorian – Architect unknown

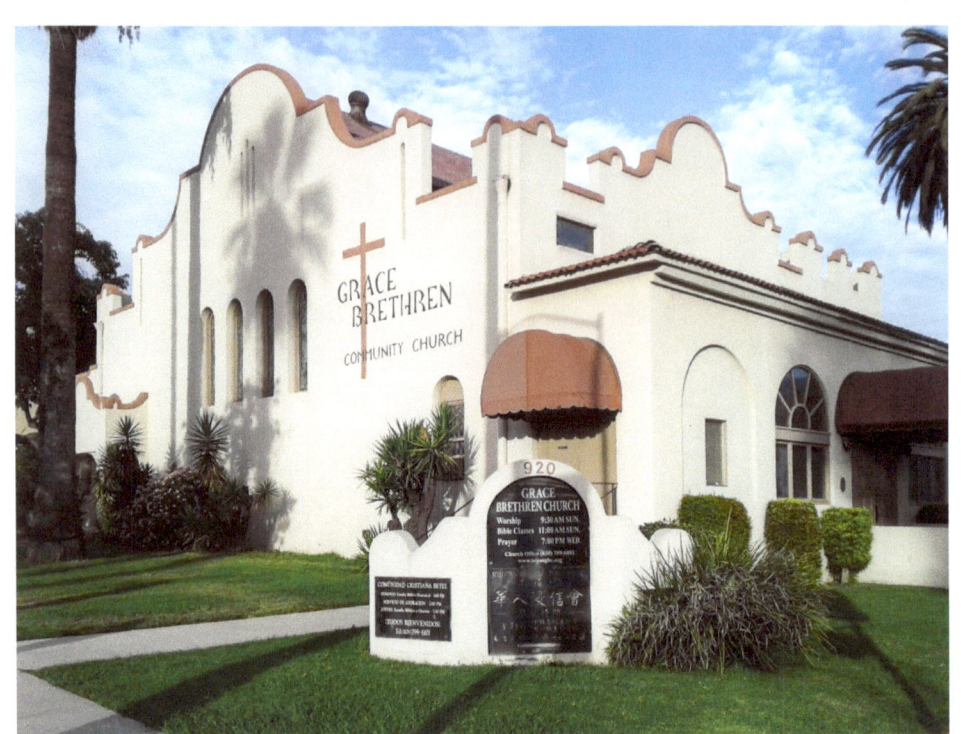
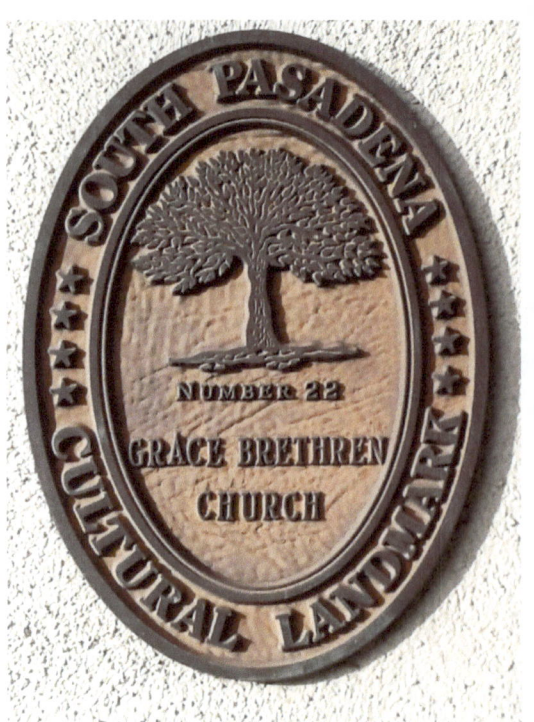

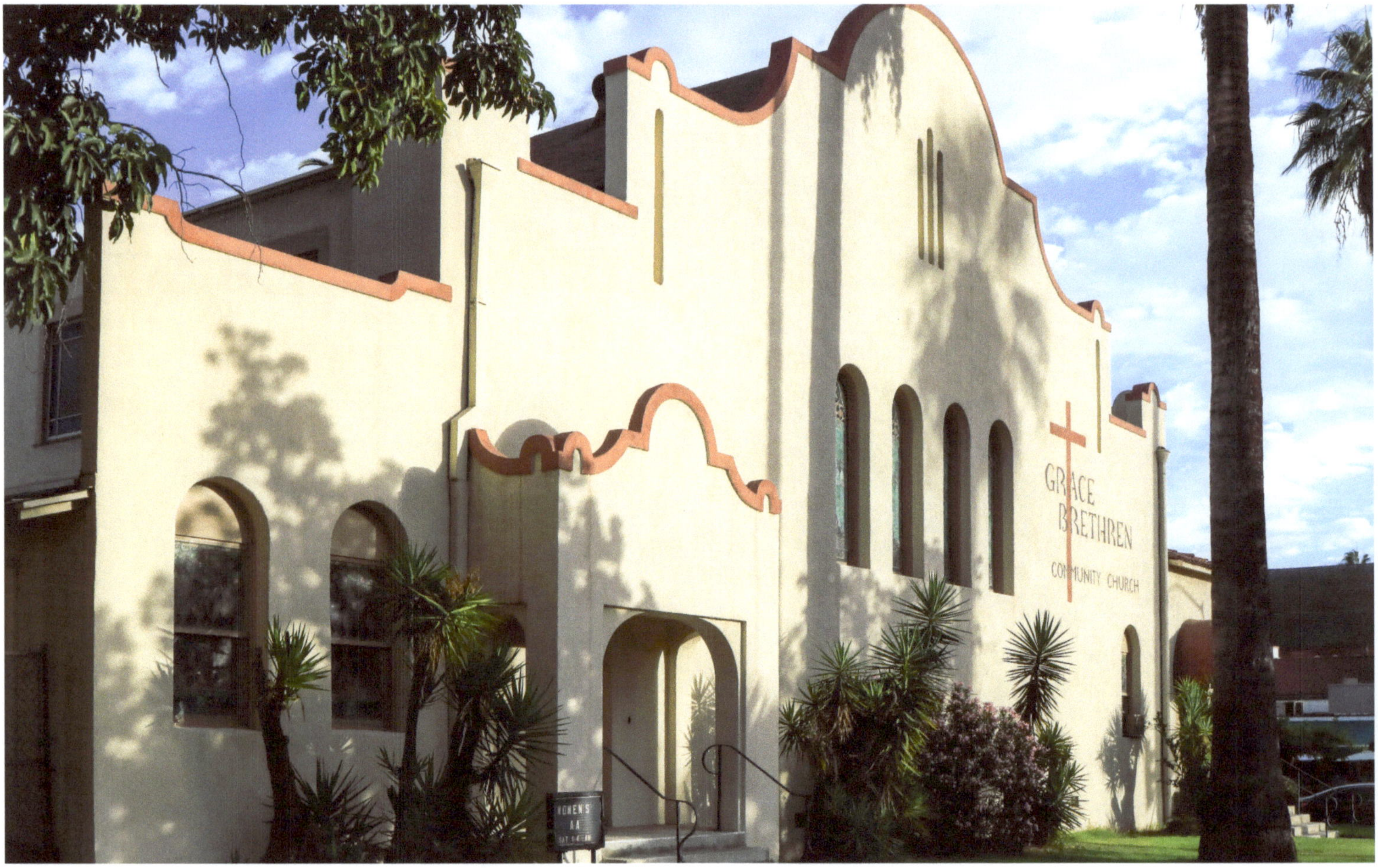

22 Grace Brethren Church – 1907

Mission Revival façade over a Victorian interior from 1887

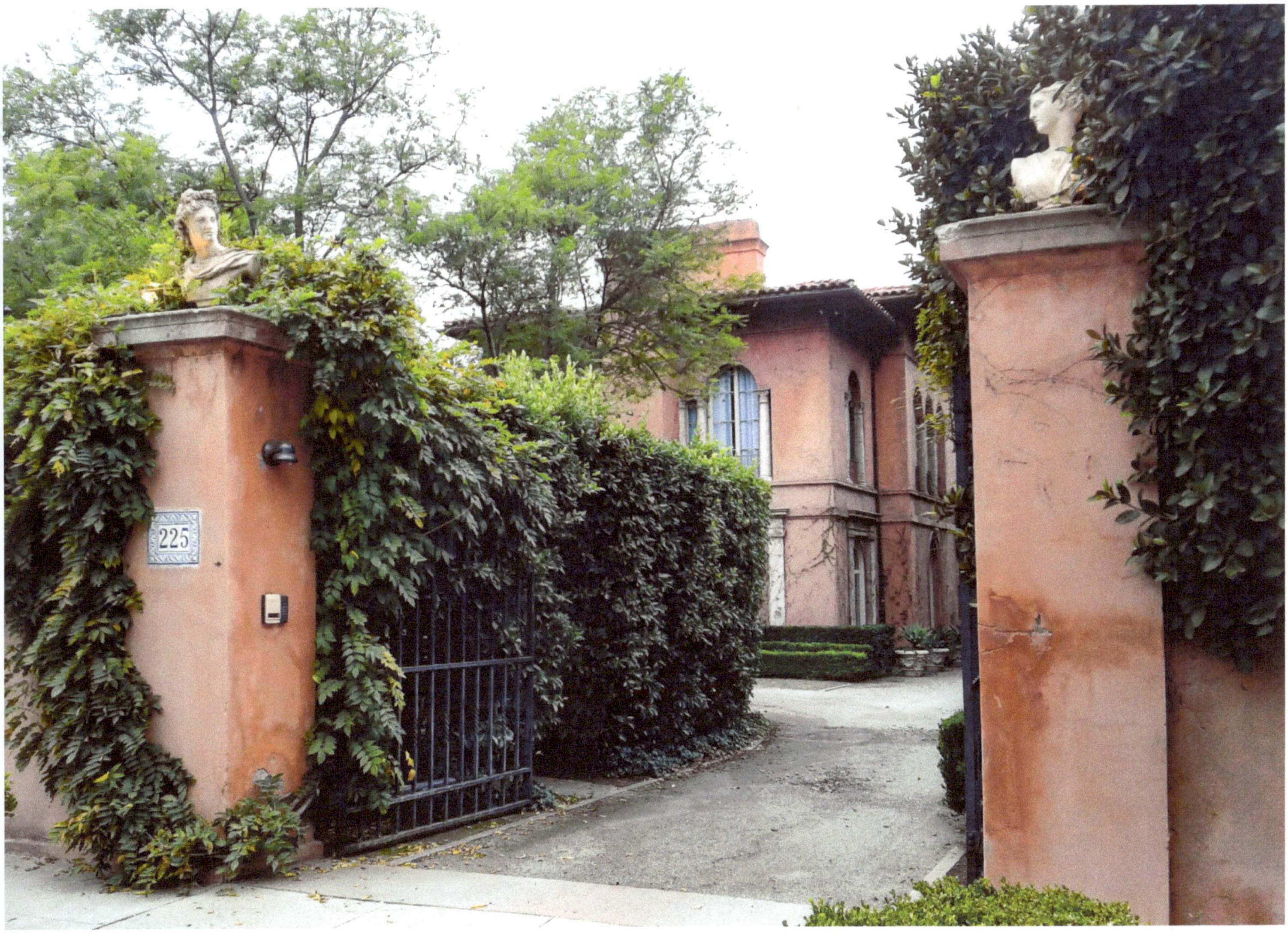

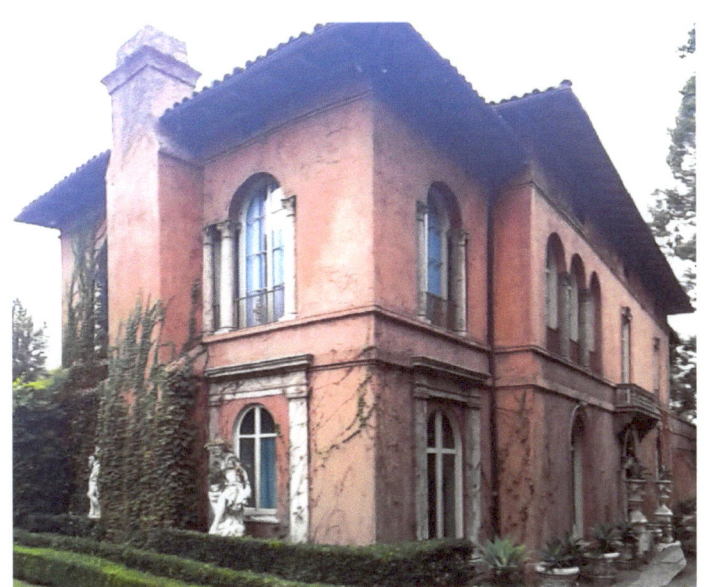
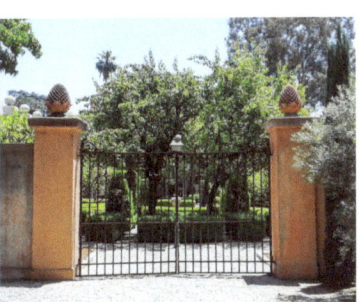
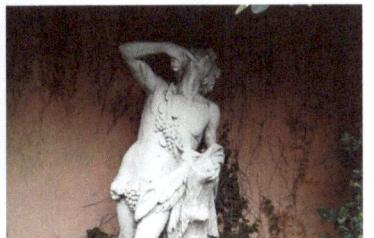
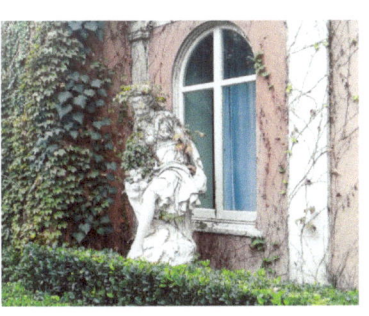
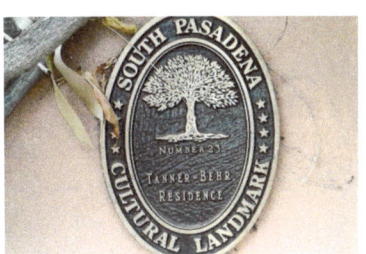
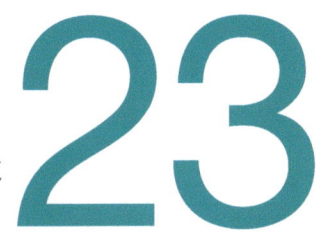

Tanner – Behr House – 1917

Italianate Mansion – Reginald Johnson, Architect

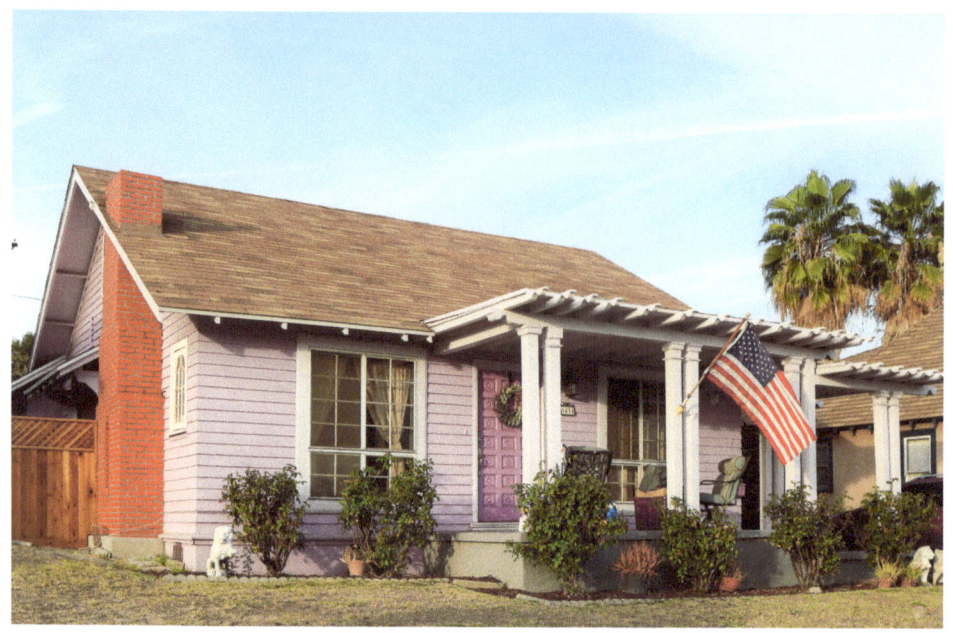
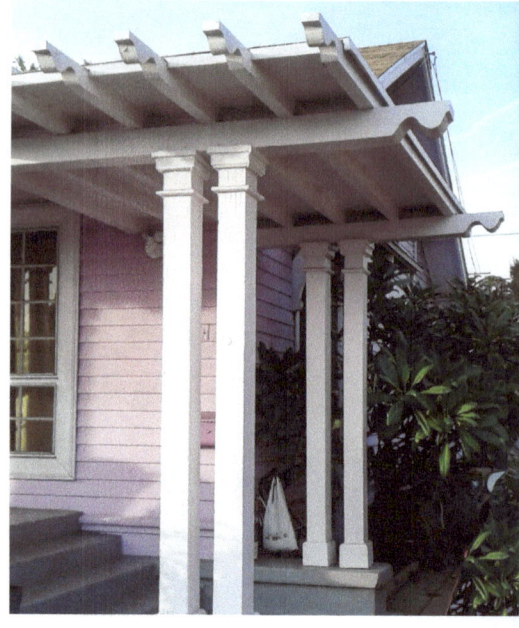

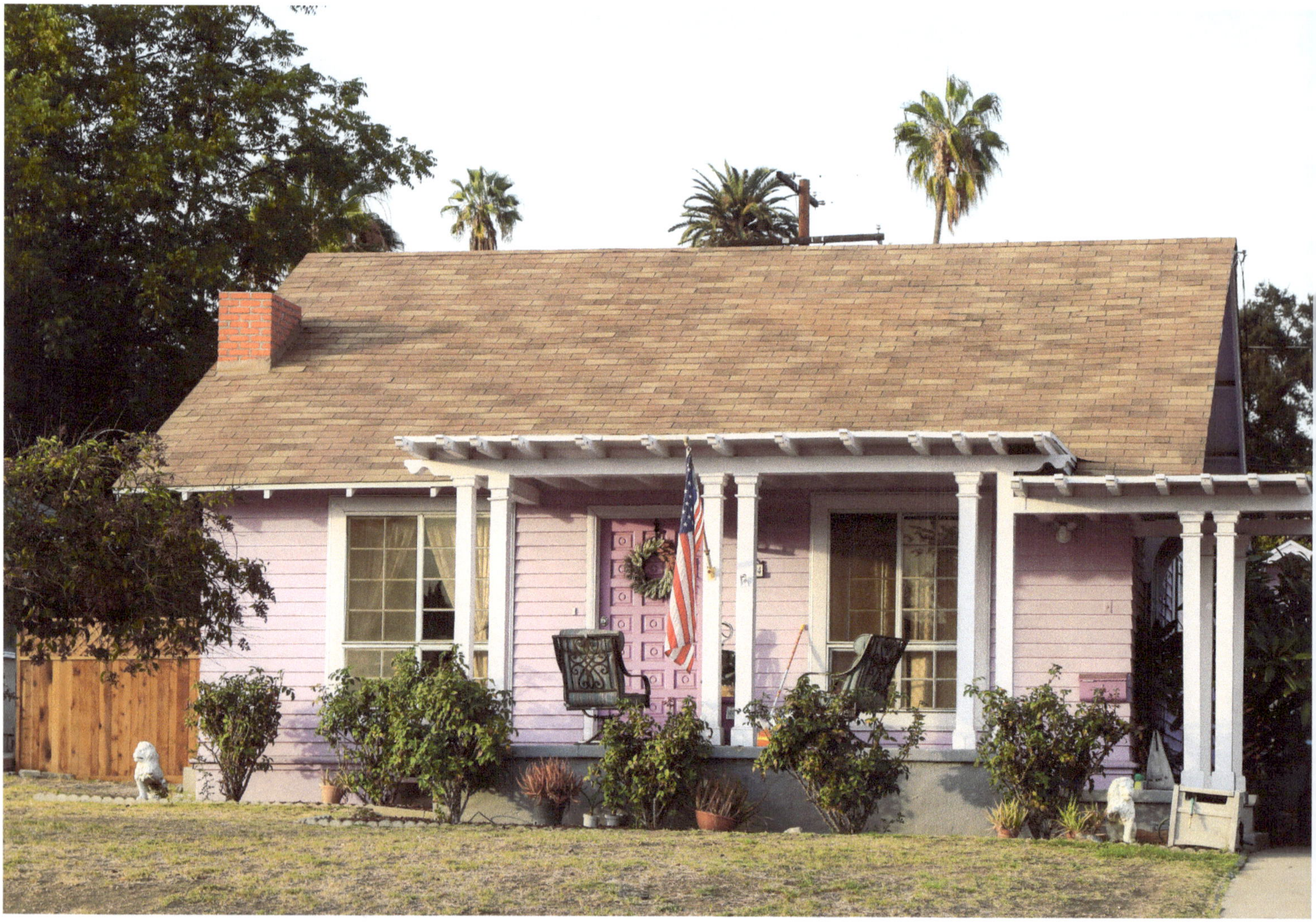

24 Lloyd Morrison House – 1925

Contemporary style – Henry Green, Architect

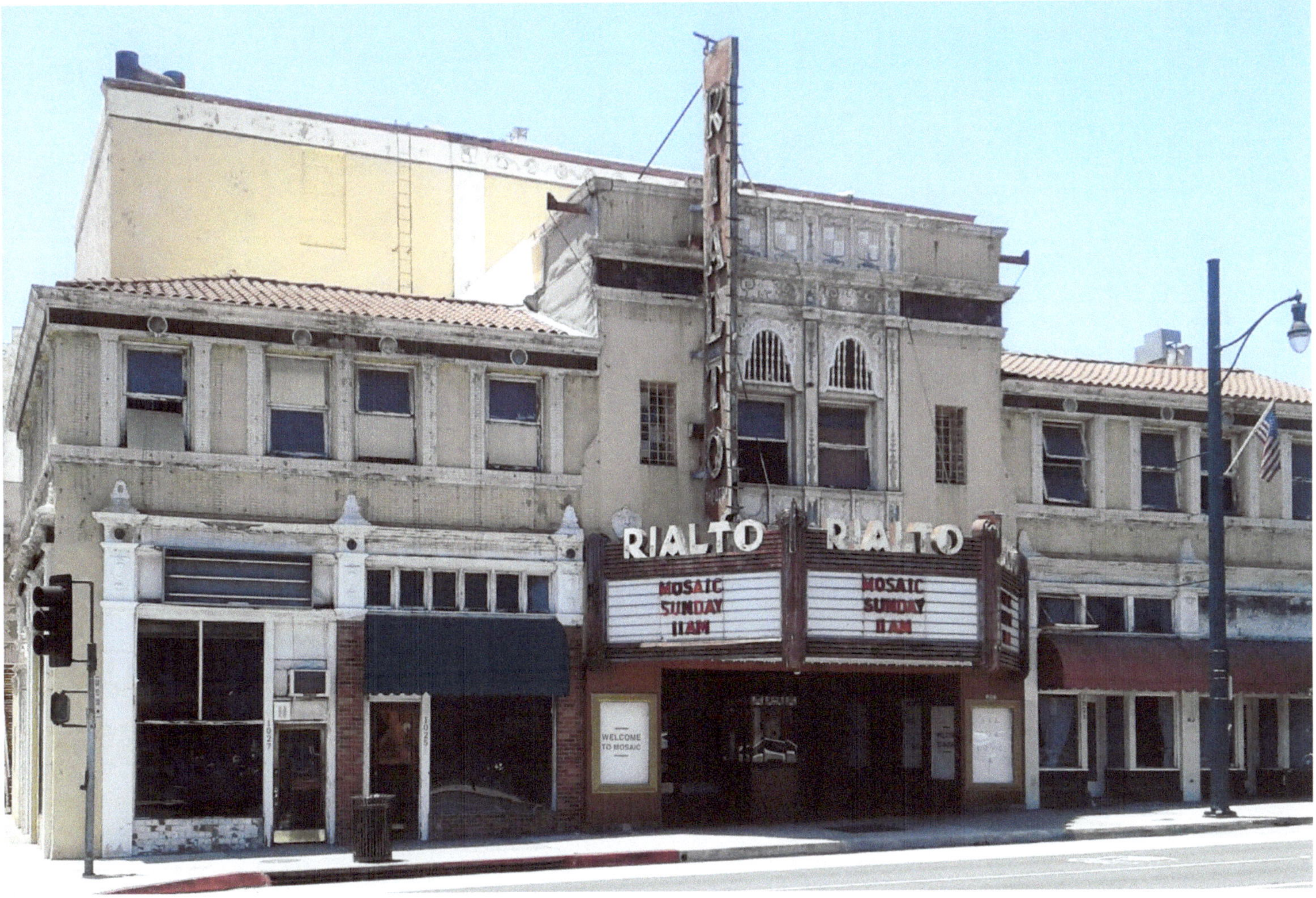

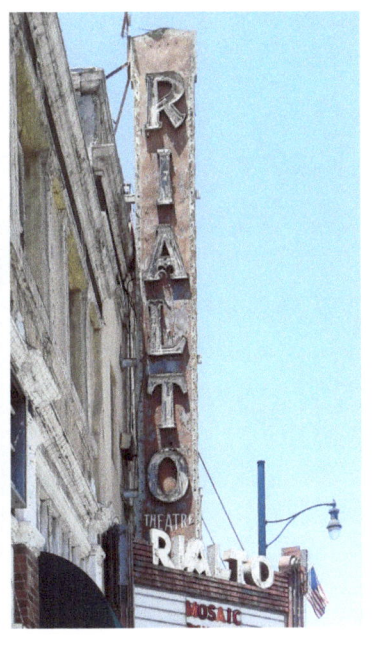
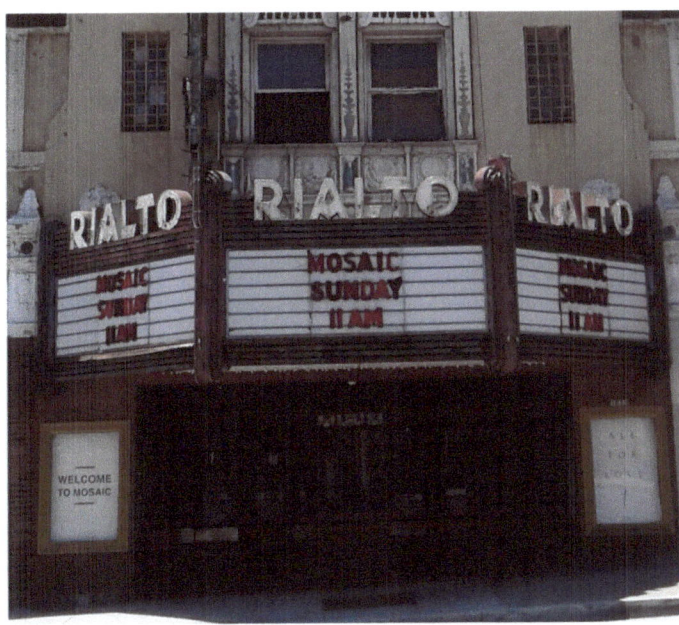
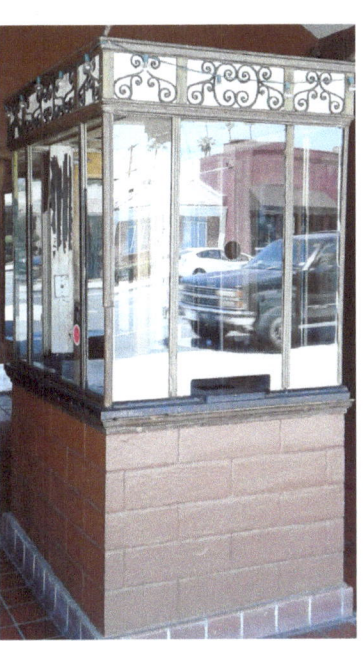

Rialto Theatre – 1925

Movie Palace – L. A. Smith, Architect

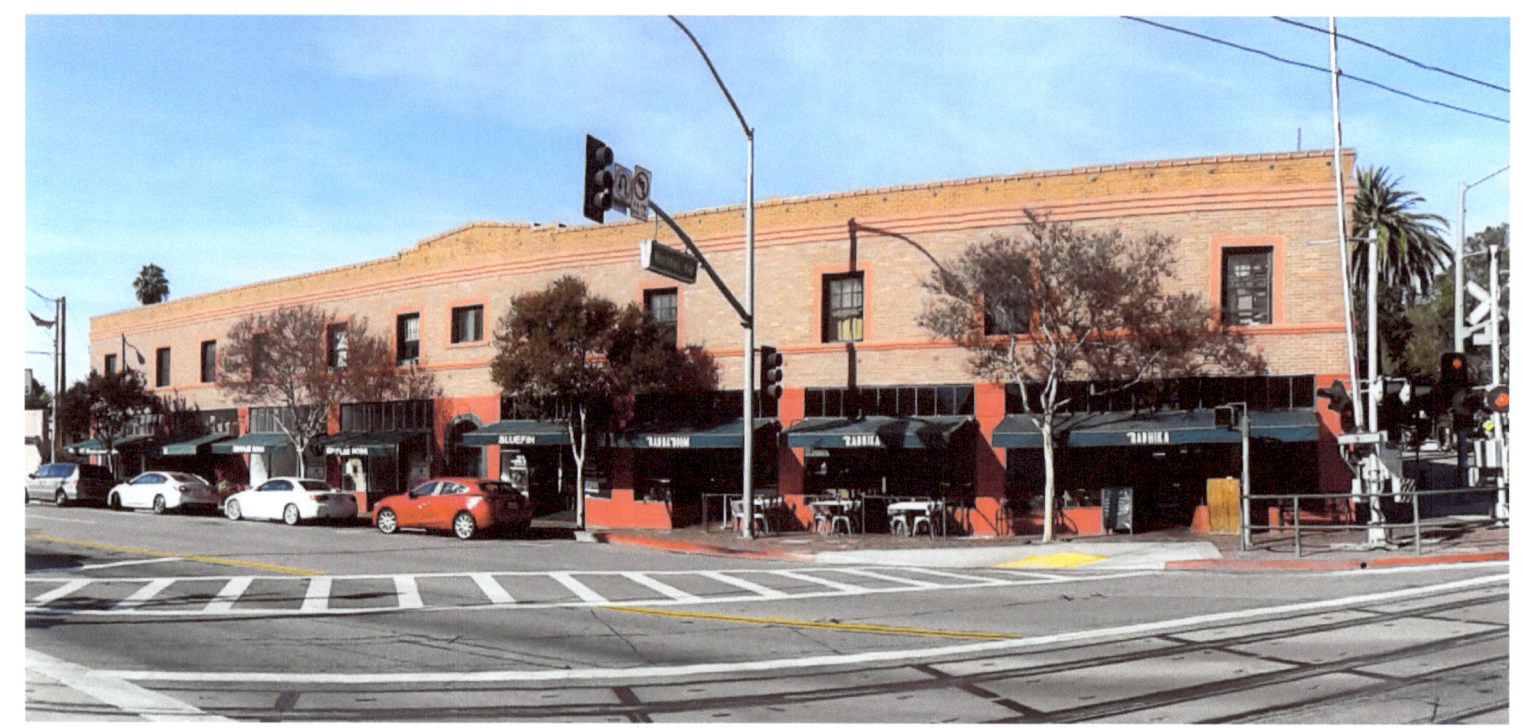

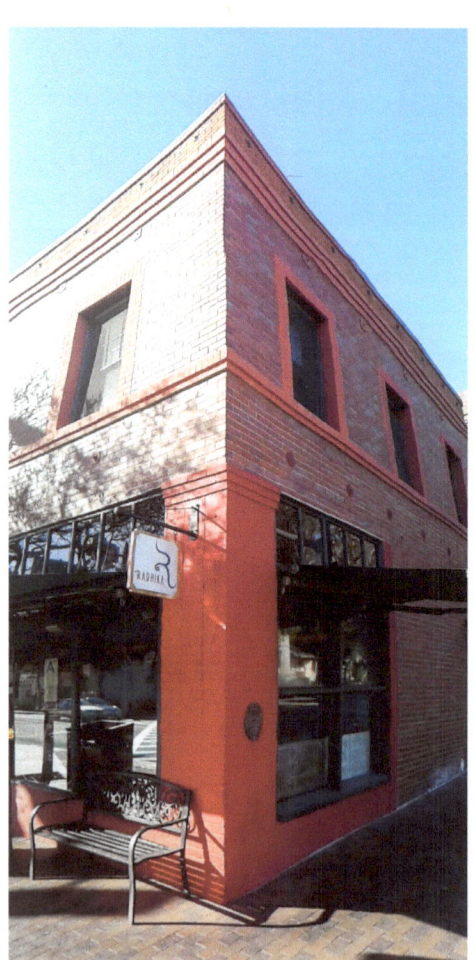

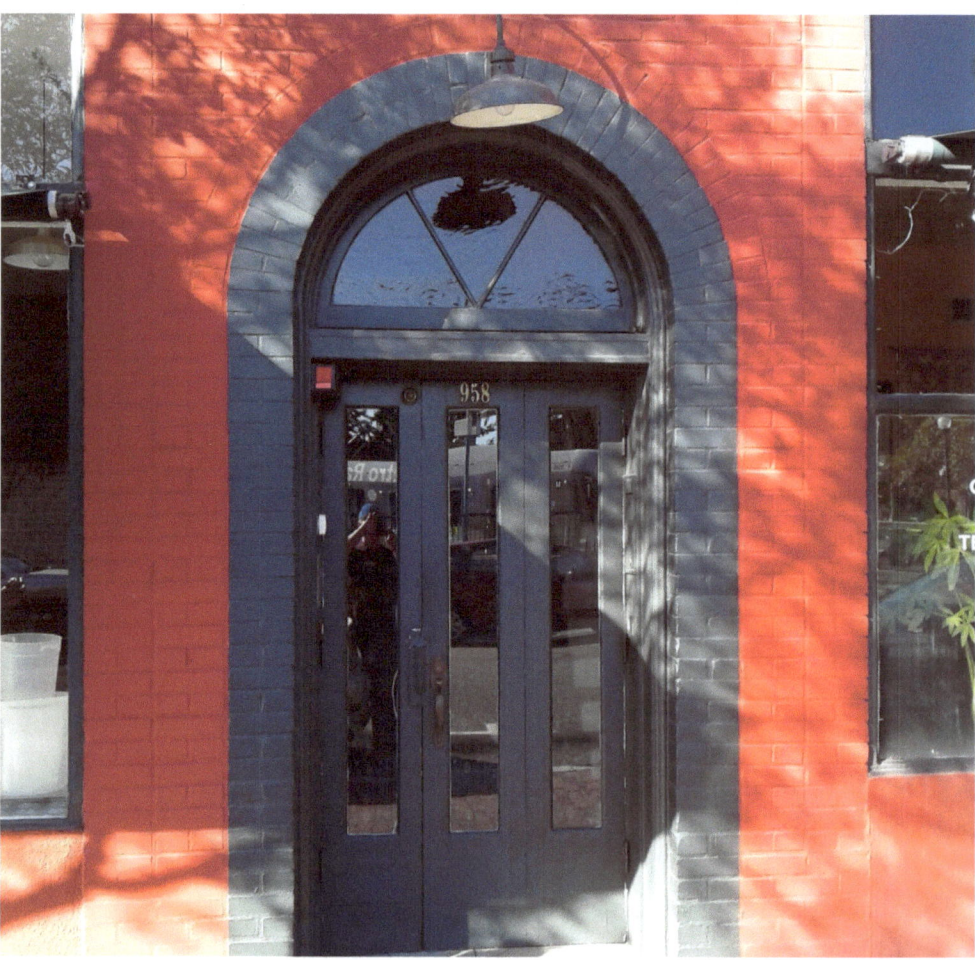

26

Mission Hotel – 1923

Two story brick structure – Architect unknown

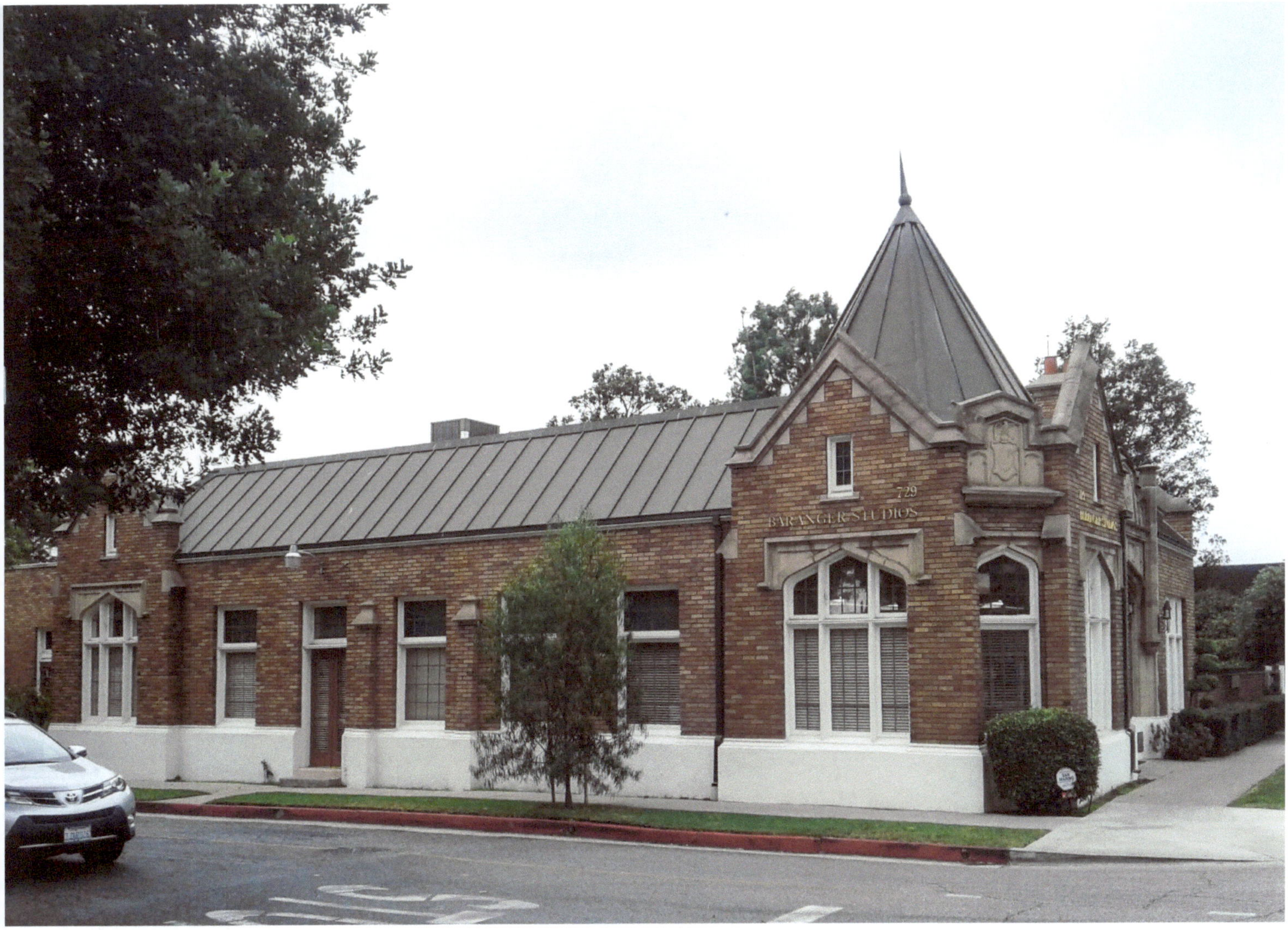

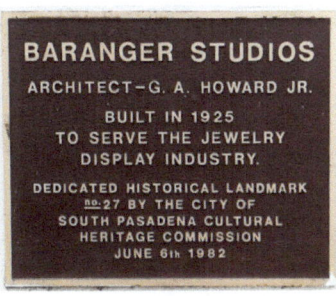
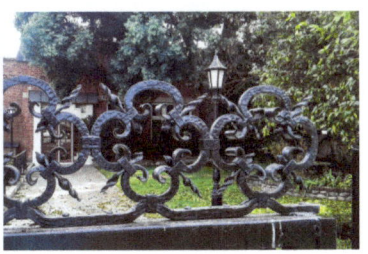
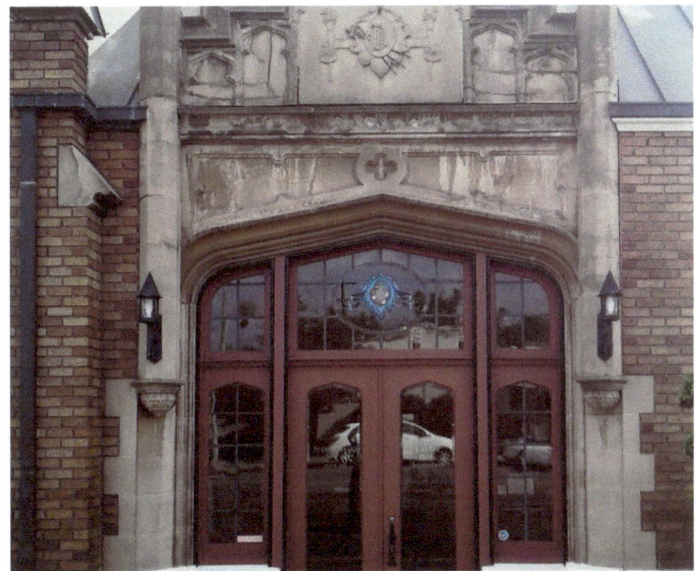
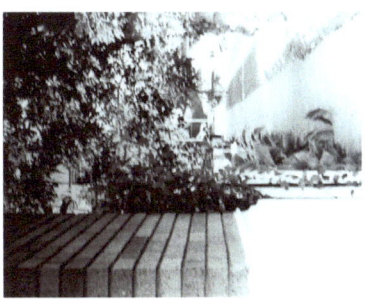
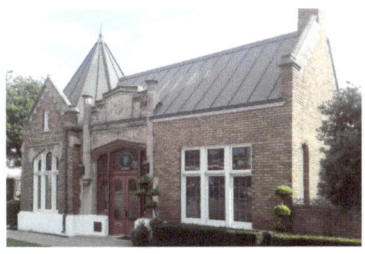

Baranger Studios – 1925

Brick Gothic – G. A. Howard, Architect

27

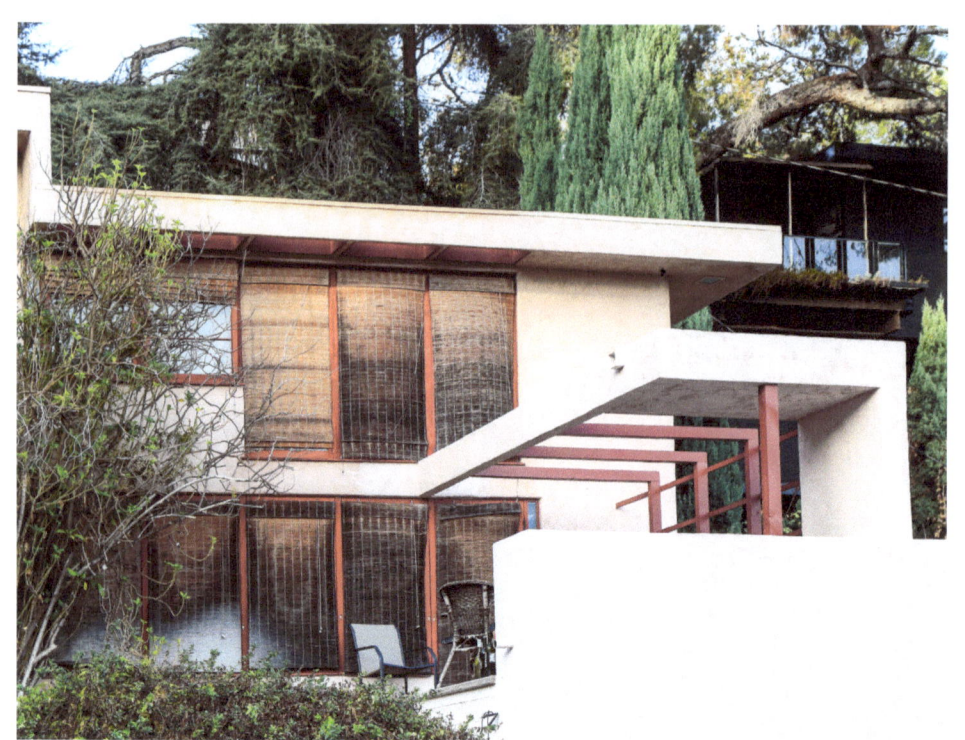
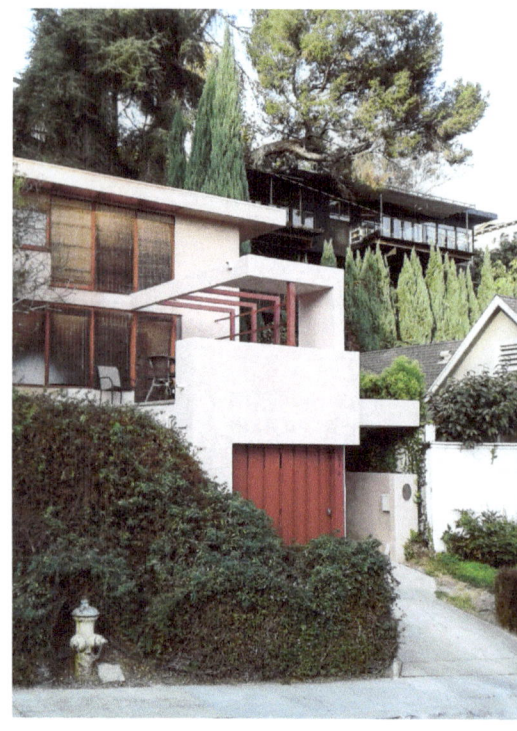
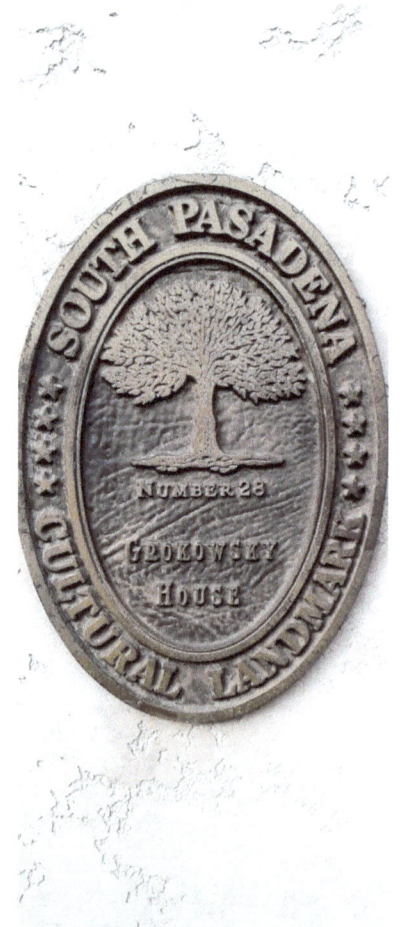
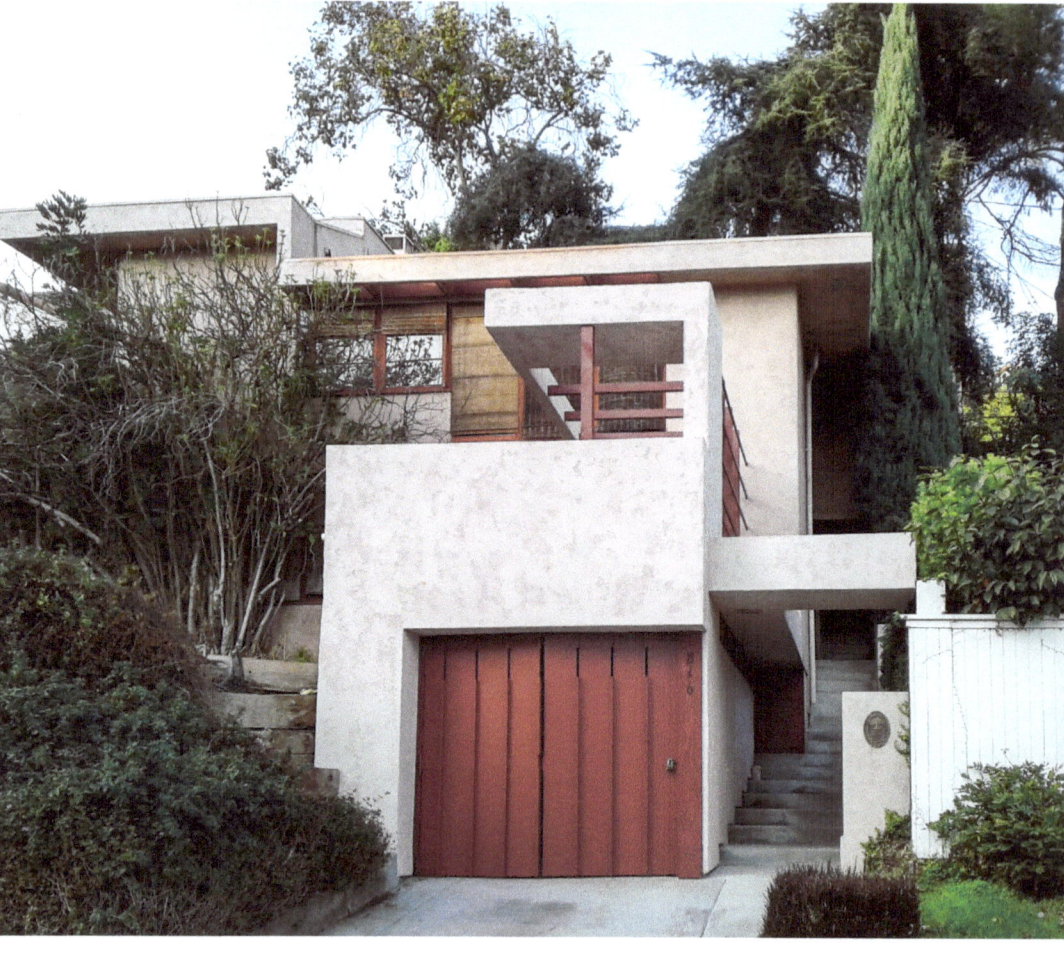

28
Grokowski House 1928

International Style - Rudolph Schindler, Architect

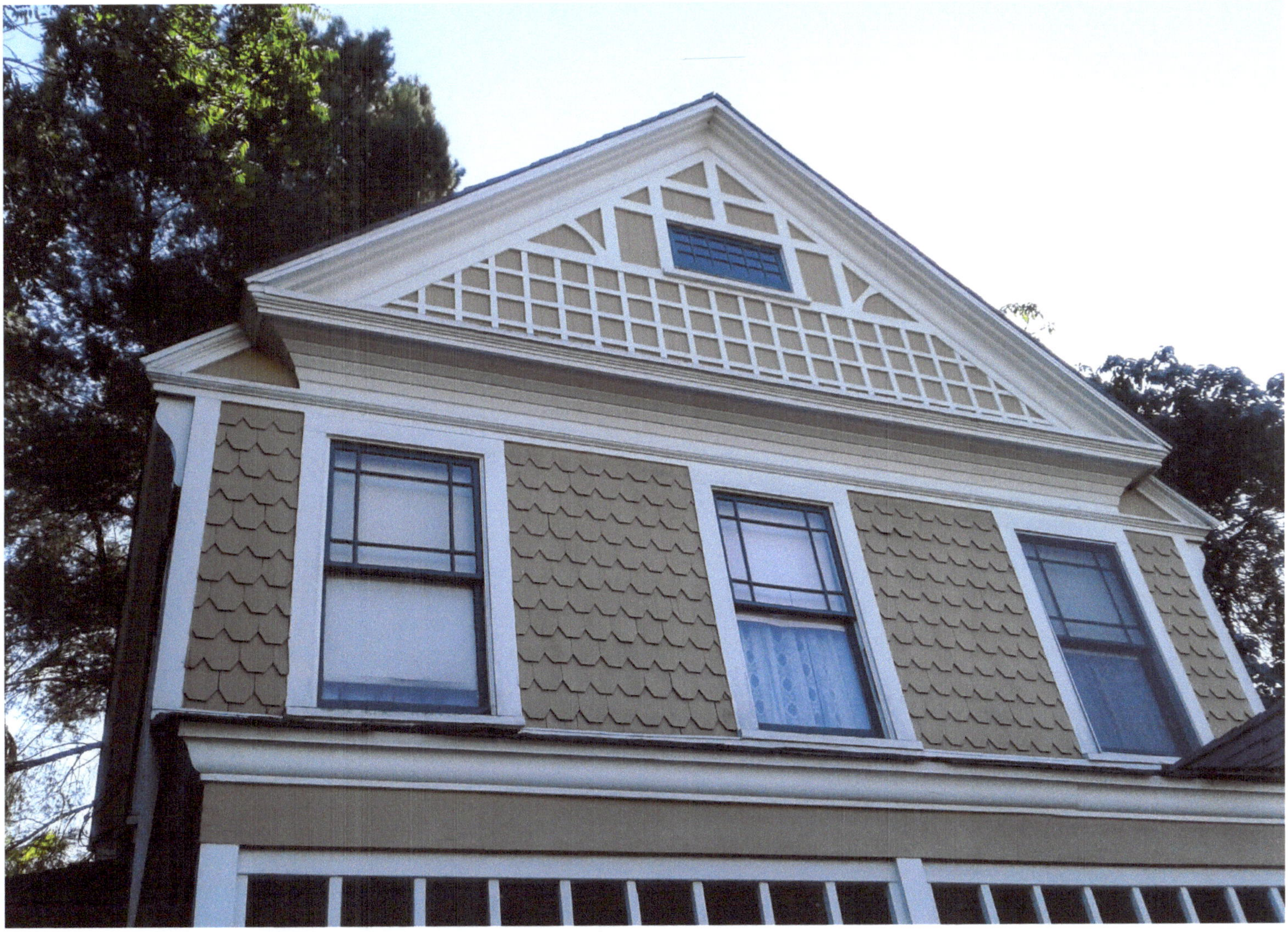

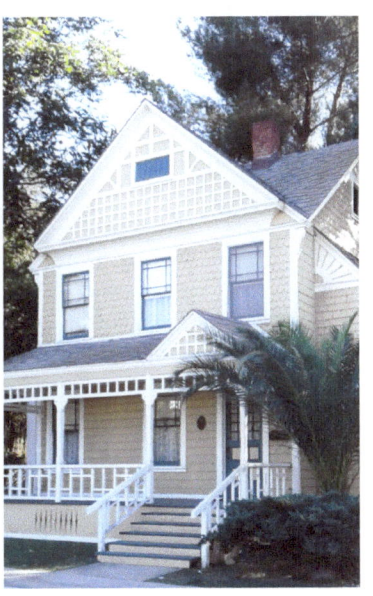
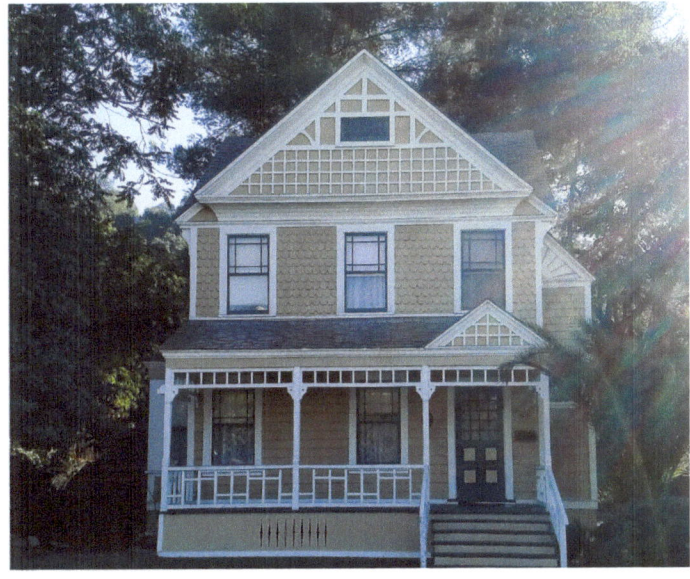
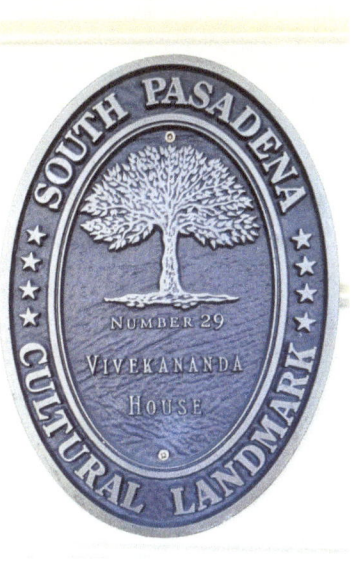

Vivekananda House – circa 1880

Front Gabled Victorian – Architect unknown

29

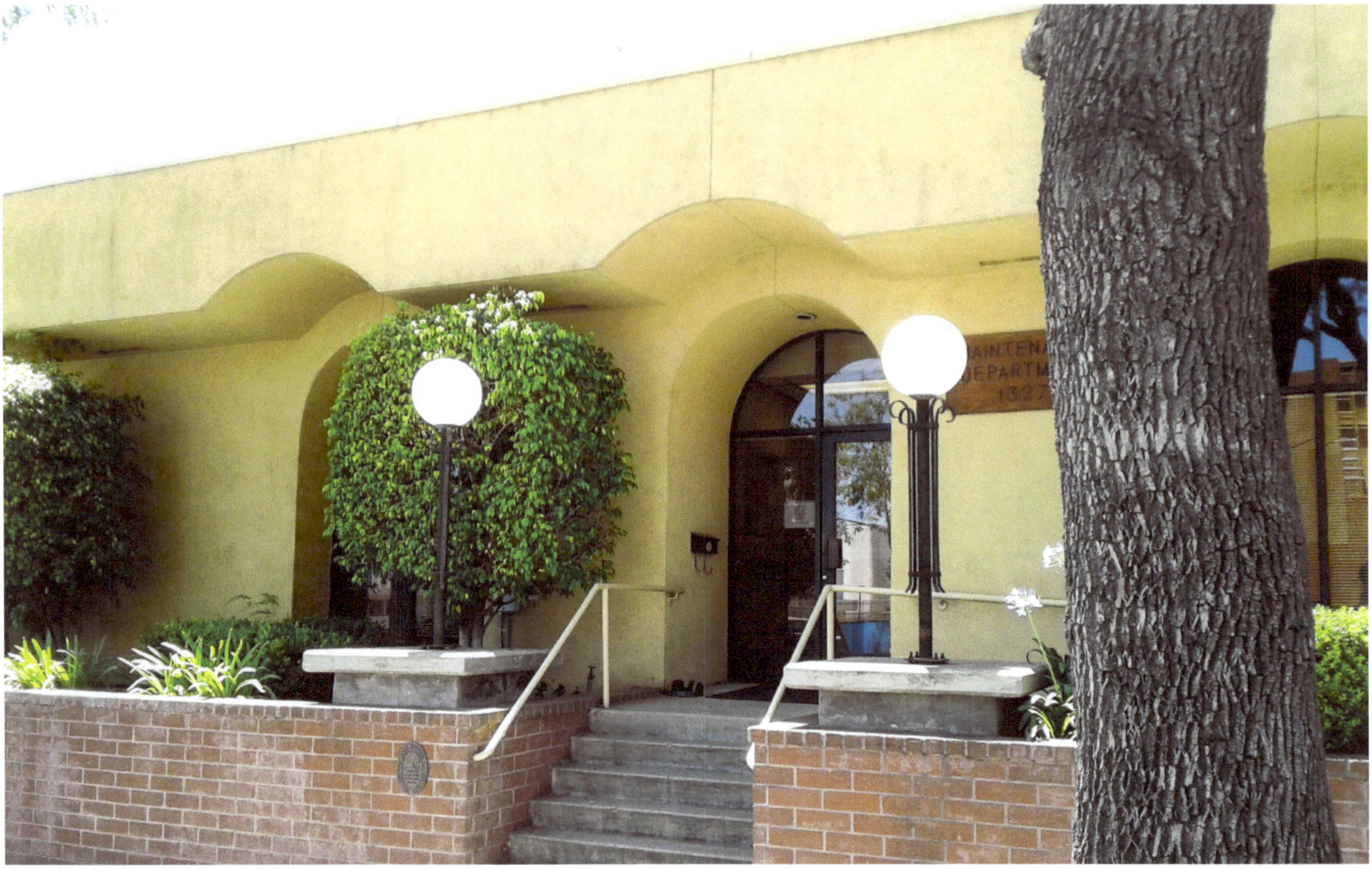

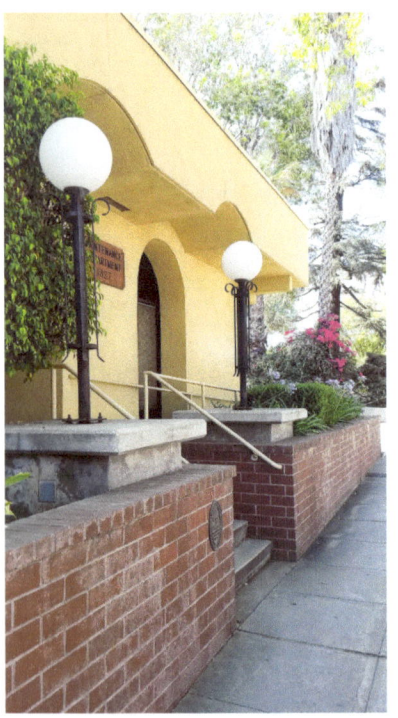
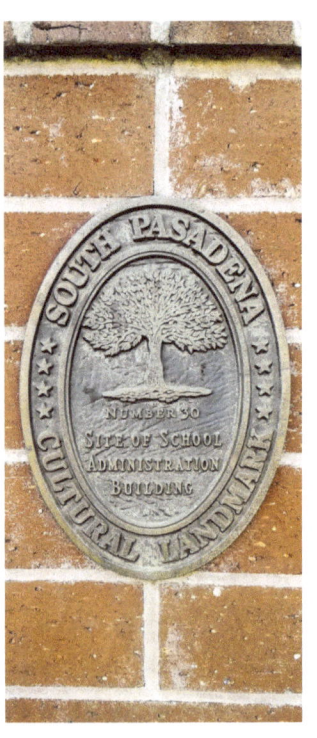
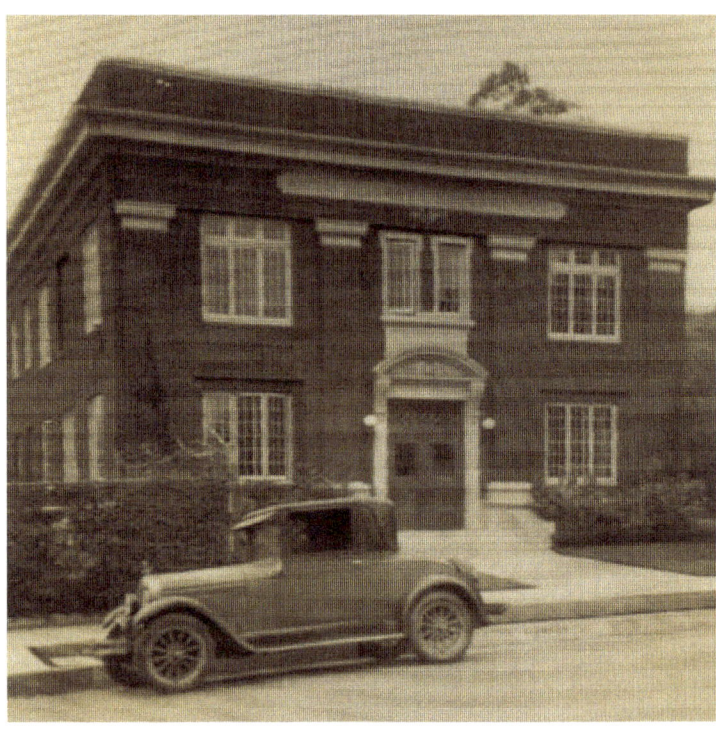

30

School Administration Building –

1925 demolished 1985

Brick Georgian – Norman Marsh, Architect

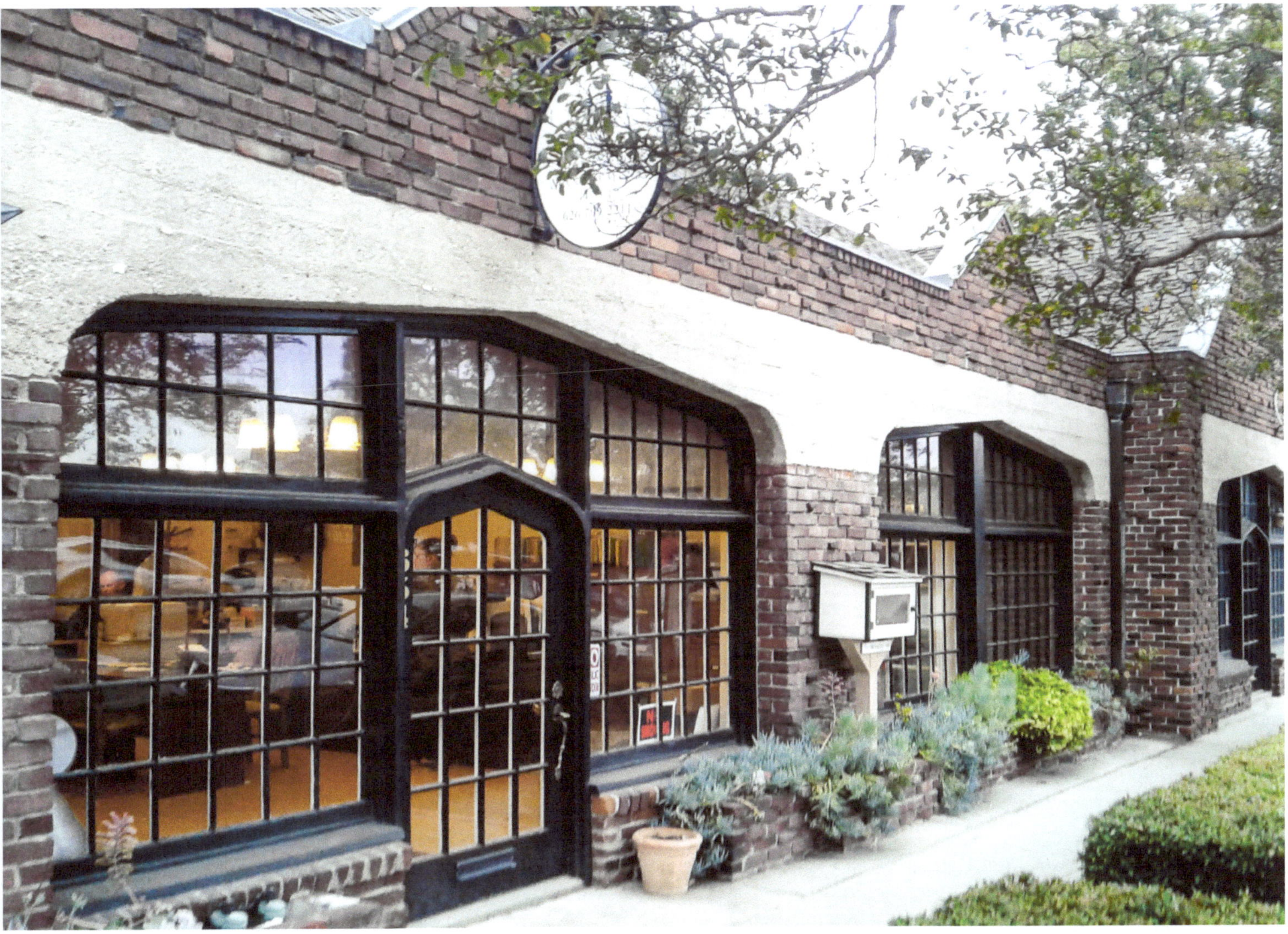

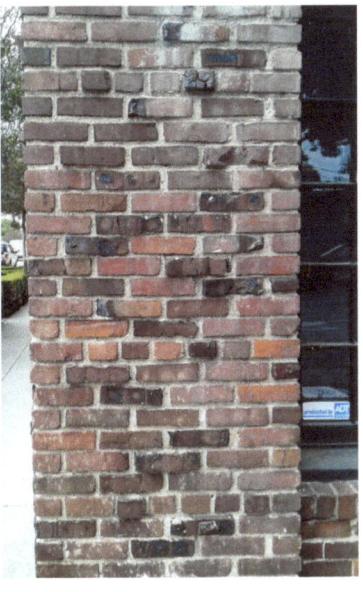
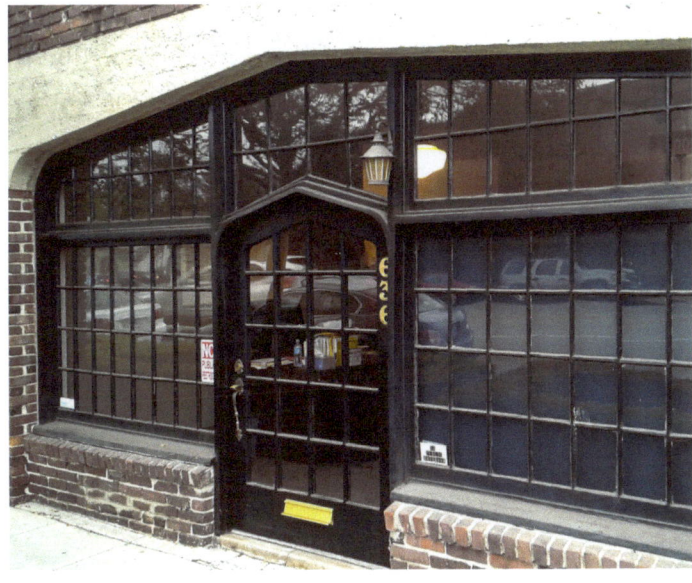
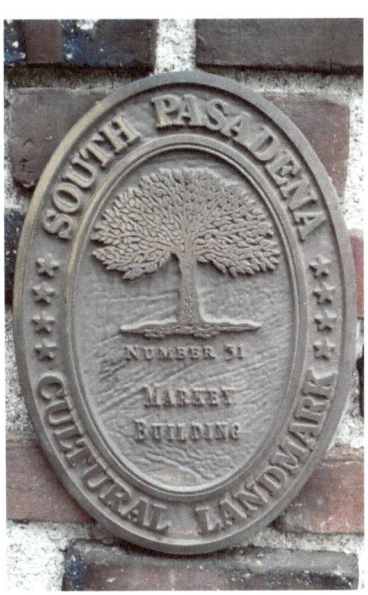

Lewis-Markey Building – 1928

Clinker Brick Gothic – Architect unknown

31

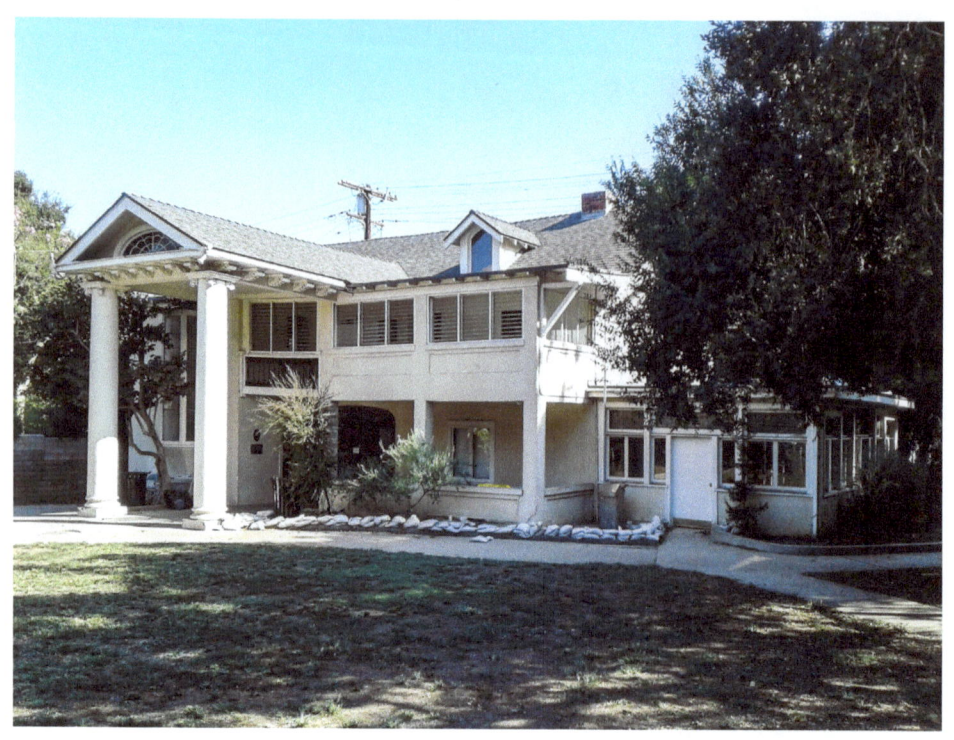
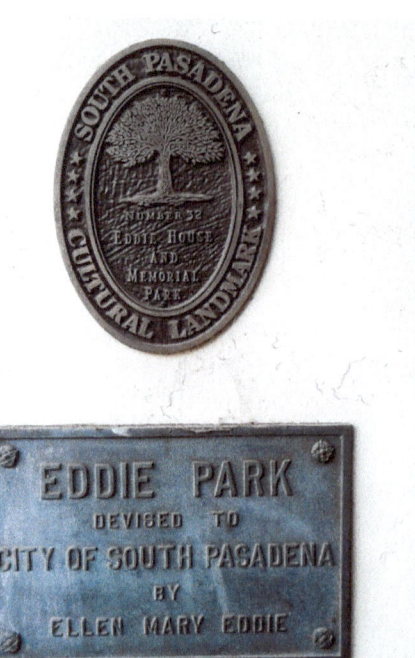
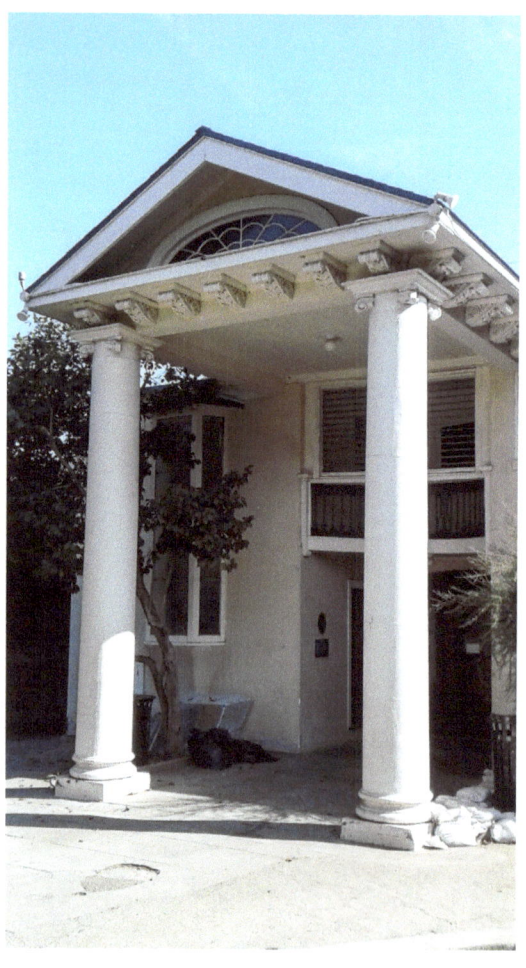
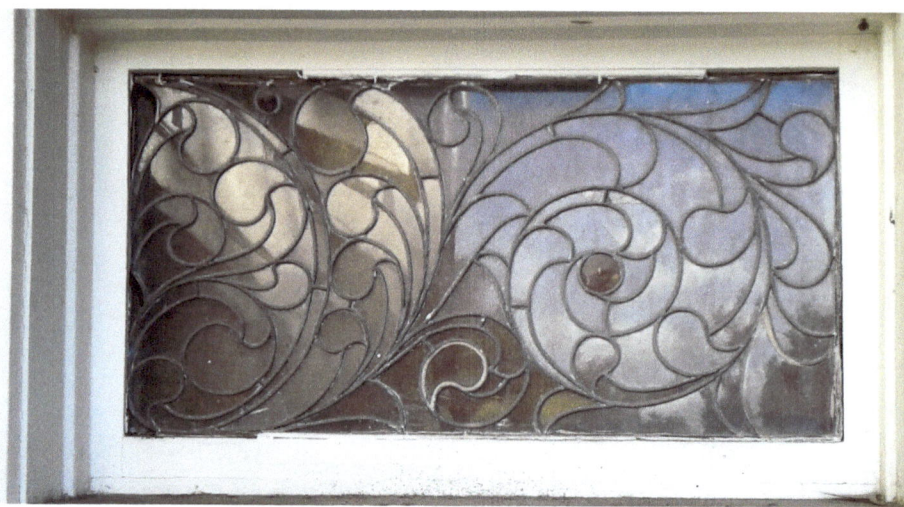
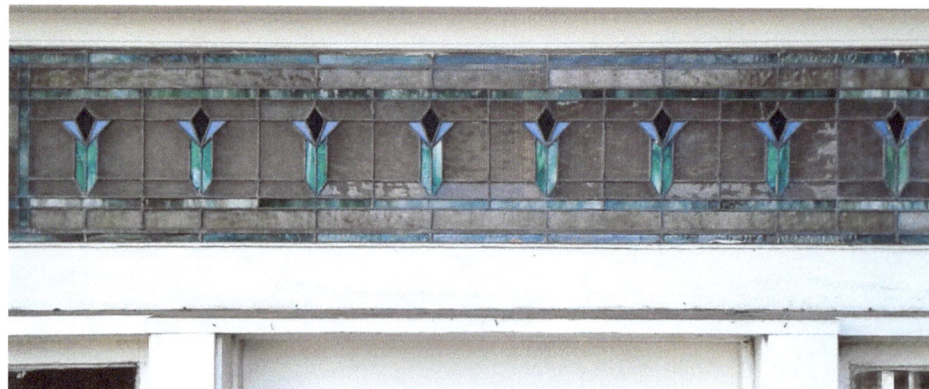

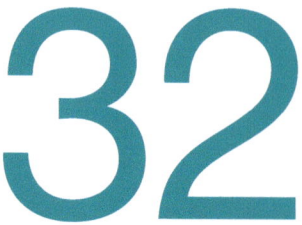

Eddie House and Memorial Park – 1910

Greek Revival - Architect unknown

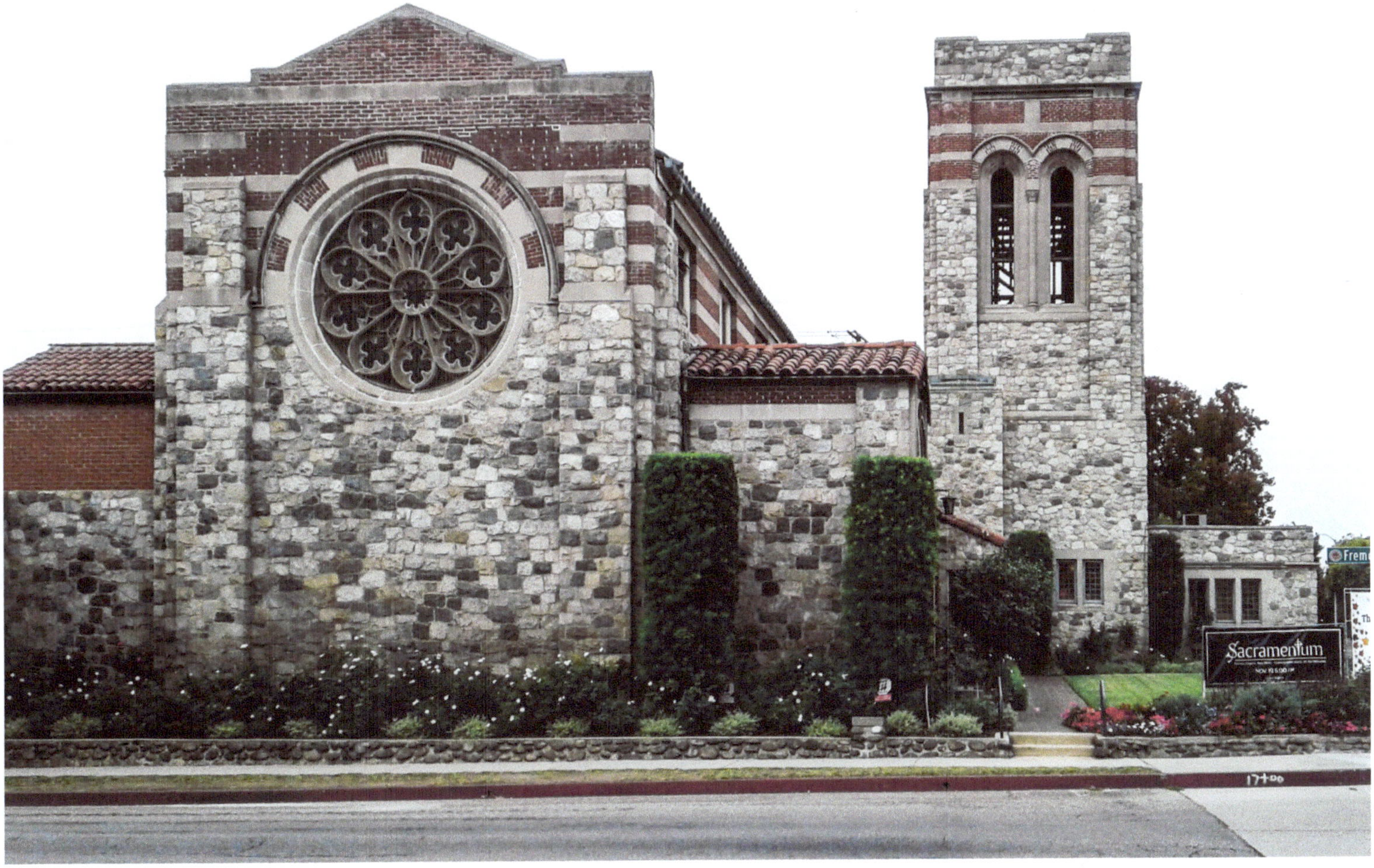

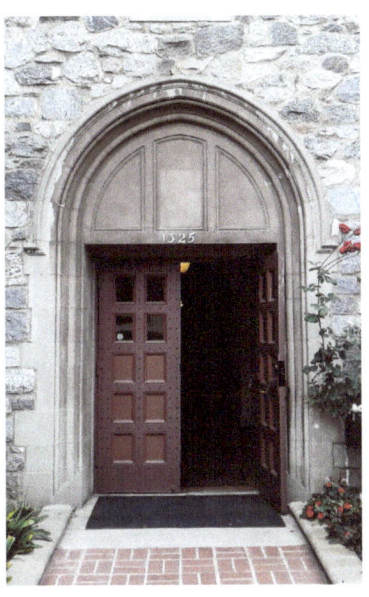
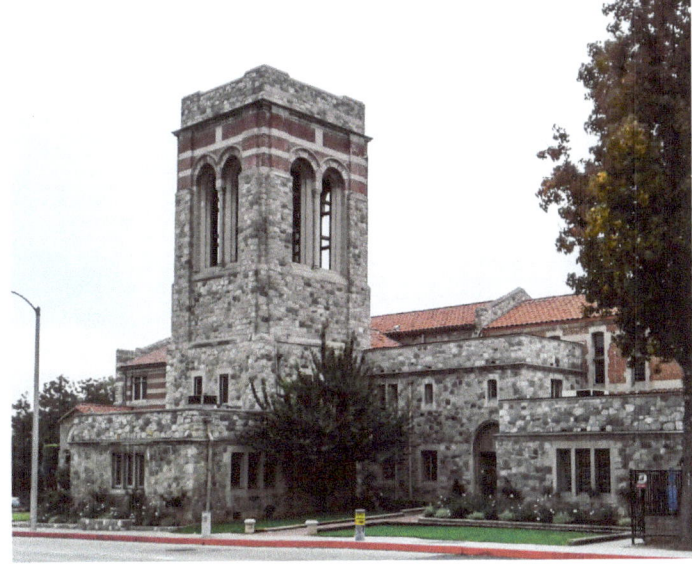
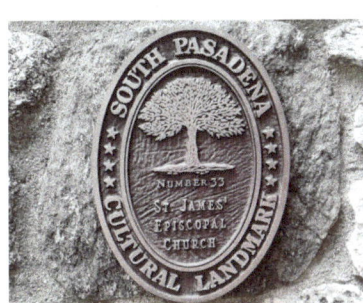
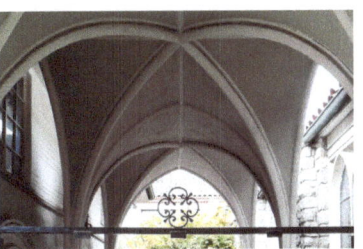

St. James Episcopal Church – 1907

English Norman Style – Bertram Goodhue, Architect

33

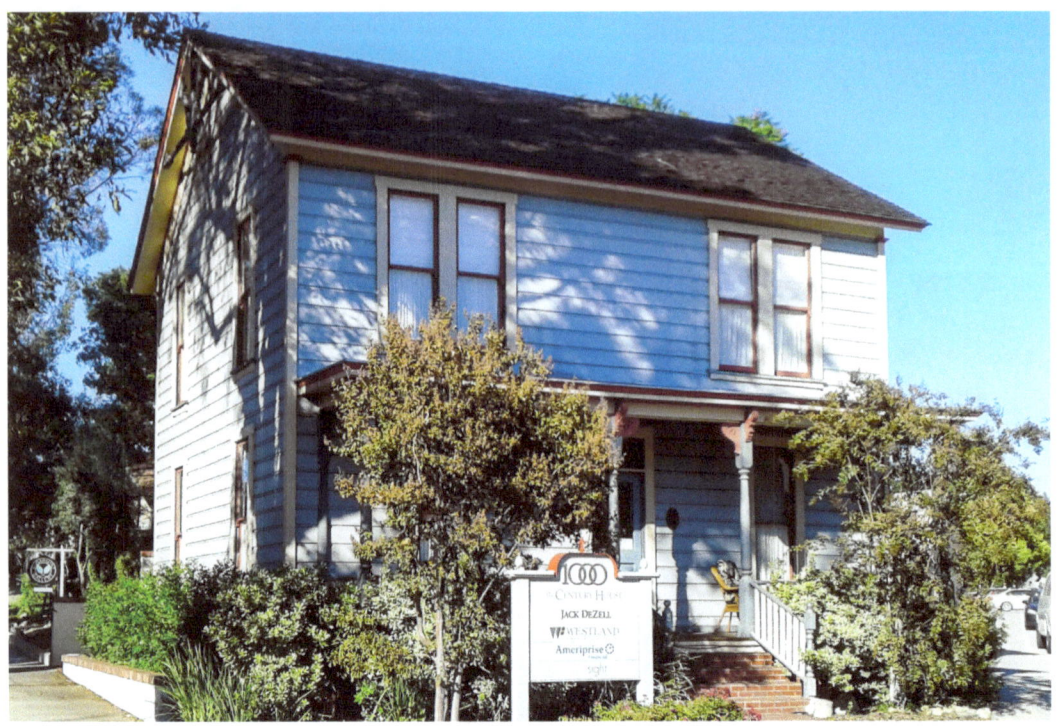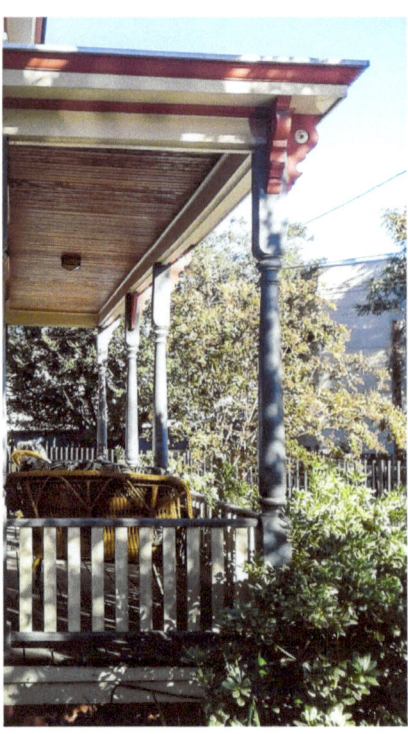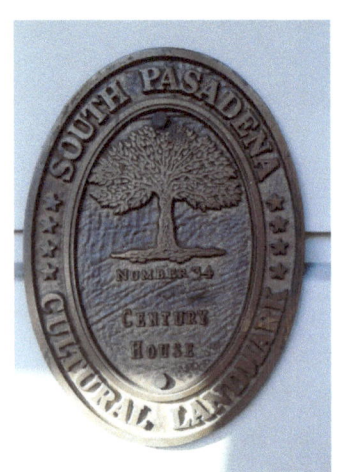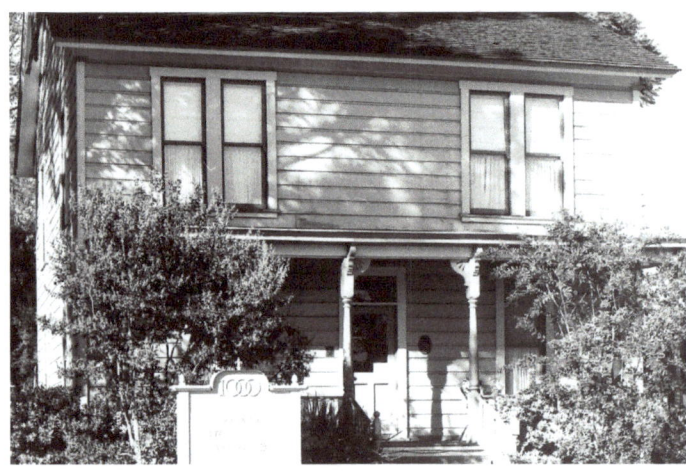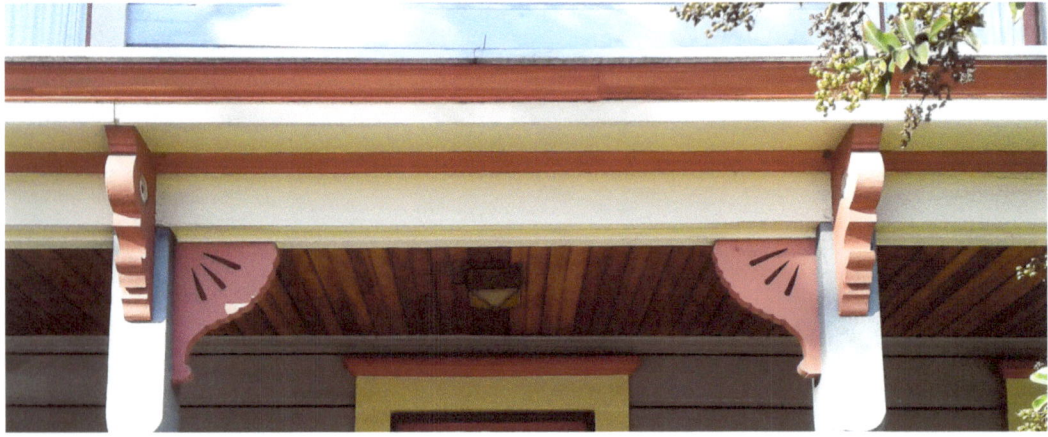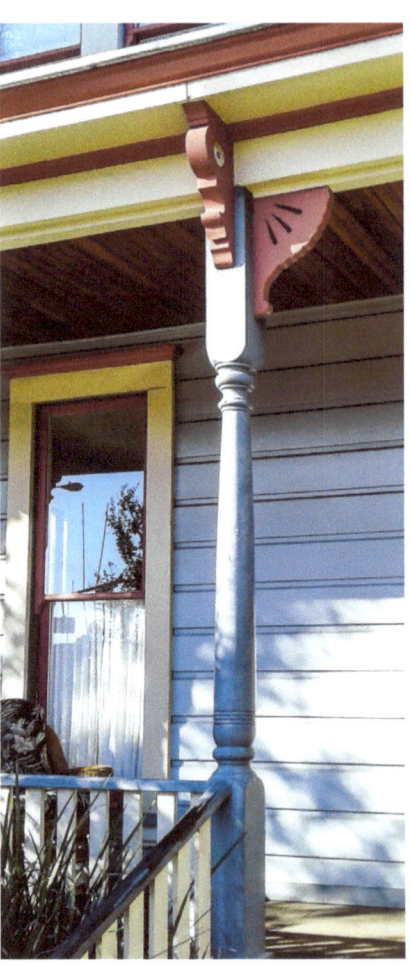

34

Century House – 1888

Folk Victorian – Architect Unknown

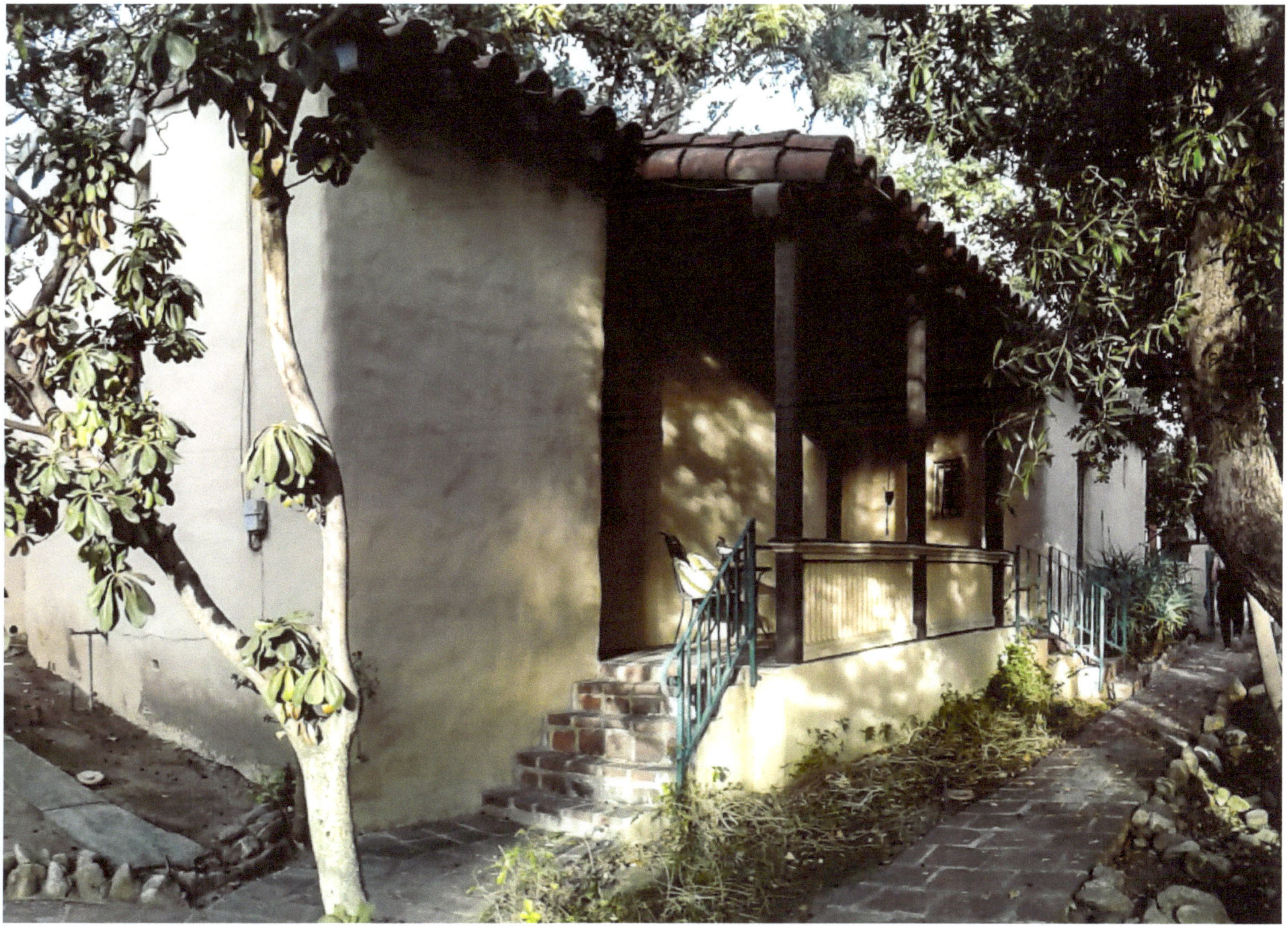

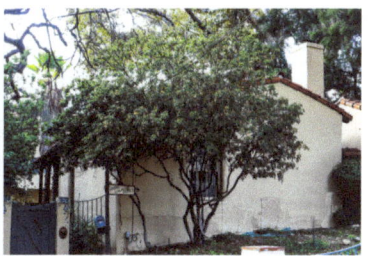
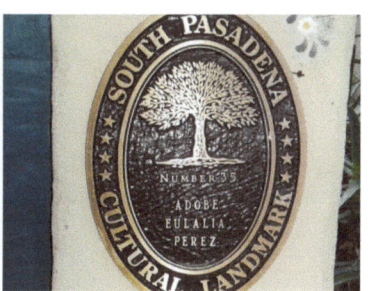
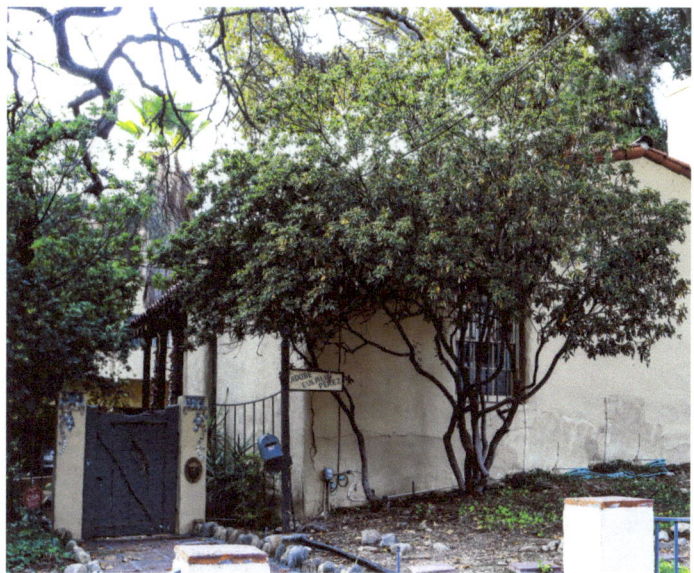
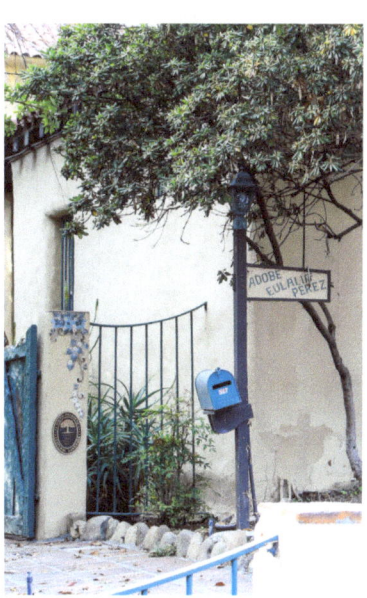

Adobe Eulalia Perez – 1924

Spanish Revival Adobe - Carlton Winslow, Architect

35

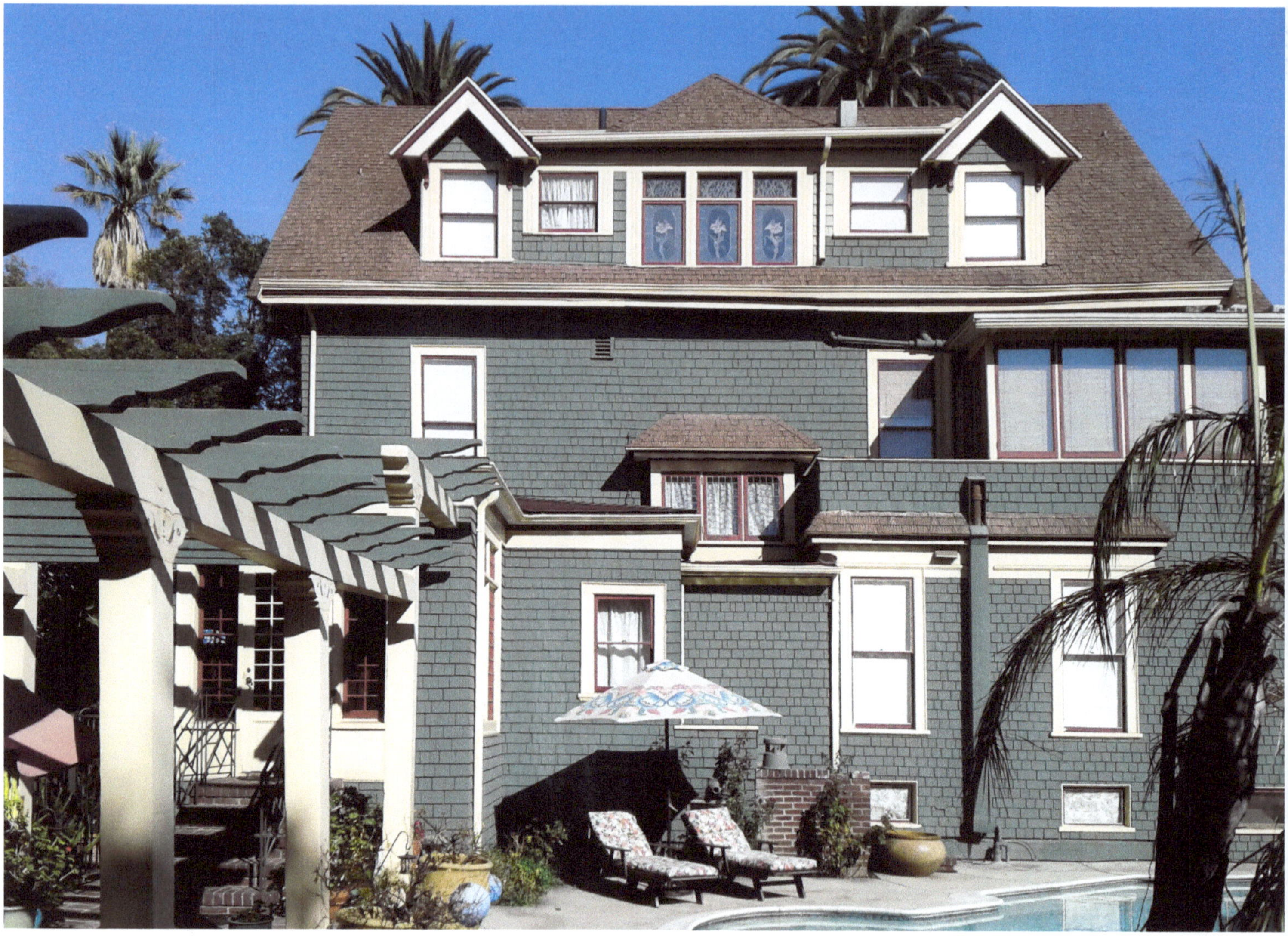

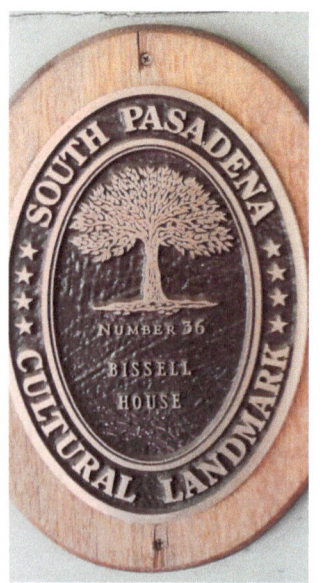
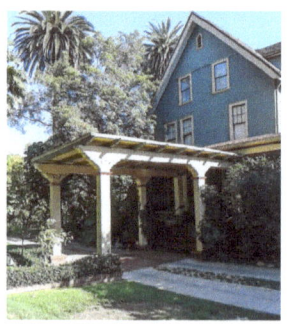
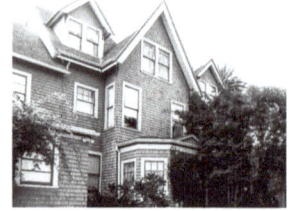
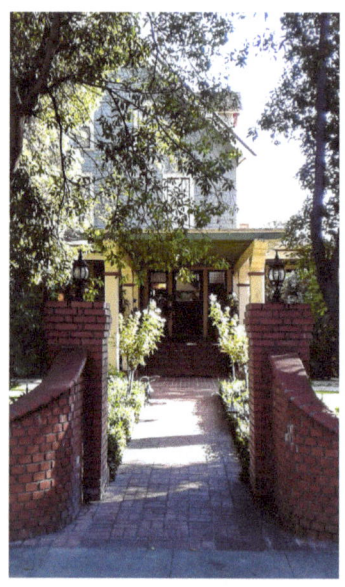
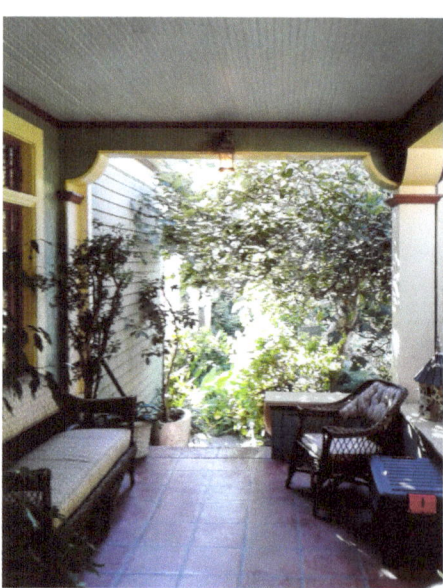

36

Bissell House – 1887

Gabled Victorian – Architect unknown

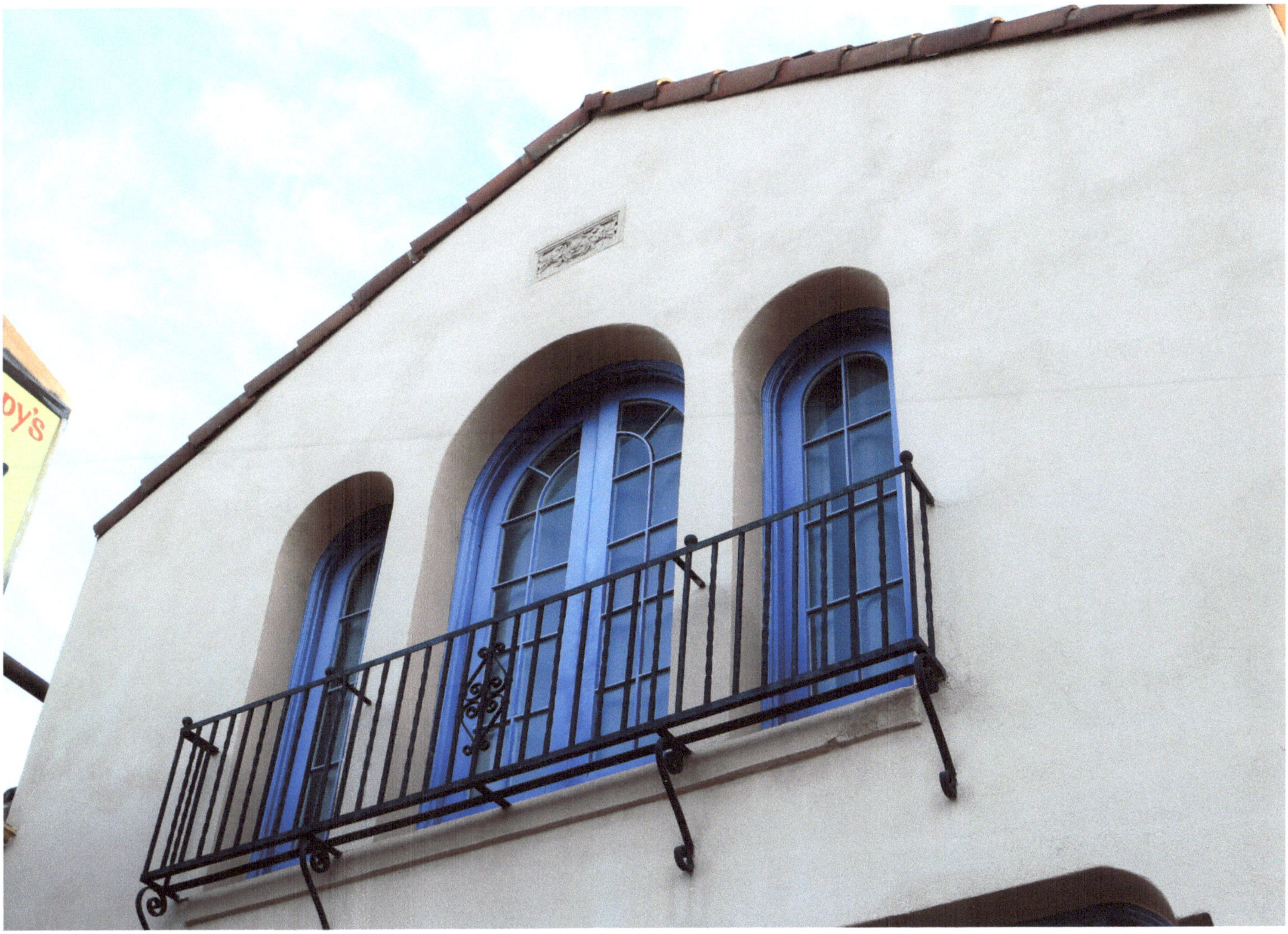

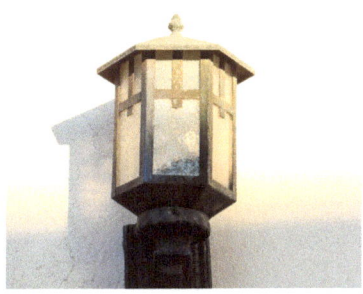
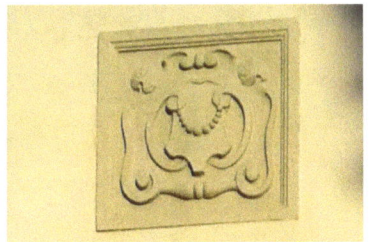
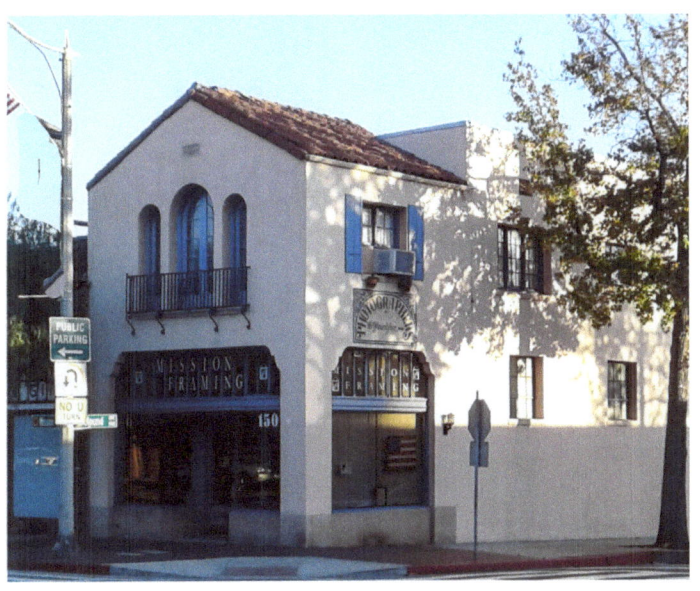
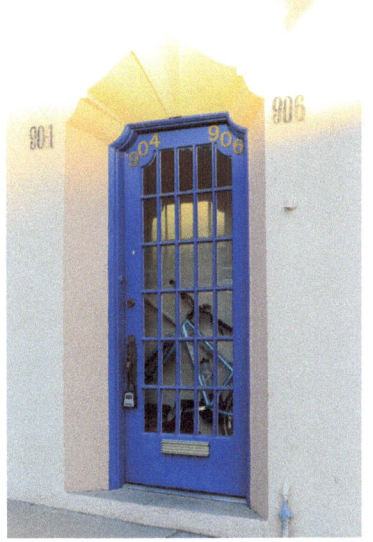

Pettee Building – 1933

Spanish Revival - Architect unknown

37

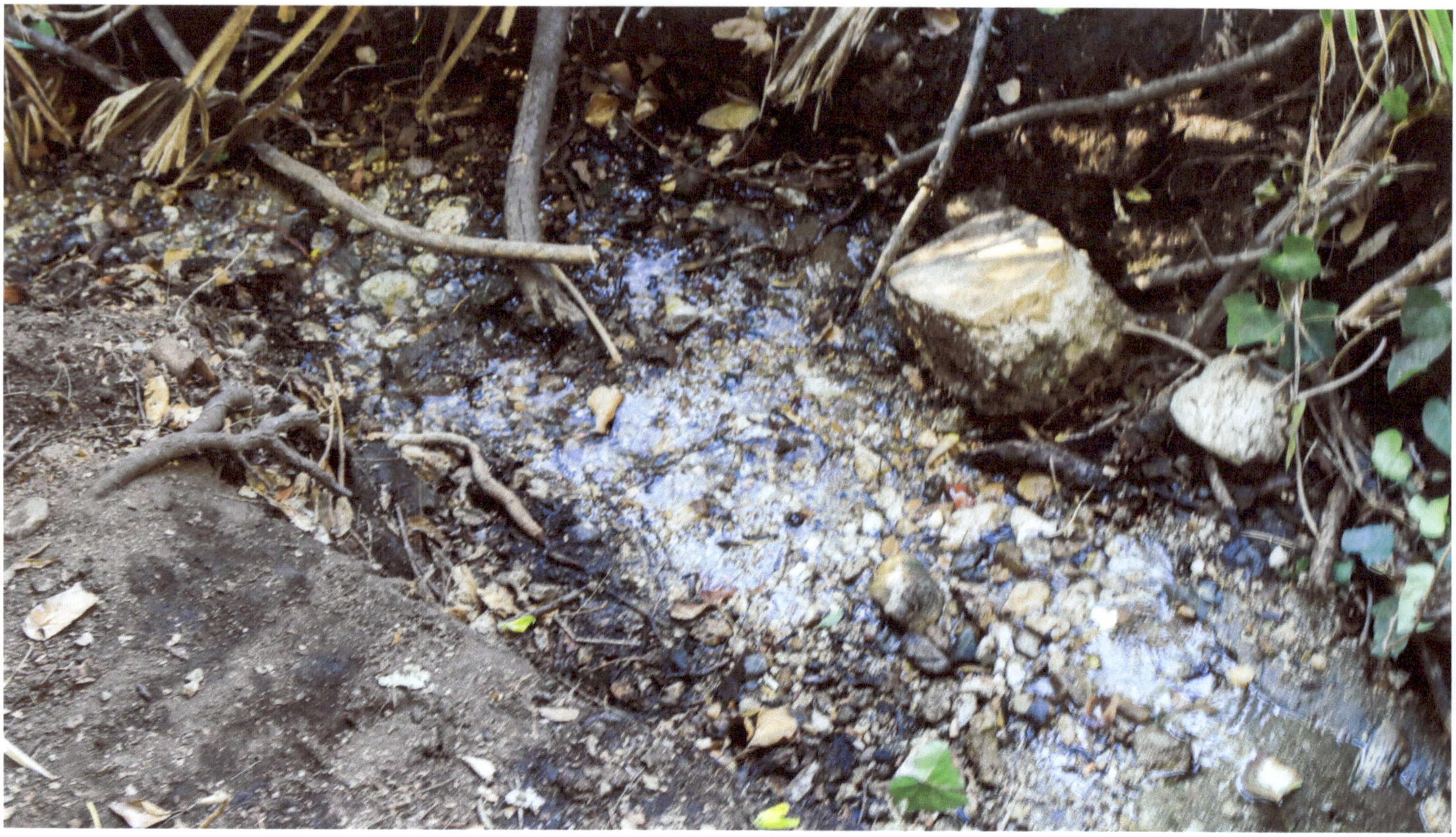

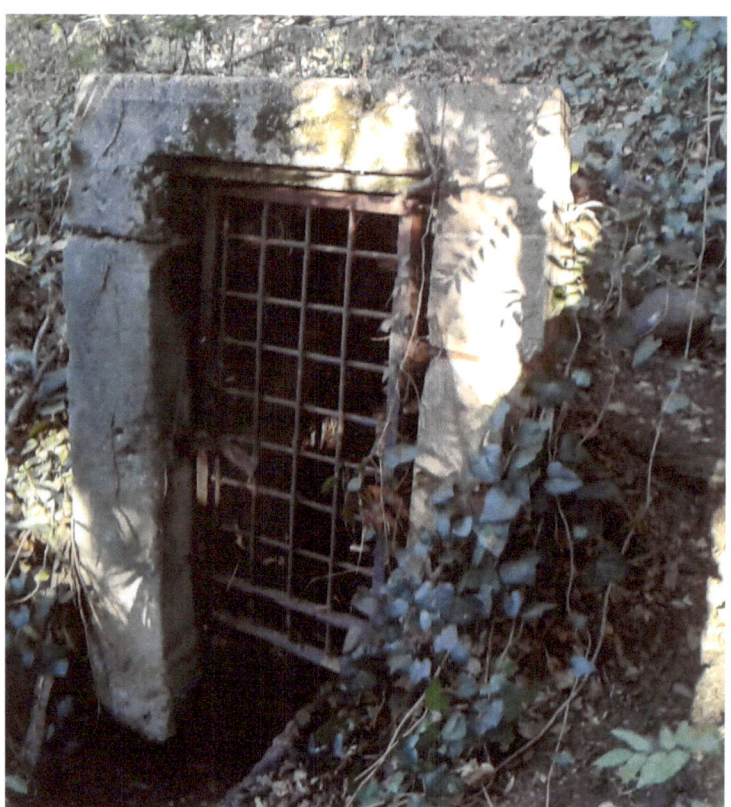
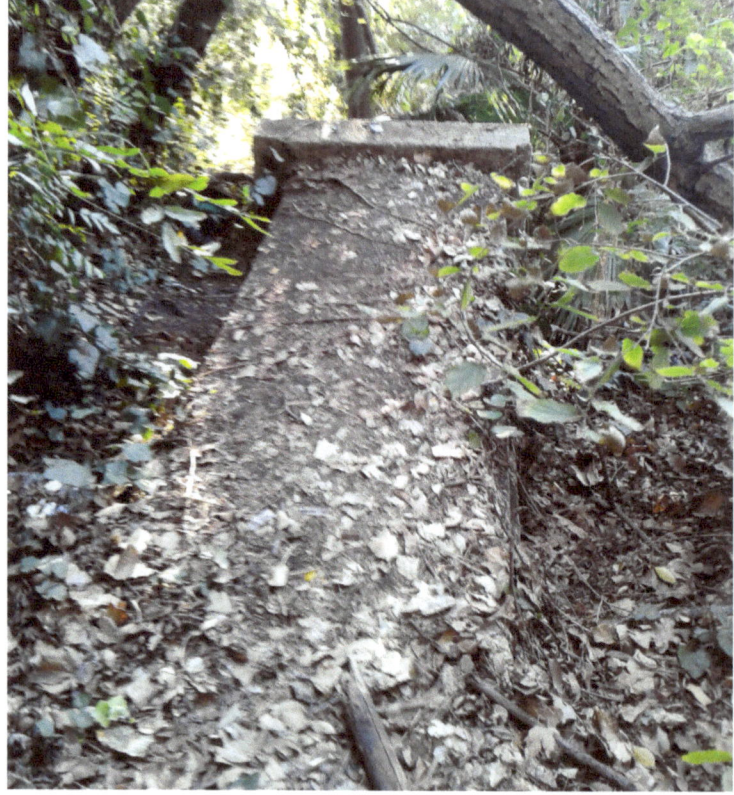

38

Garfias Spring

Ancient Artesian Spring

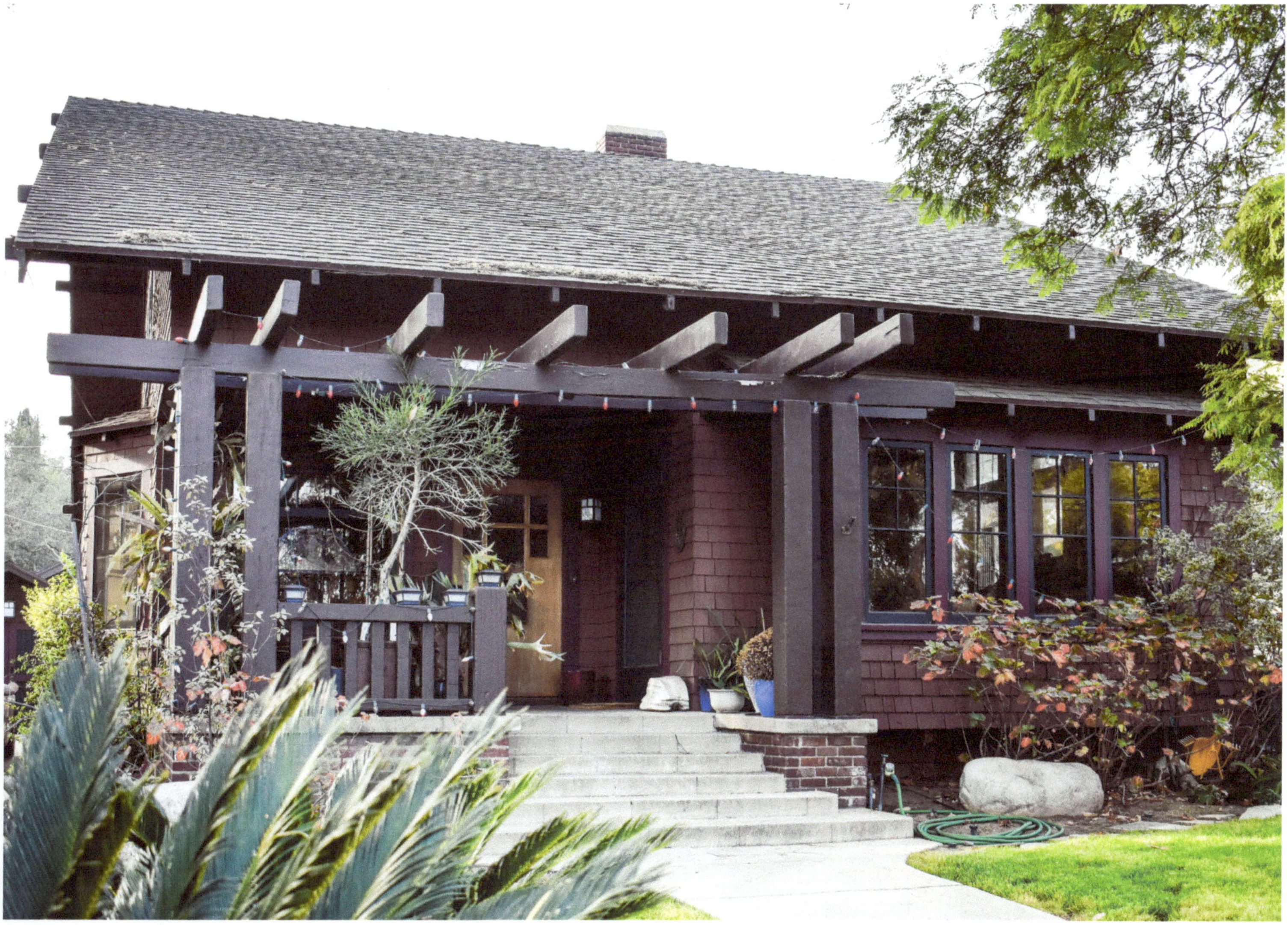

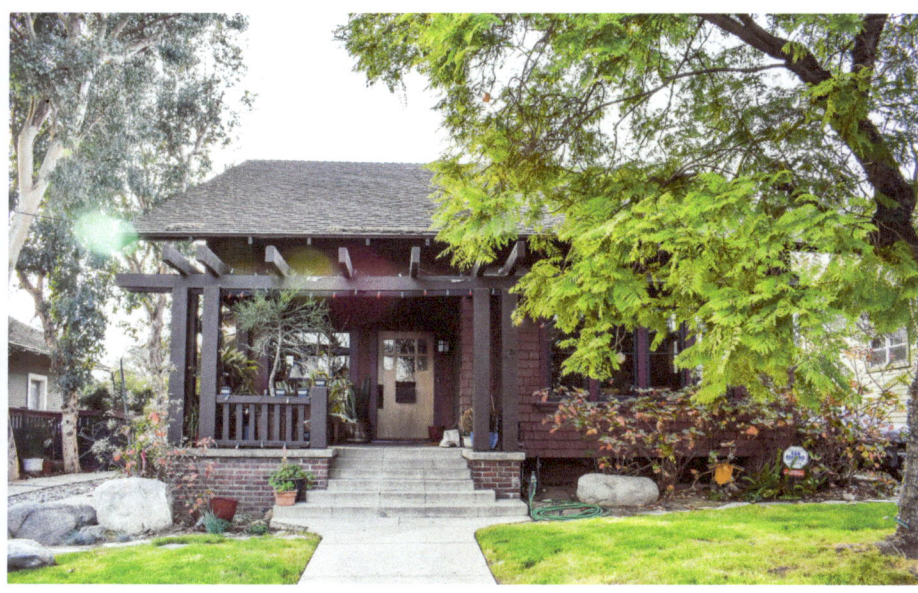
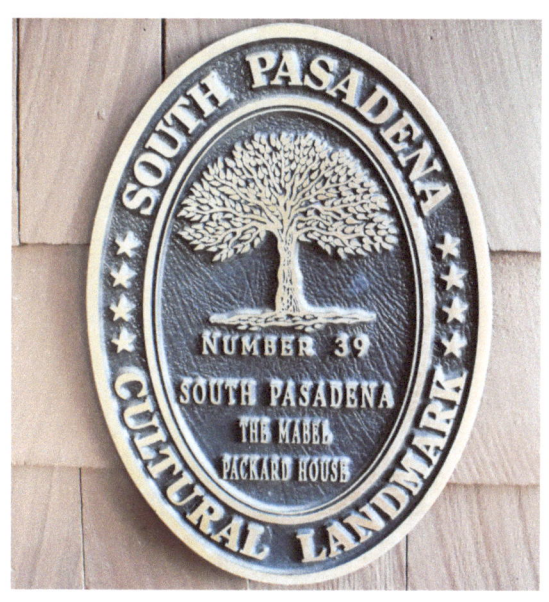
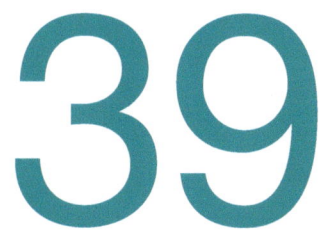

Mabel Packard House – 1914

Craftsman Artist Studio – Architect unknown

39

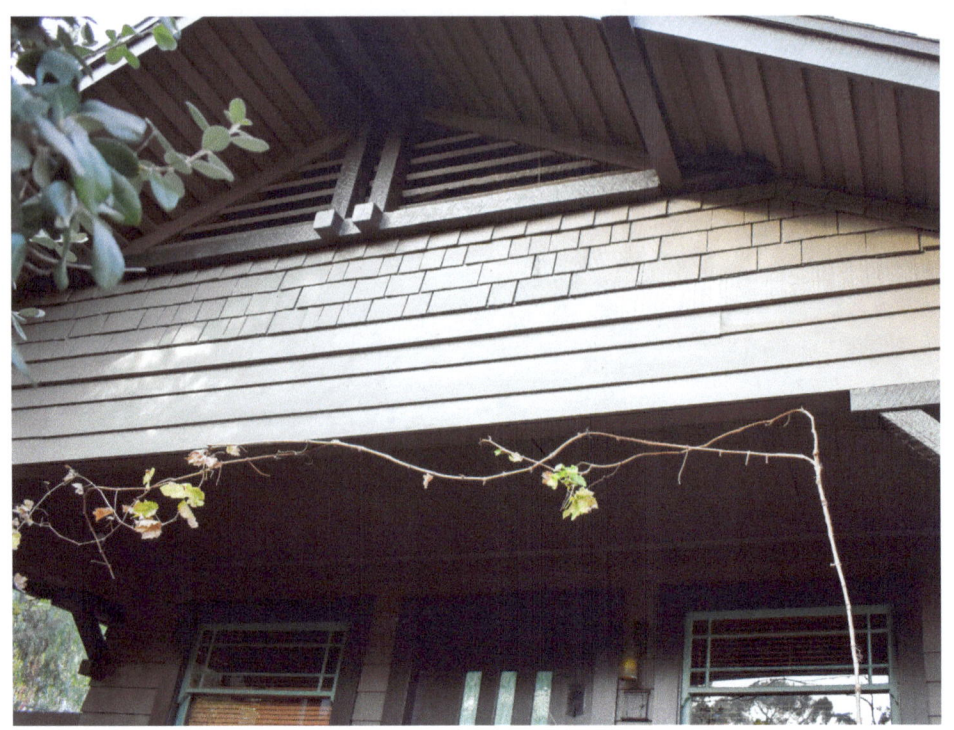
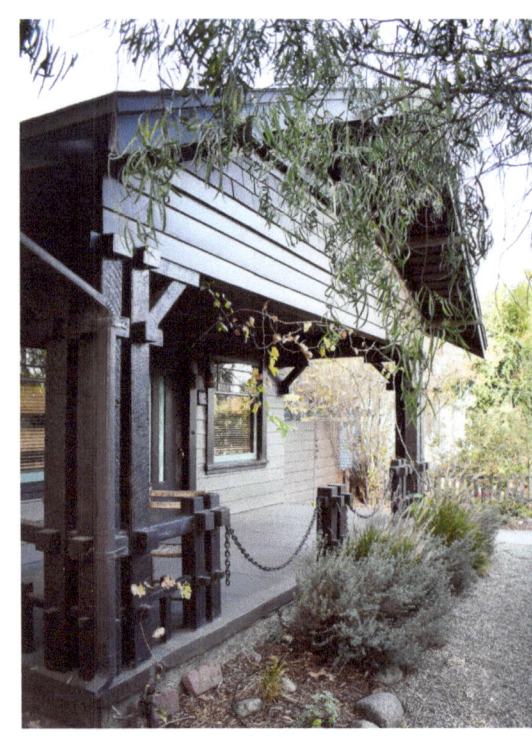
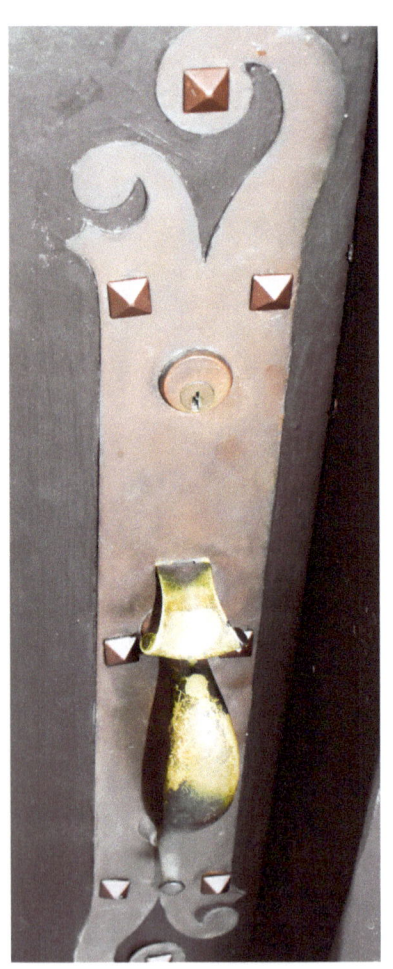
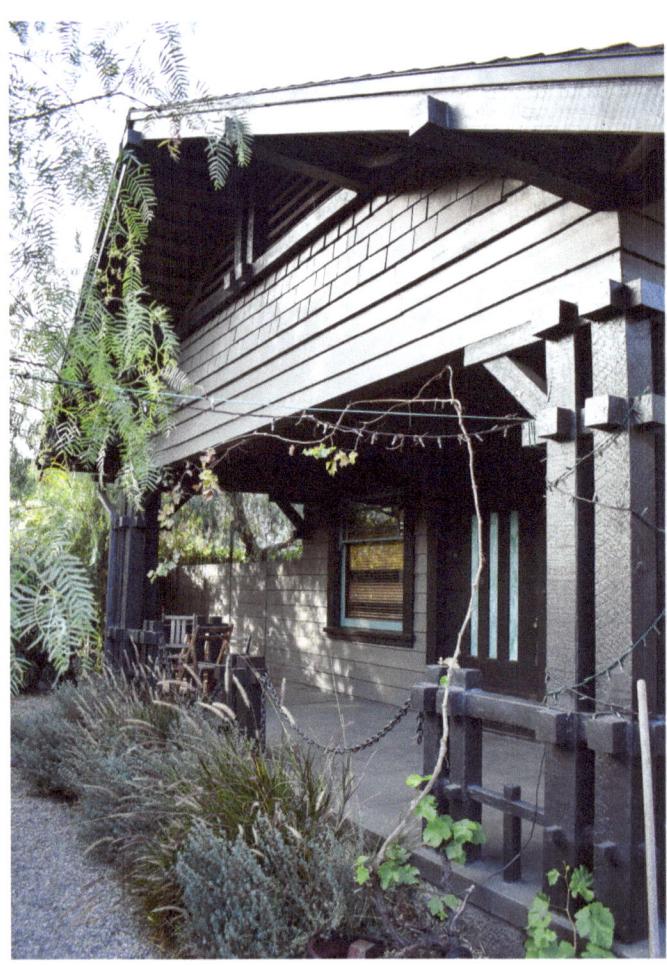
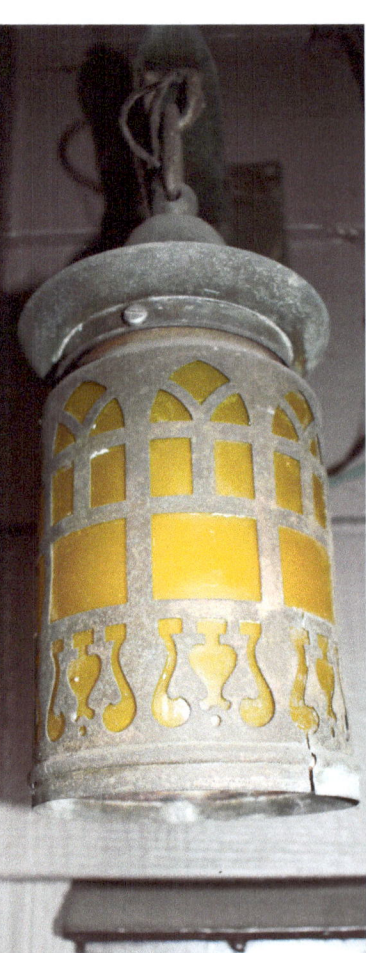

40

Washburn House – 1910

Craftsman bungalow – Bliss Washburn, Architect

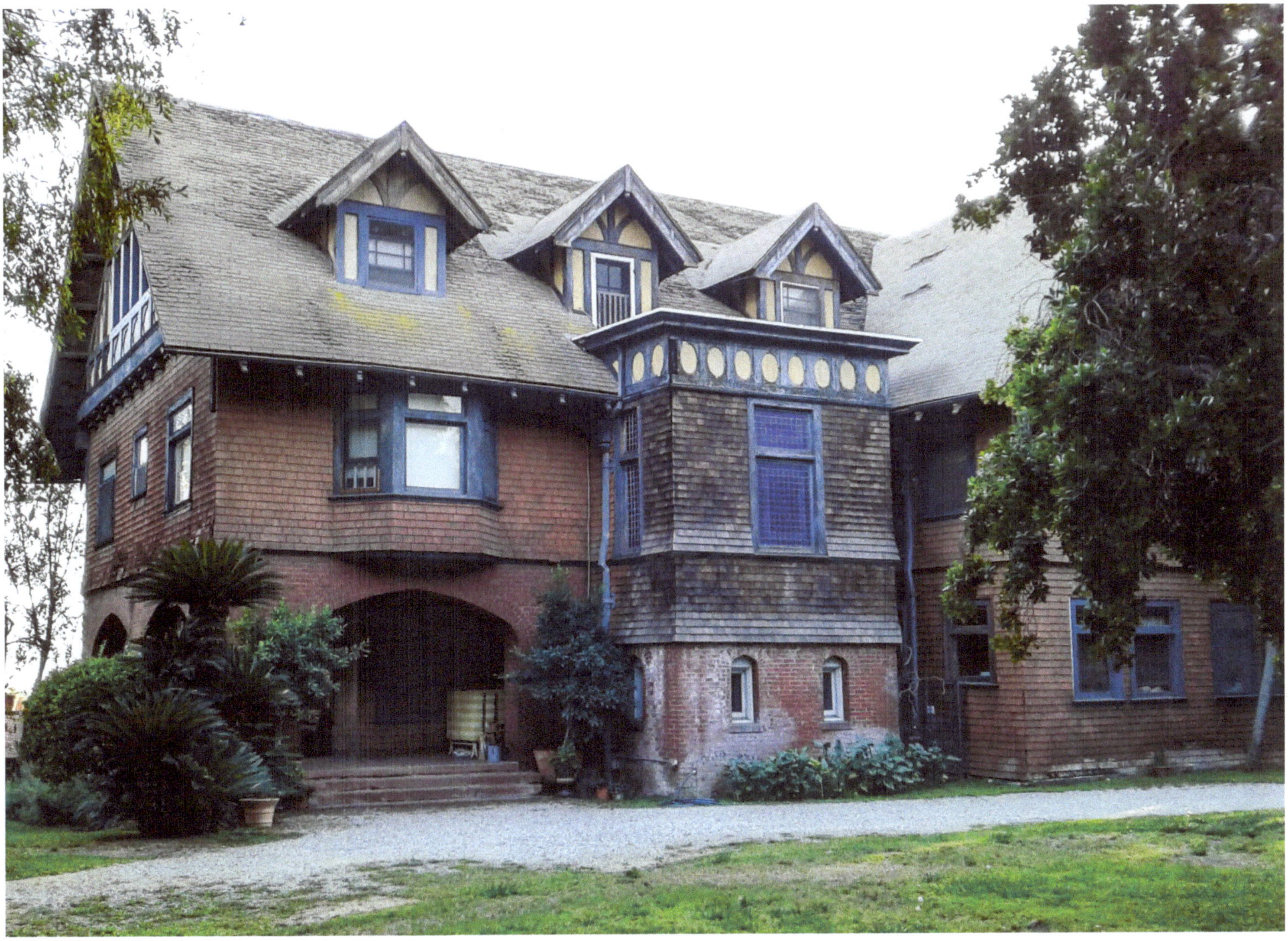

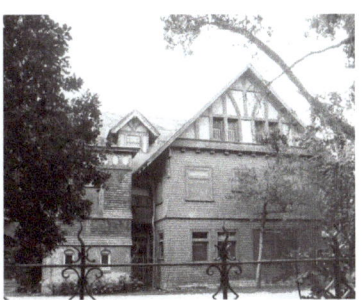
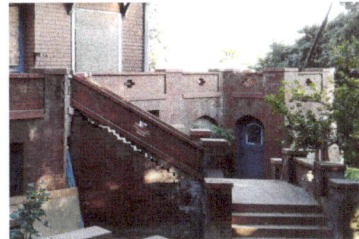
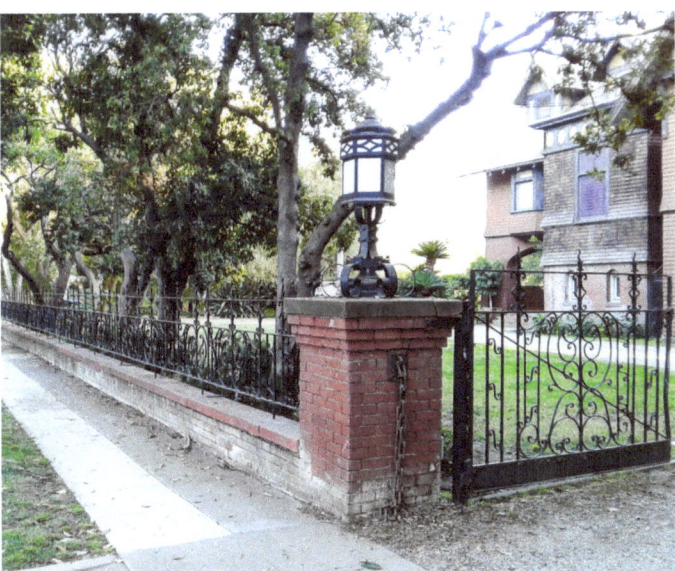
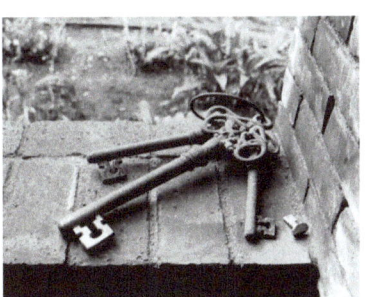
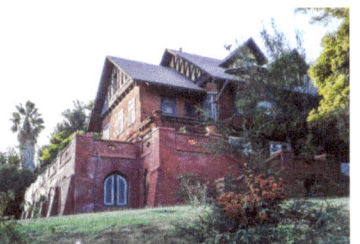

Torrance-Childs House - 1903

Tudor Revival – Charles Buchanan, Architect

41

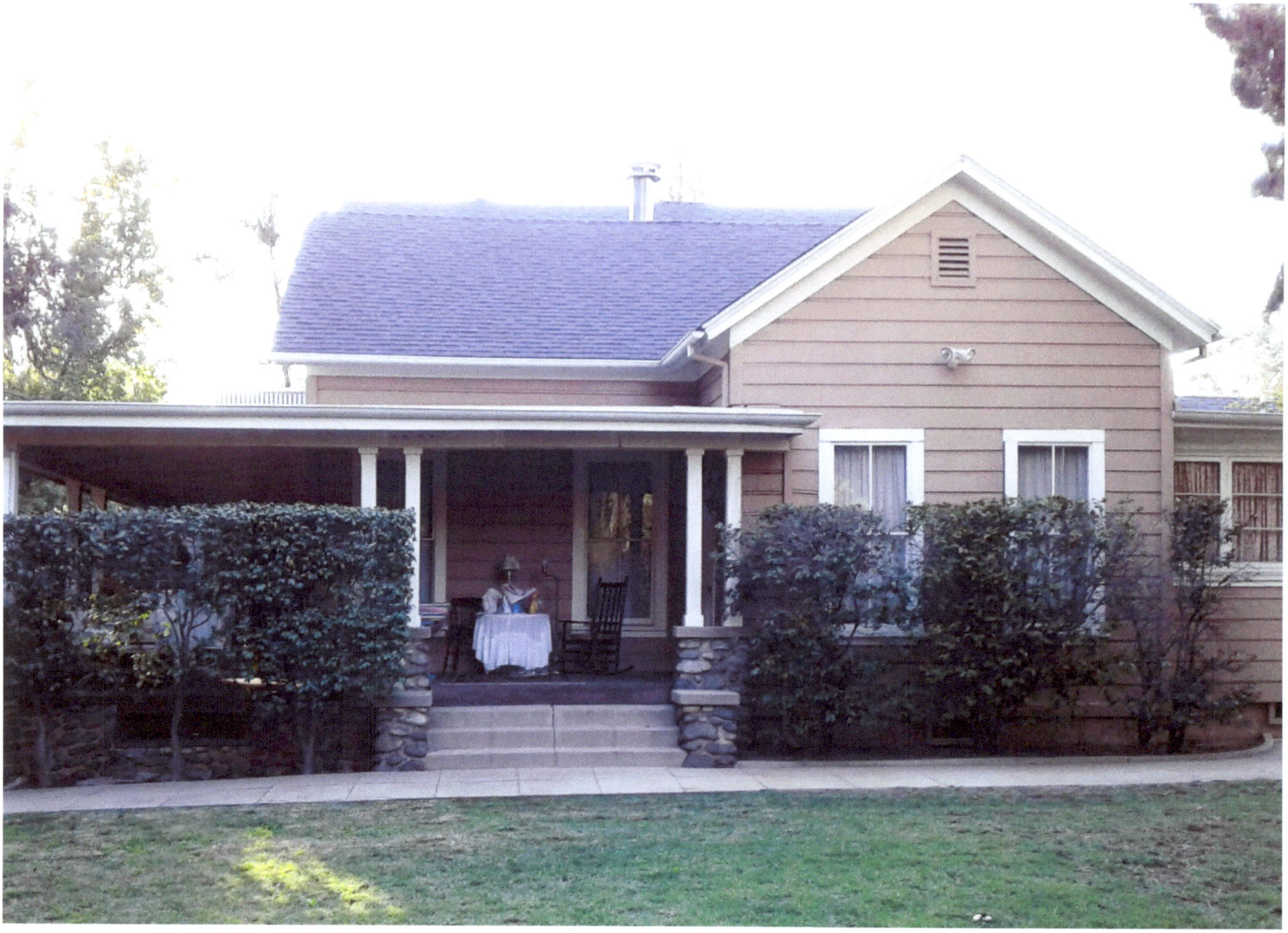

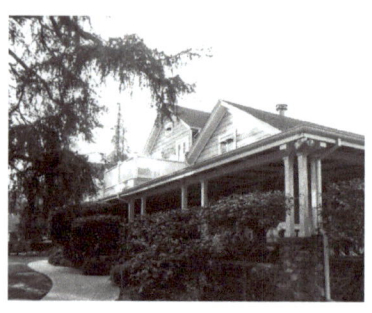
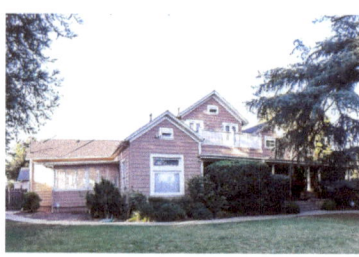
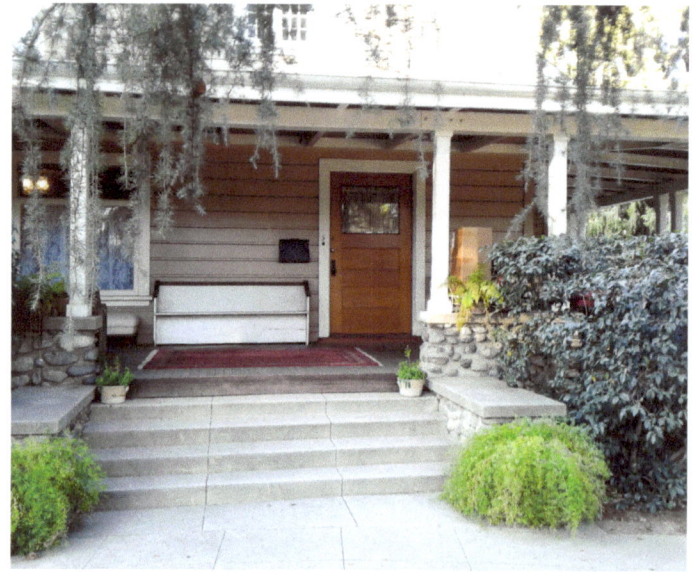
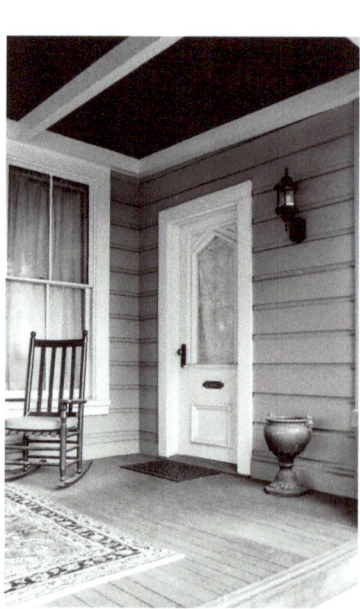

42 Knox-Merwin - Porter House - circa 1875

Folk Victorian – Architect unknown

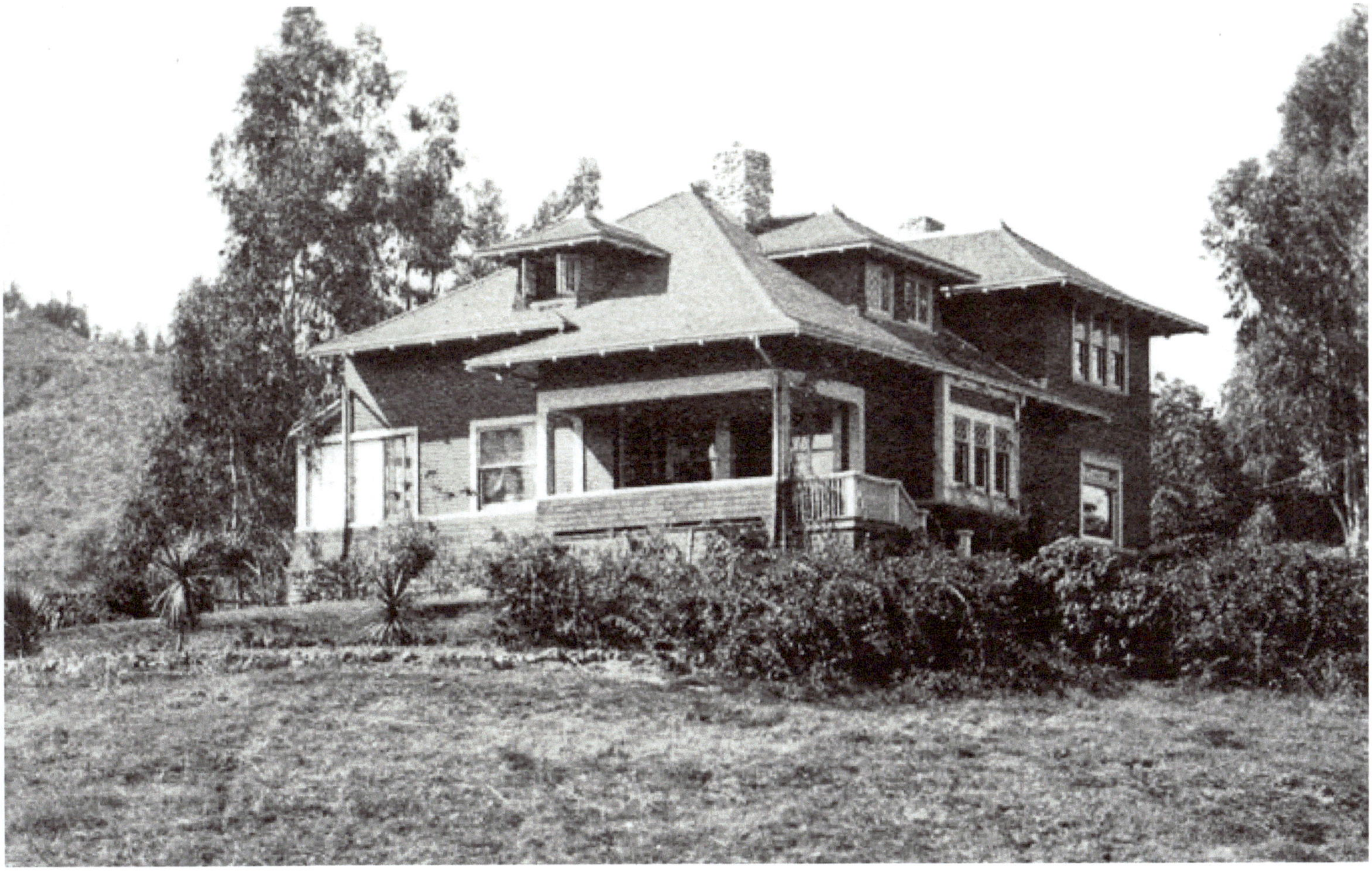

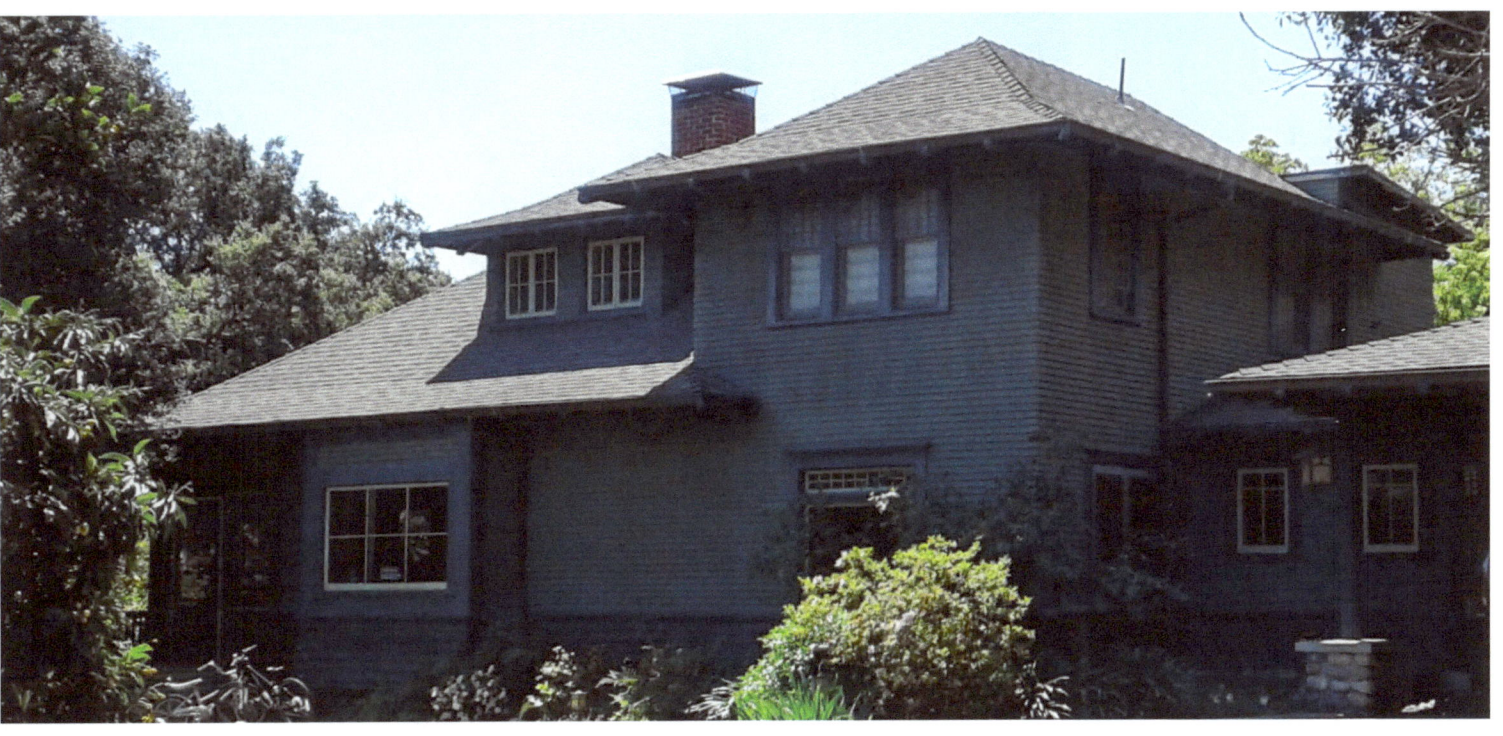

East Wynyate - 1896
Eclectic Victorian - Frederick Roehrig, Architect

43

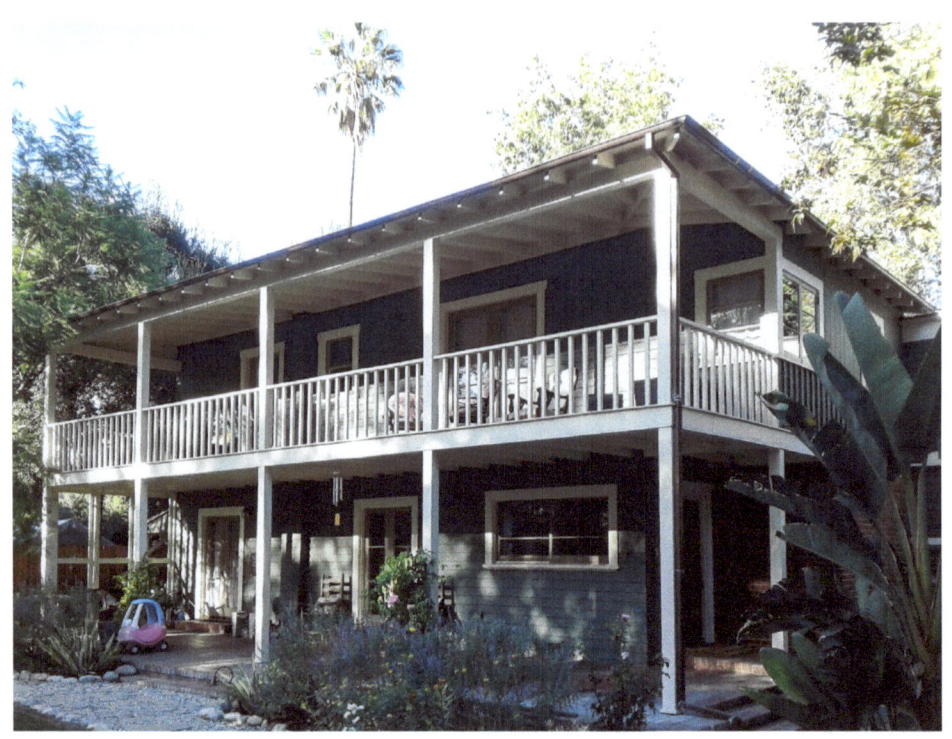
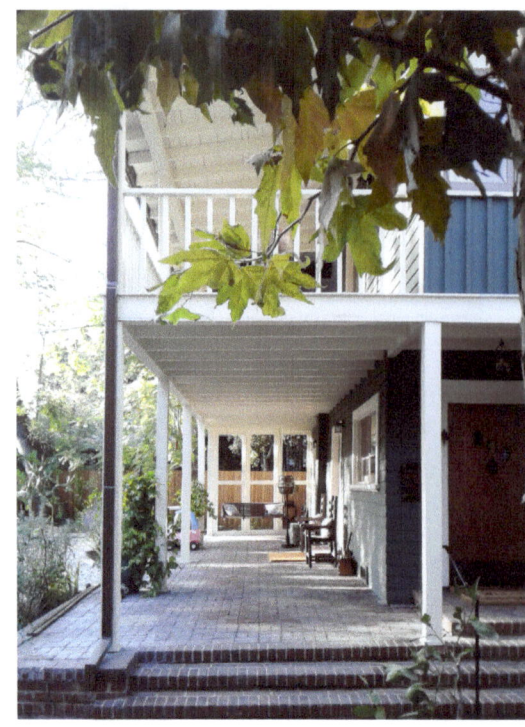
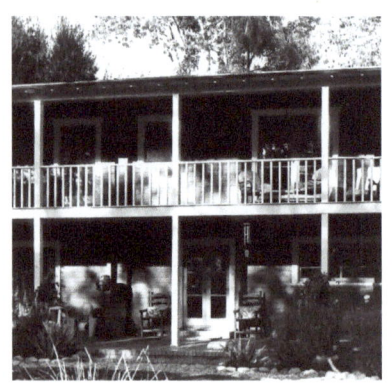
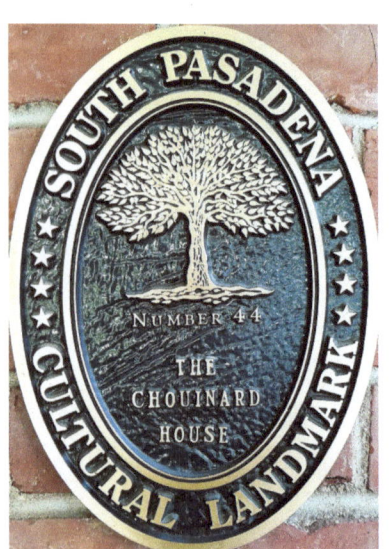
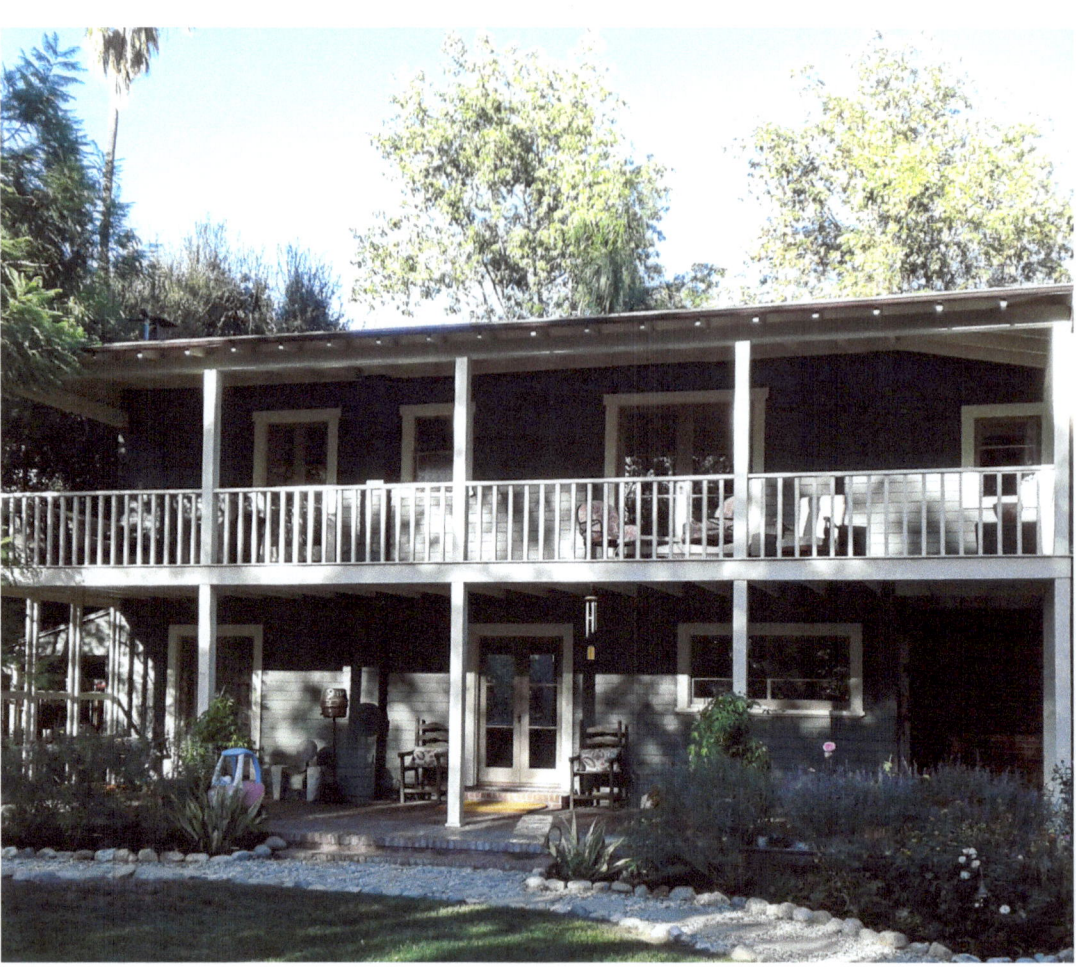

44
Chouinard House – 1907

Monterey Spanish Revival - Architect unknown

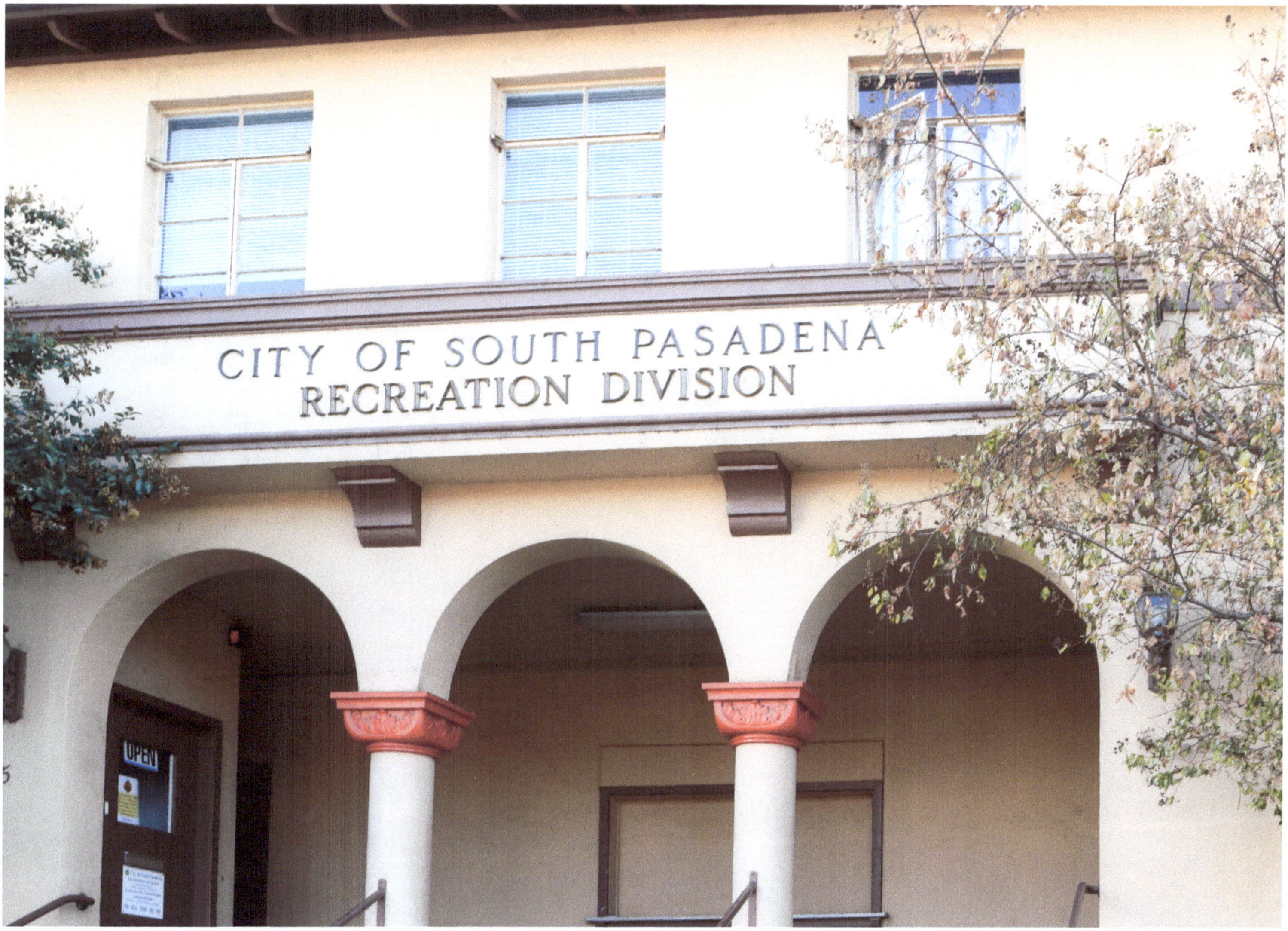

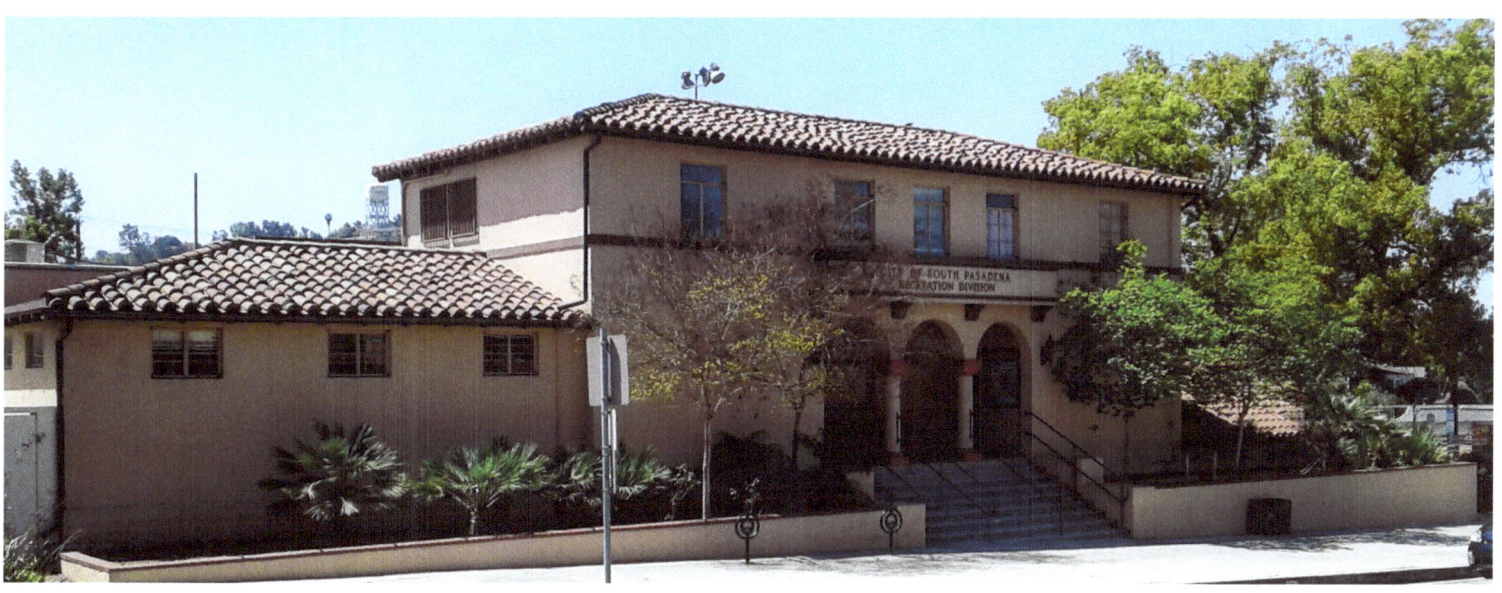

Municipal Plunge Building – 1936

Spanish Revival - Harry L. Pierce, Architect

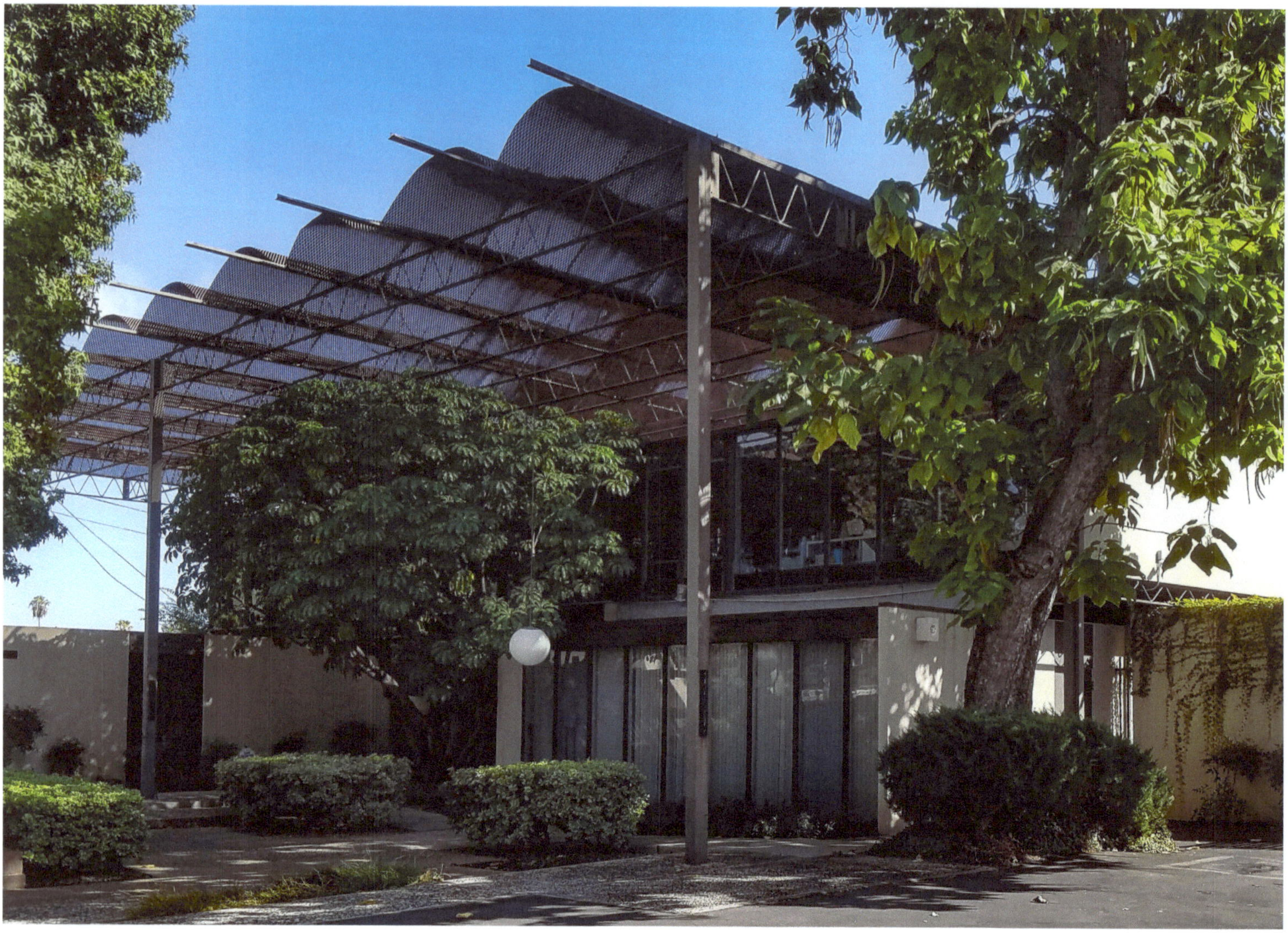

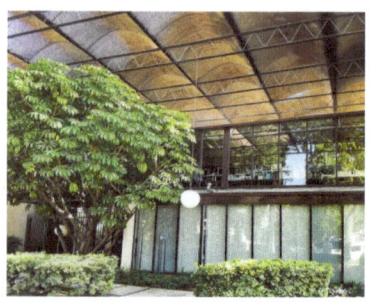
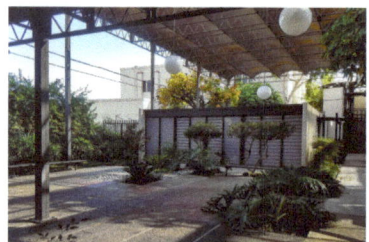
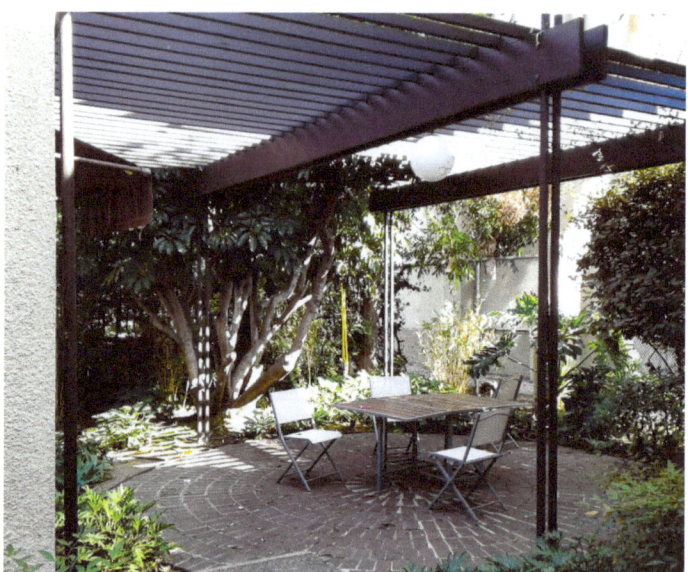
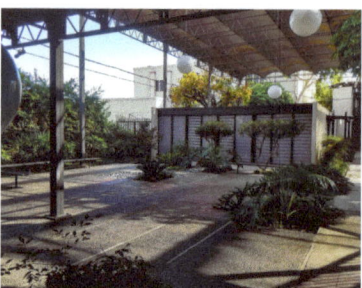
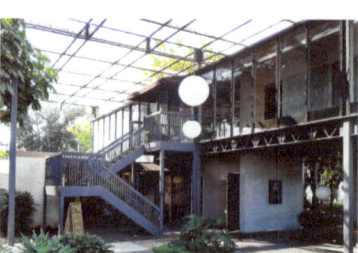

46

Smith & Williams Building – 1958

Mid-Century Office Complex –

Whitney D Smith, Wayne Williams, Architects

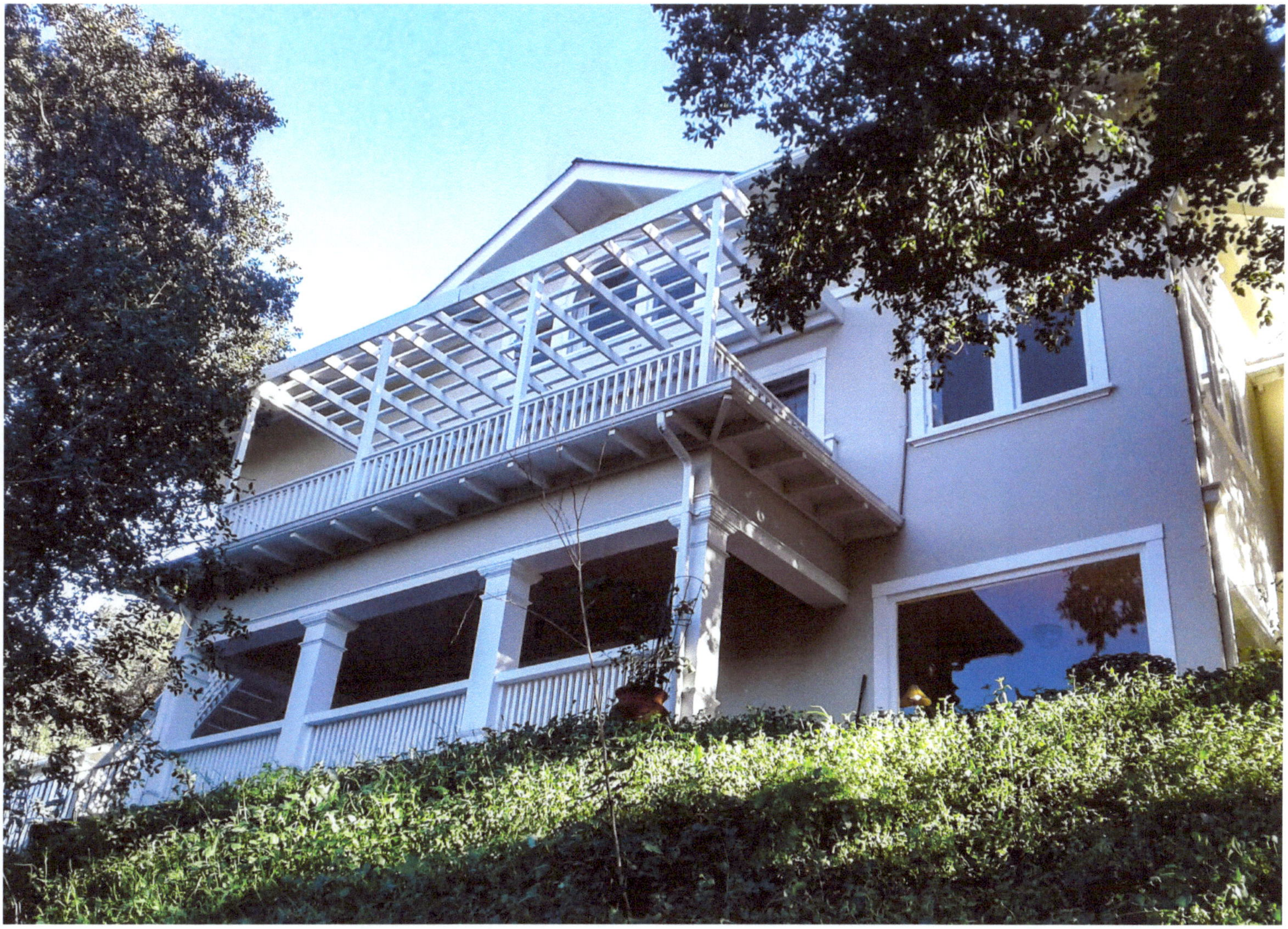

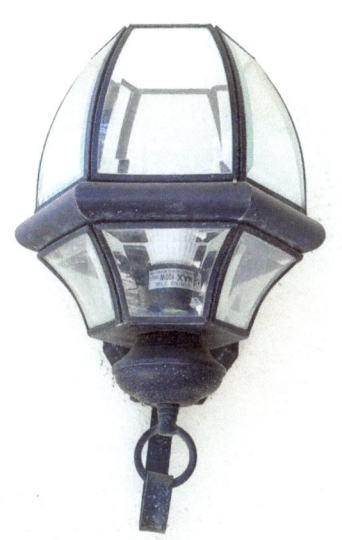
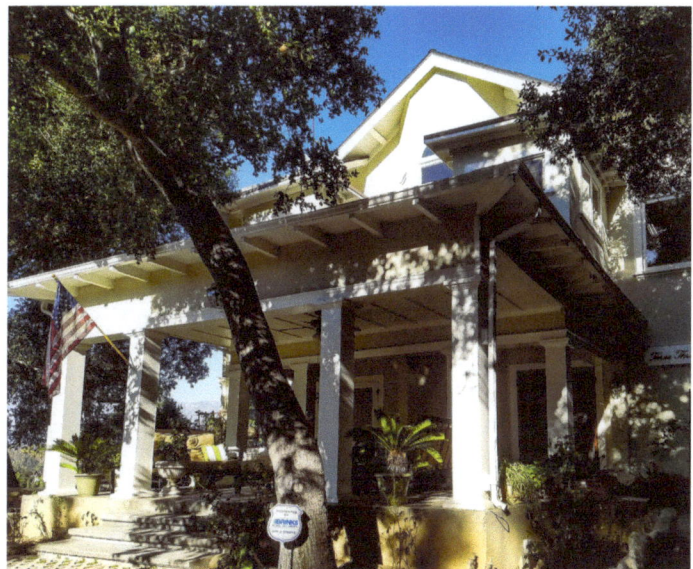
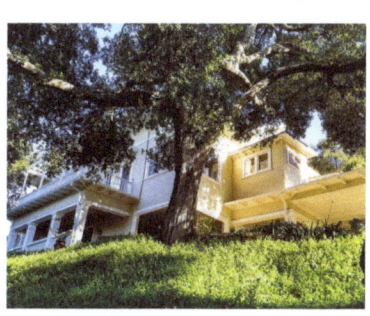
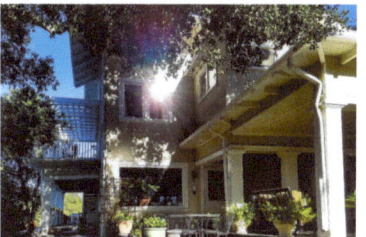

Burwood – 1910

Craftsman – Lester Moore, Architect

47

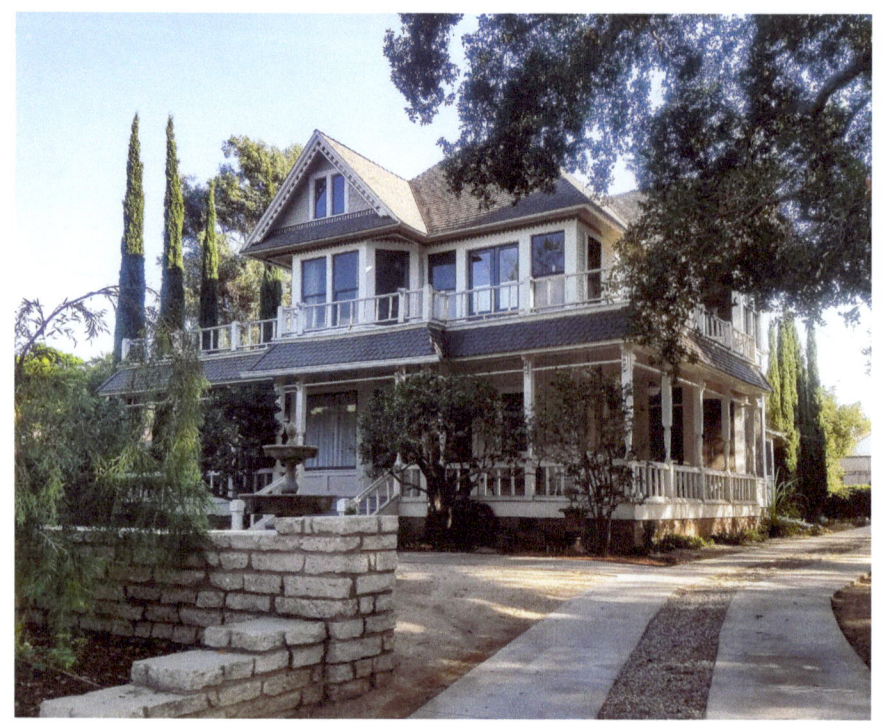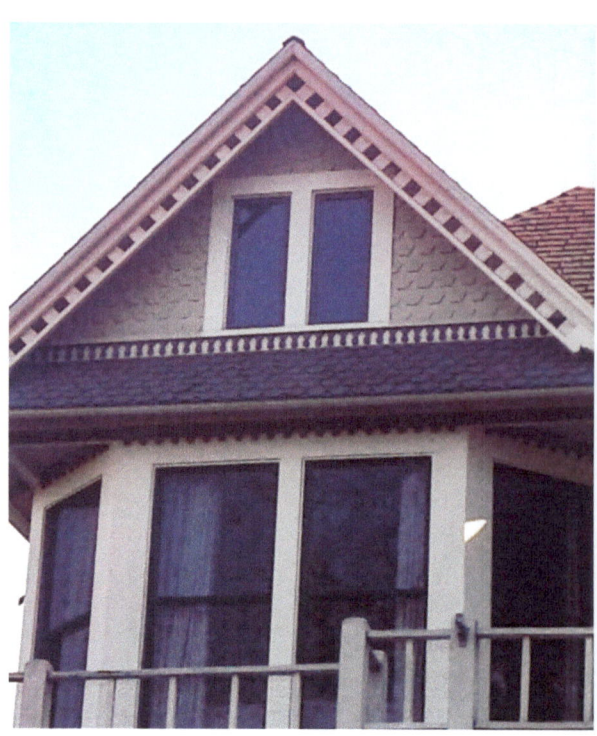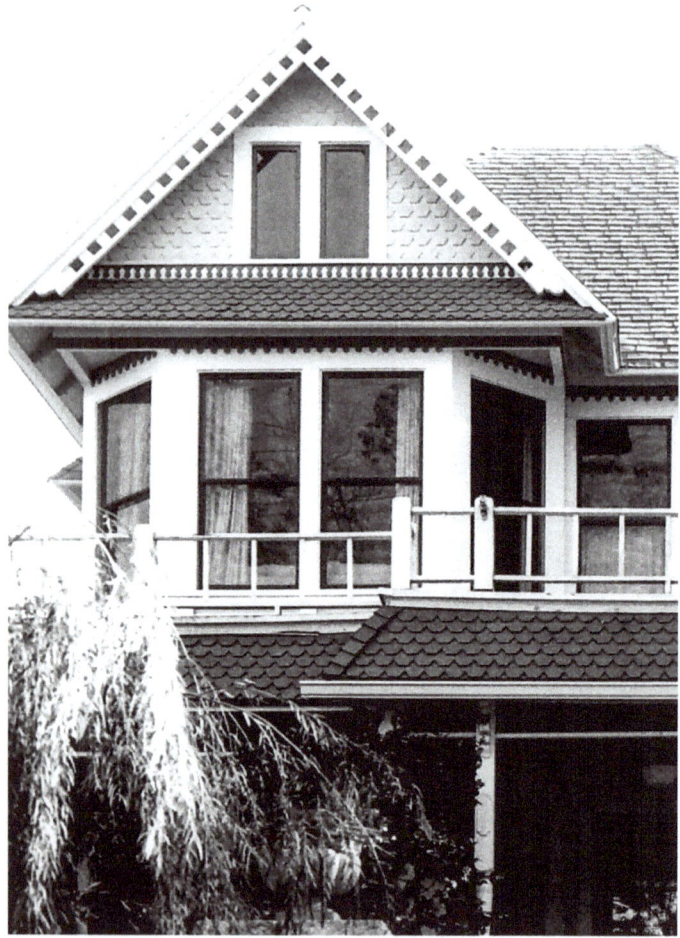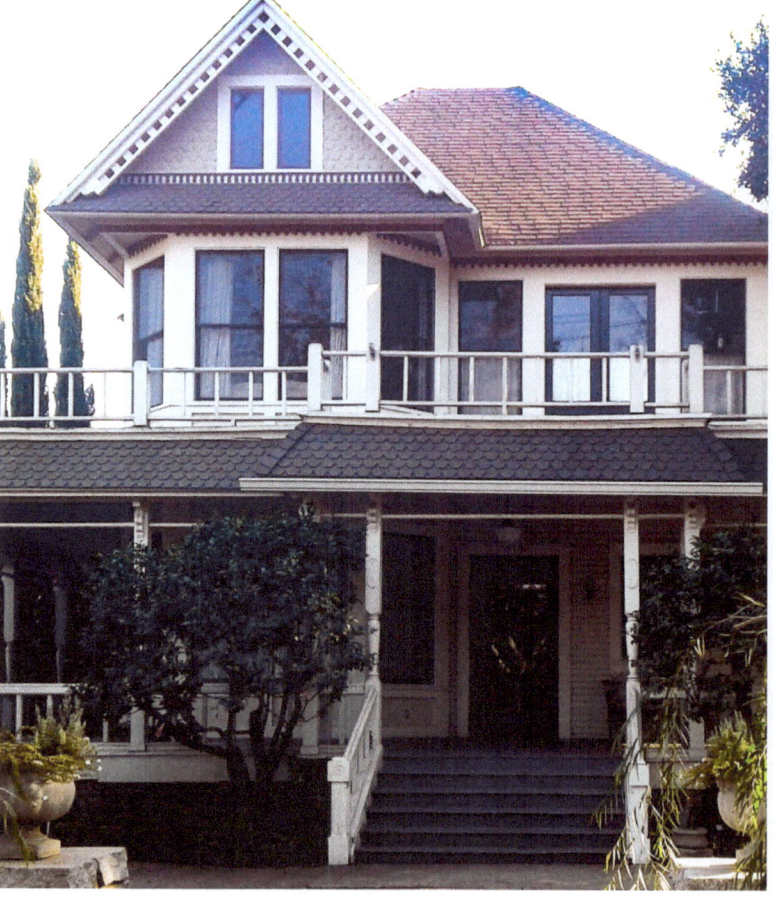

48

Riggins House – 1885

Queen Anne Victorian – Architect unknown

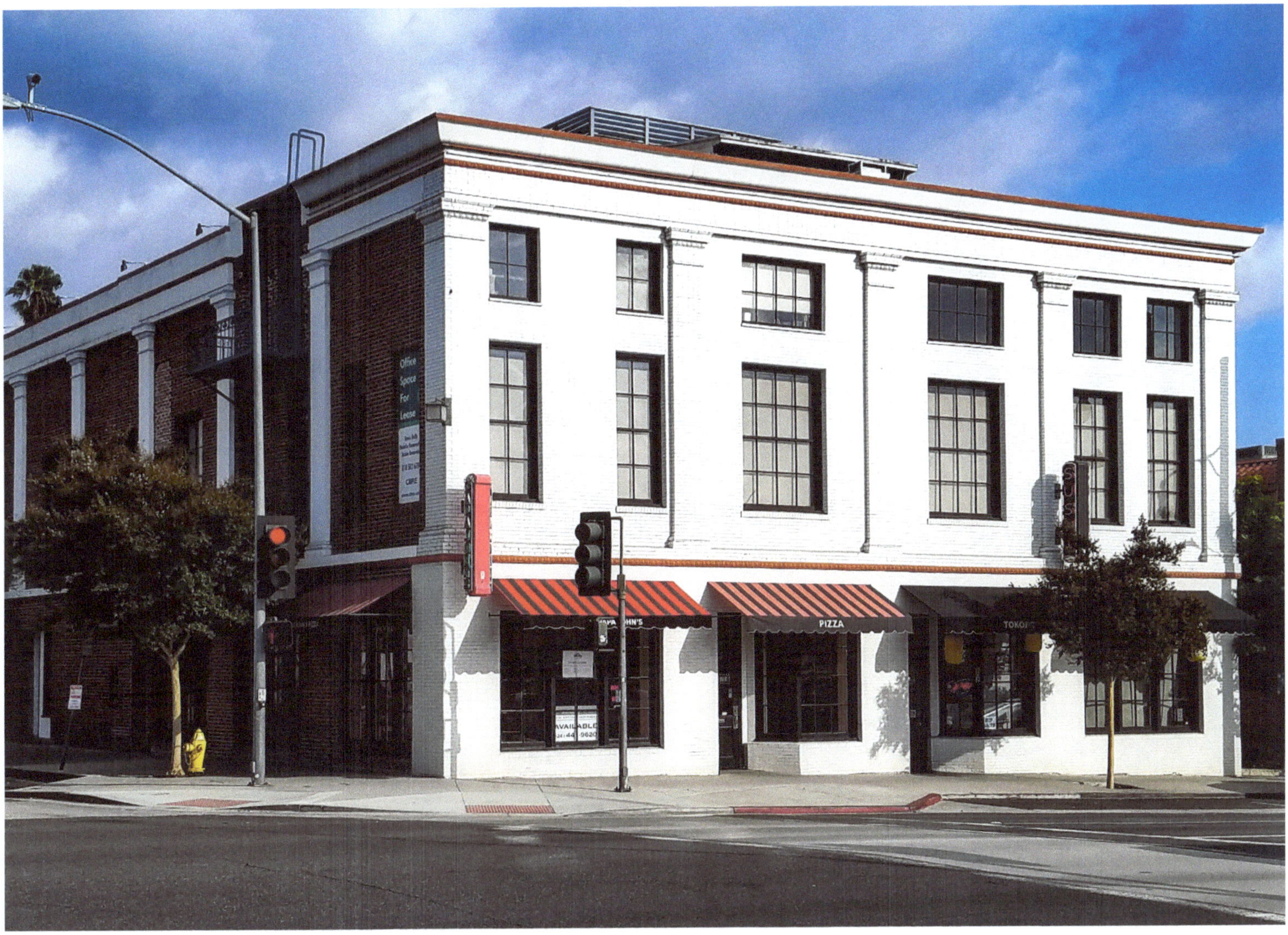

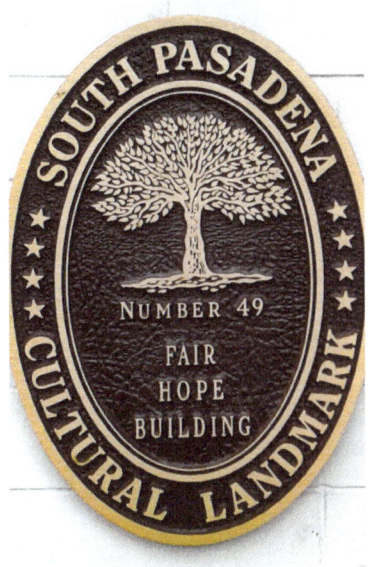
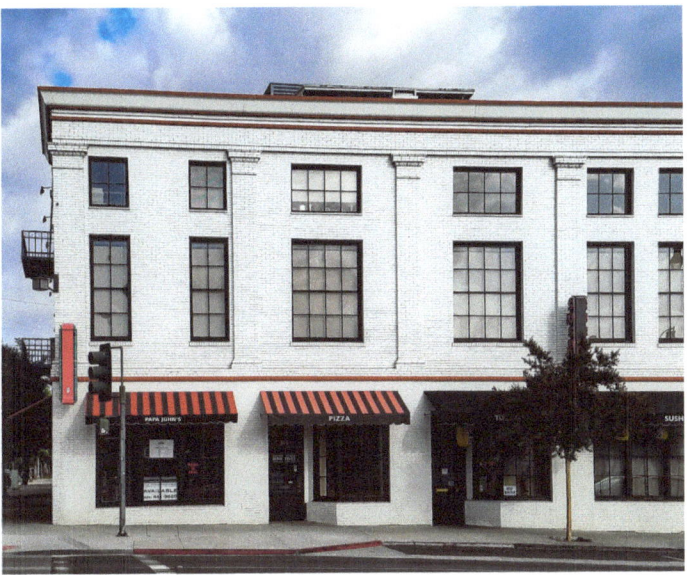
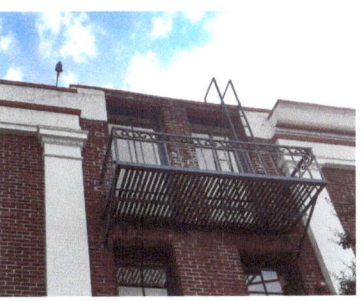
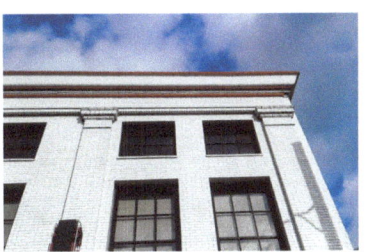

Fair Hope Building – 1911

Brick Commercial Building – Architect unknown

49

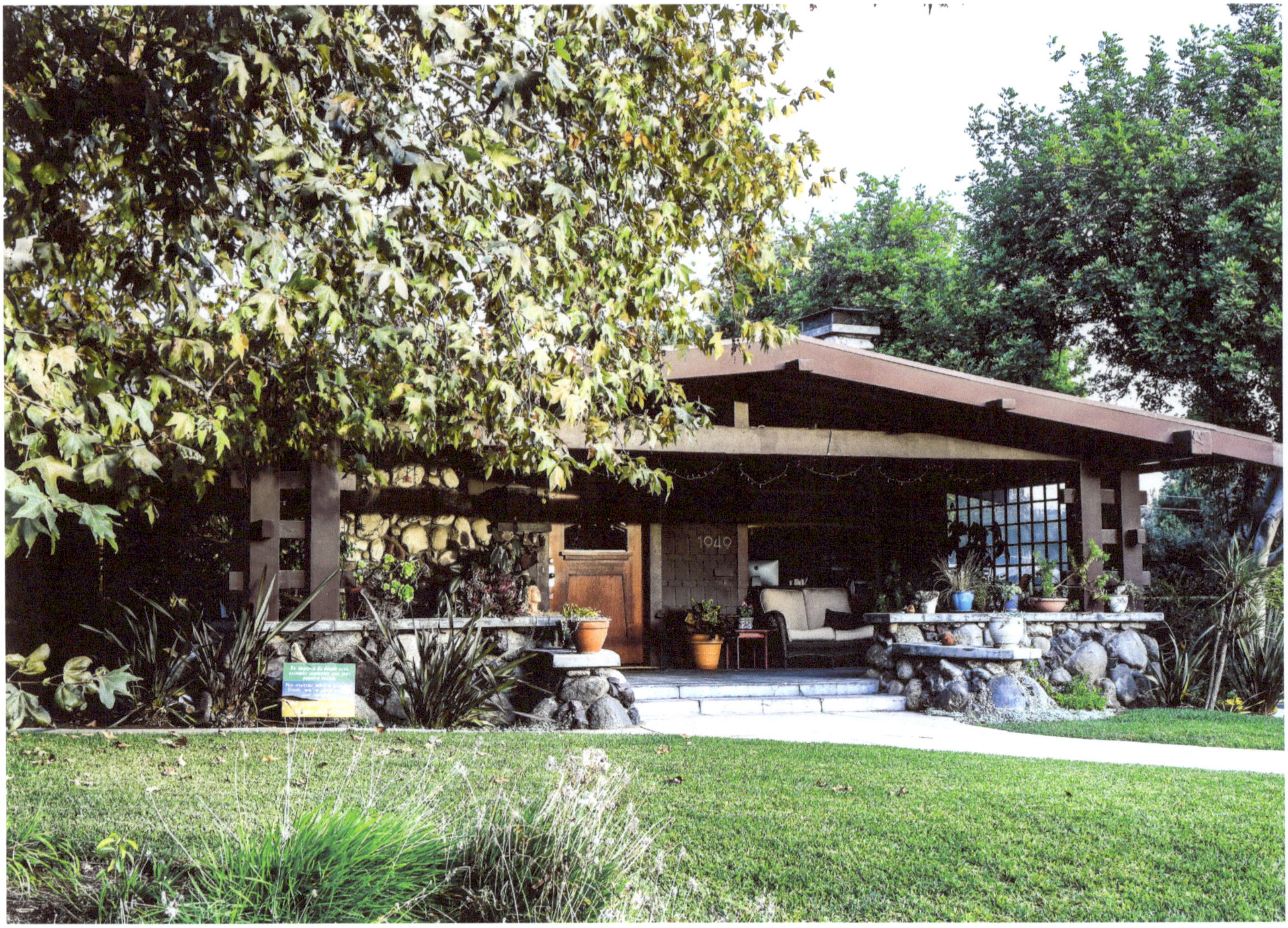

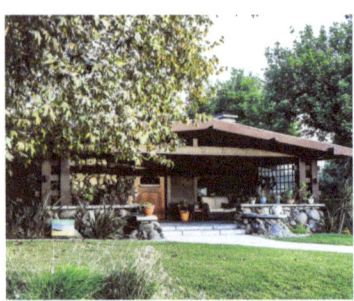
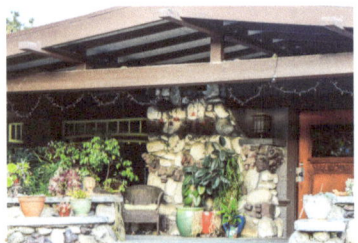
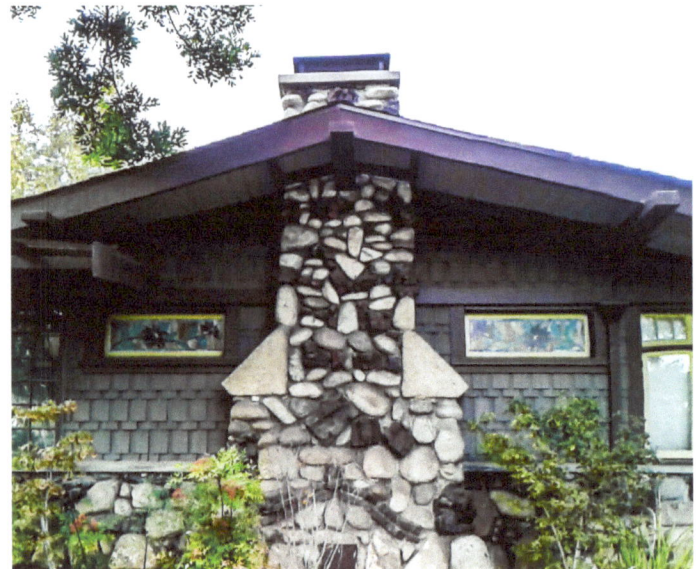
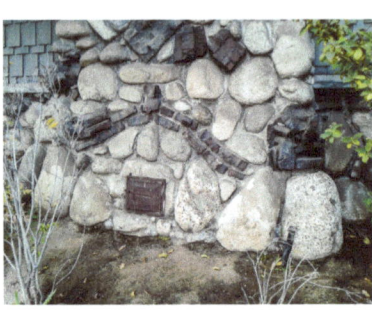
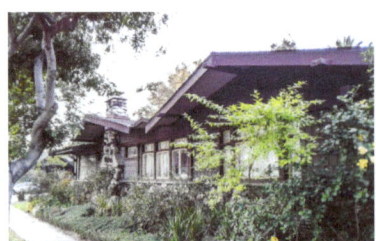

50

Huntzinger House – 1910

Craftsman Bungalow – Designed and built
by Edward Sweet Building Co.

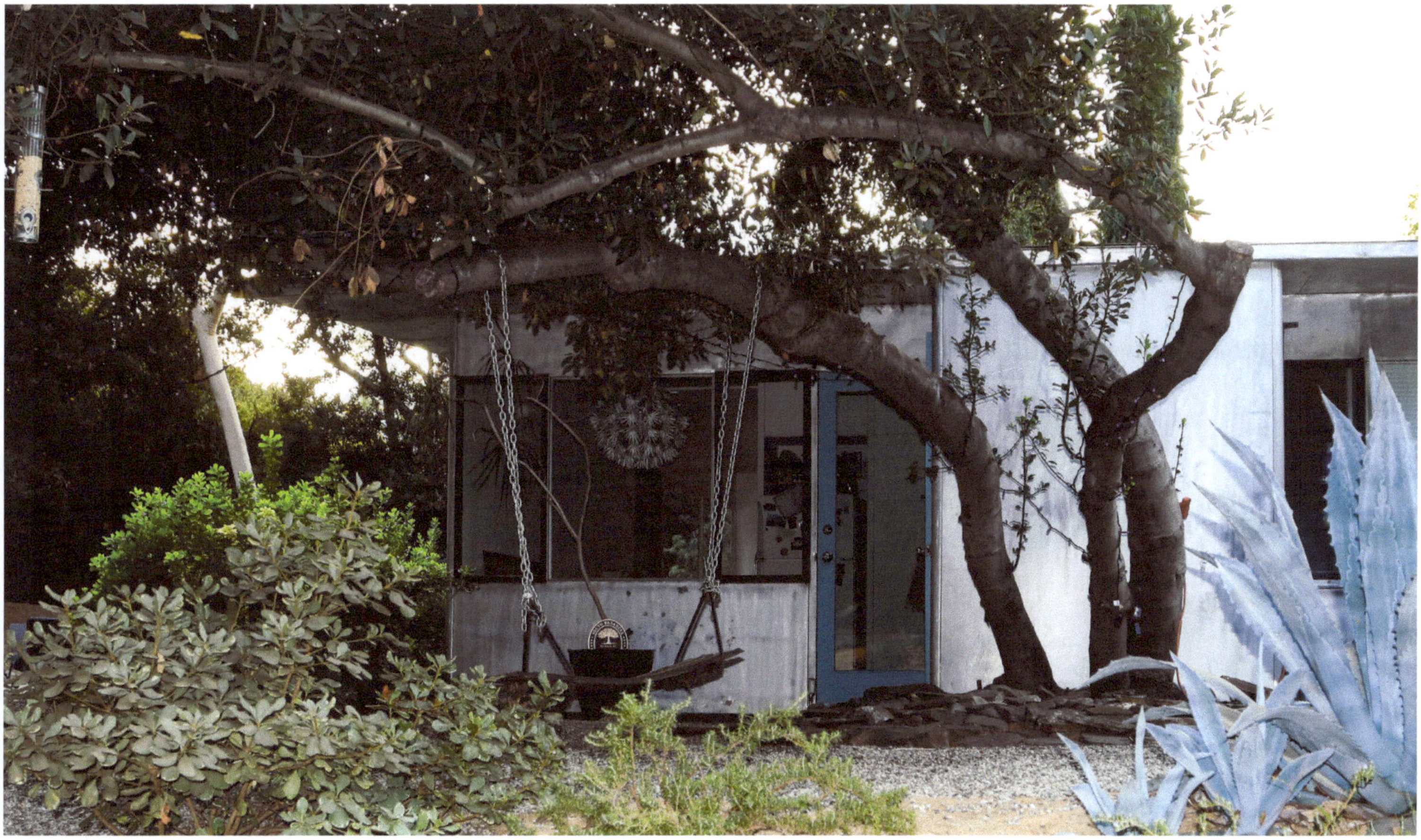

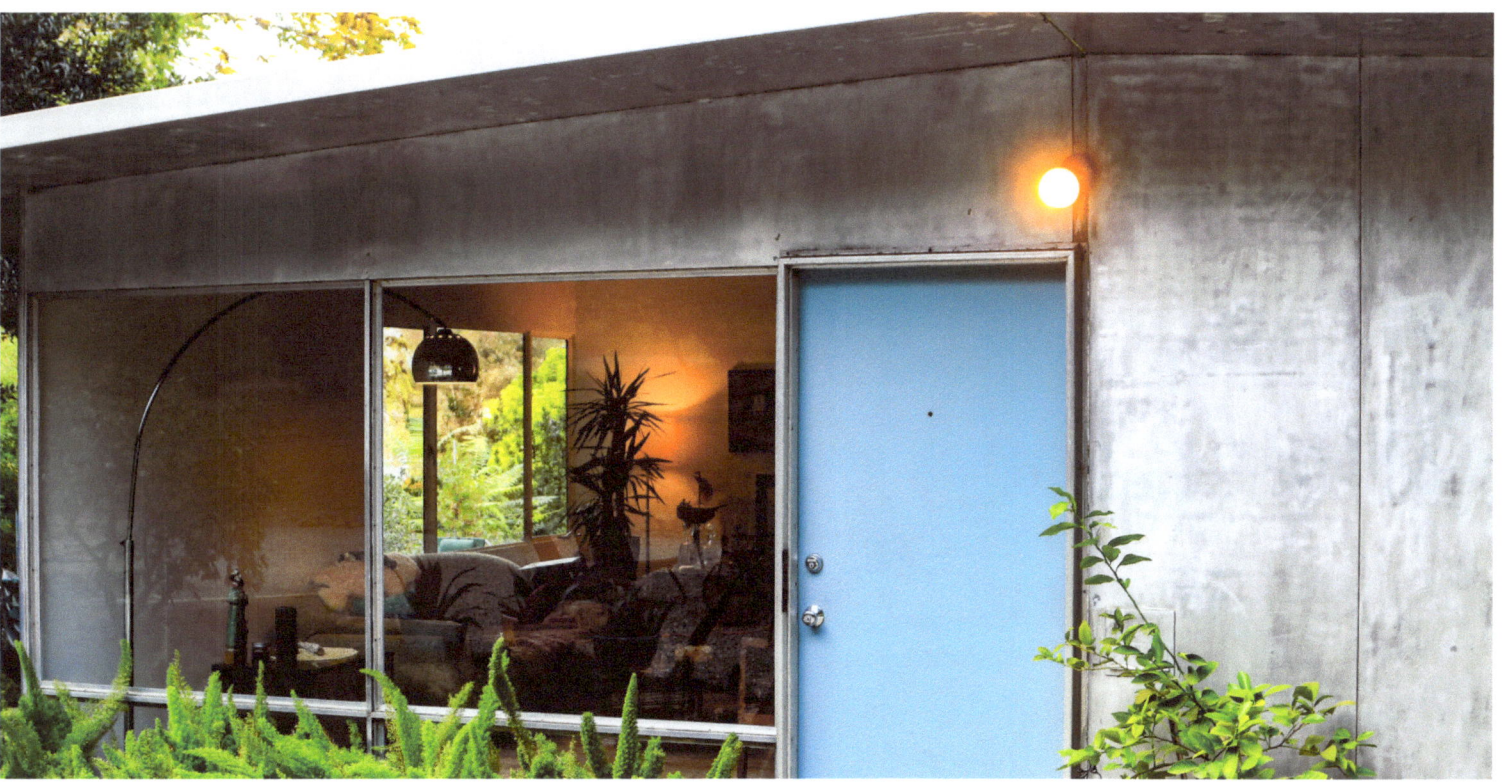

Fleet House -1947

Mid Century Pre-fab house – Henry Dreyfuss, Edward L. Barnes, Architects

51

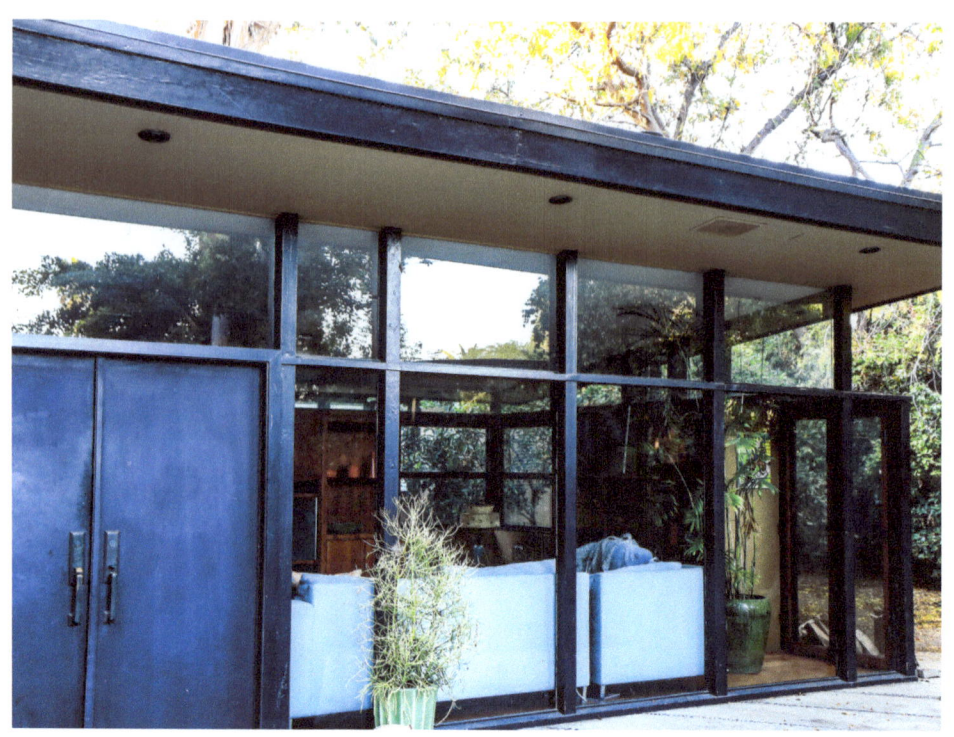
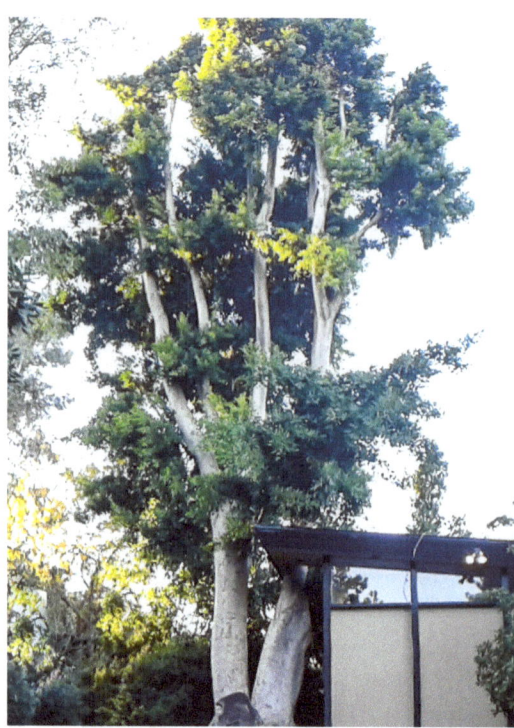
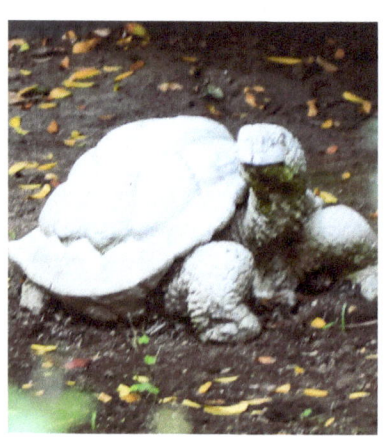
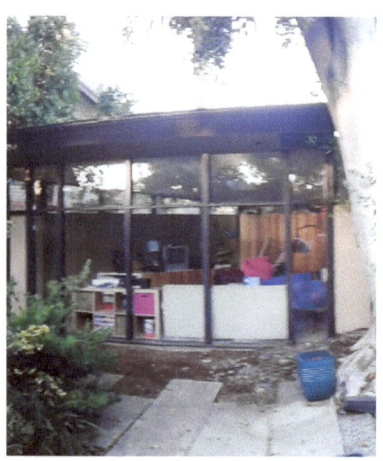
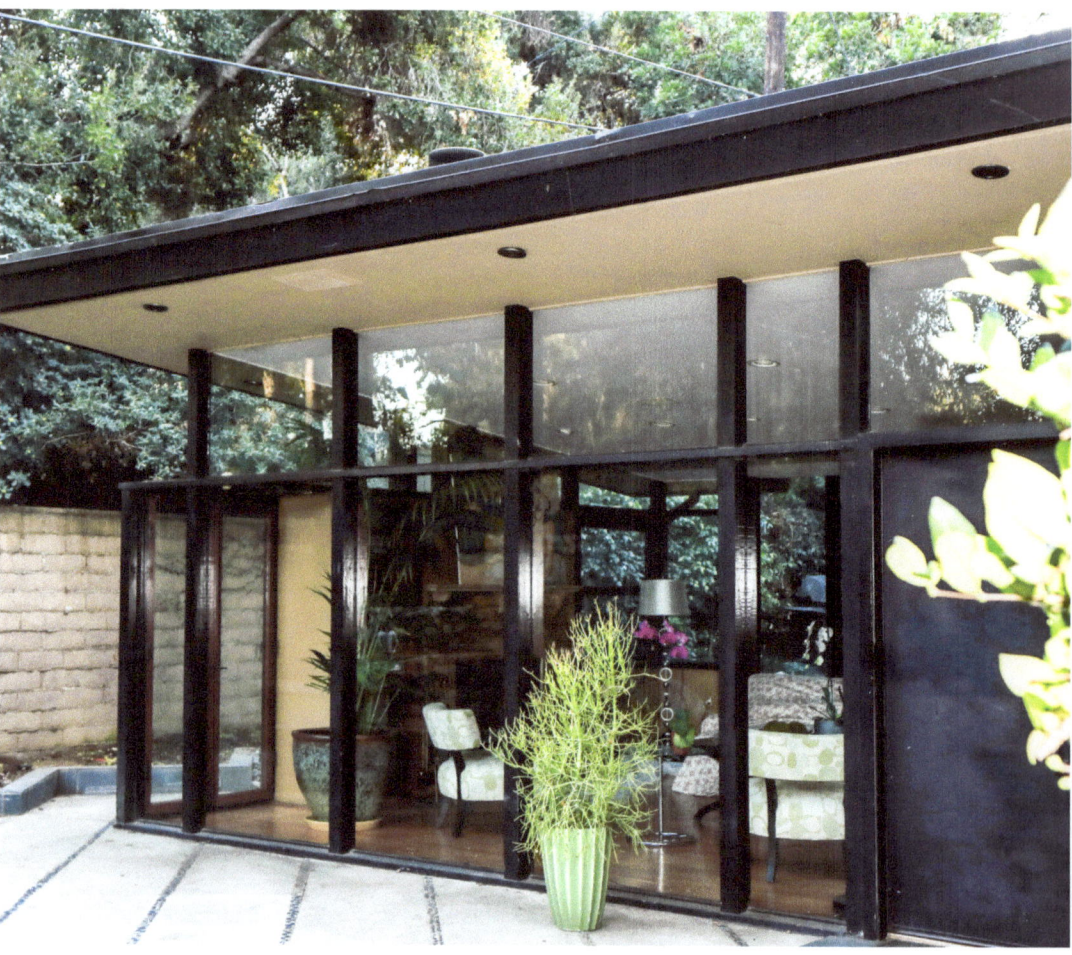

52

Whit Smith House - 1947

Mid Century House – Whitney R. Smith, Architect

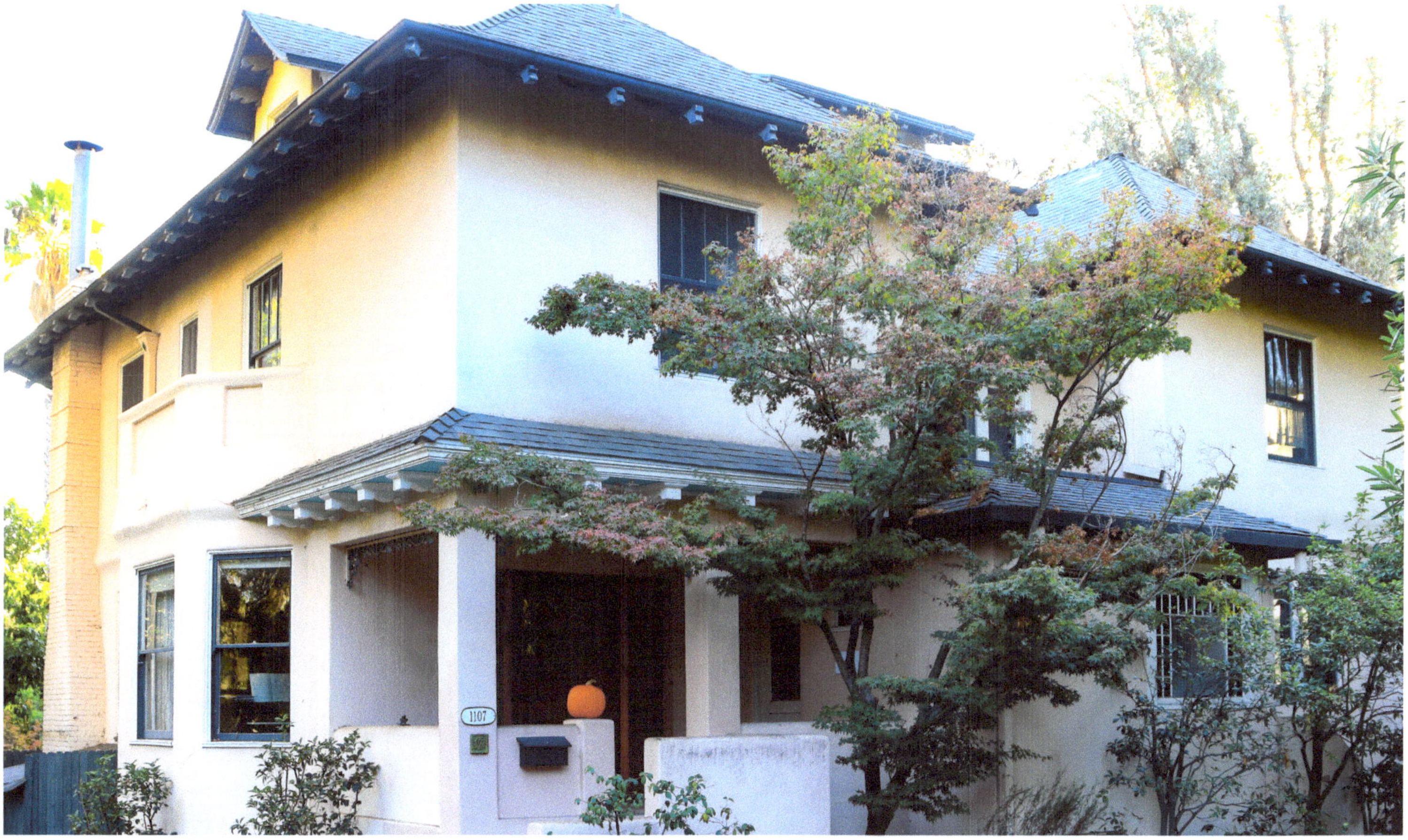

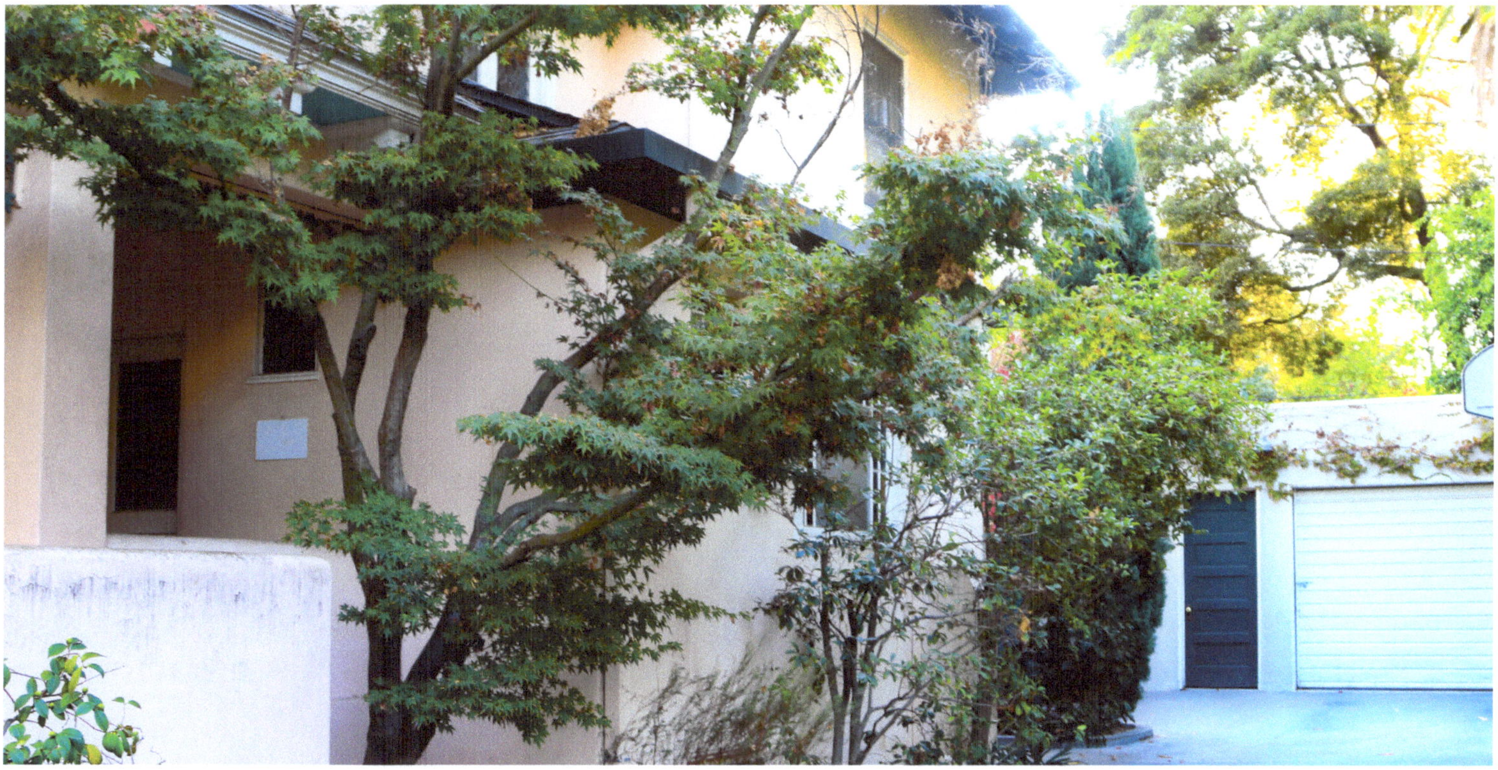

Raab Family Homestead – Circa 1875

Eclectic Victorian – Architect unknown

53

the

end

www.ingramcontent.com/pod-product-compliance
Lightning Source LLC
Chambersburg PA
CBHW051210220526
45473CB00003B/981